£33·50

33-50

00002763

KT-444-956

Natural Landscaping

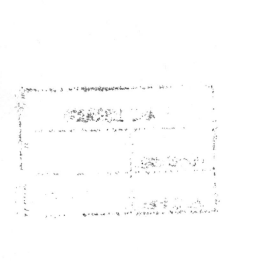

Natural Landscaping

DESIGNING WITH NATIVE PLANT COMMUNITIES

John Diekelmann, M.S.L.A.

Robert Schuster, M.A.

Illustrations by Renee Graef

D.A.C. LIBRARY

CLASS No. 710

ACC. No. 84306

McGRAW-HILL BOOK COMPANY

New York   St. Louis   San Francisco   Auckland
Bogotá   Hamburg   Johannesburg   London
Madrid   Mexico   Montreal   New Delhi
Panama   Paris   São Paulo   Tokyo
Singapore   Sydney   Toronto

Library of Congress Cataloging in Publication Data

Diekelmann, John.
  Natural landscaping.

  Includes index.
  1. Landscape gardening— Northeastern States.
  2. Wild flower gardening—Northeastern States.
  3. Landscape gardening.   4. Wild flower gardening.
  I. Schuster, Robert M.   II. Title.
  SB472.32.U6D53   715   81-13686
  ISBN 0-07-016813-X   AACR2

Copyright © 1982 by McGraw-Hill, Inc. All rights reserved.
Printed in the United States of America. Except as permitted
under the Copyright Act of 1976, no part of this publication
may be reproduced or distributed in any form or by any means,
or stored in a data base or retrieval system, without the
prior written permission of the publisher.

234567890   VHVH   898765432

ISBN 0-07-016813-X

I.[00002763

Do   715

Date.

*The editors for this book were Joan Zseleczky and Christine M. Ulwick,
the designer was Naomi Auerbach, and the production supervisor
was Thomas G. Kowalczyk. It was set in Aster by University Graphics, Inc.*

Printed and bound by Von Hoffmann Press, Inc.

FRONT COVER PHOTO: *Yellow coneflower and blazing star in midsummer.*

BACK COVER PHOTOS (CLOCKWISE FROM TOP LEFT): *Prairie layer in early summer; rattlesnake
master, blazing star, and big bluestem, late summer mesic prairie;
wet prairie in early summer; penstemon, coreopsis, and sage, early summer dry prairie;
bloodroot and Dutchman's-breeches on north slope, spring; dry western prairie in early
summer; aromatic aster and northern dropseed, fall dry prairie; prairie layer in early
summer; toothwort and false rue anemone, early spring.*

Contents

Preface

Over the years, the term *natural landscaping* has been used to describe a variety of landscaping approaches, from letting areas "go wild" to planting a selection of brilliant wildflowers. This book will offer another: a community approach to naturalizing.

The attraction of creating a landscape with native plants lies in the promise of having nature's beauty at one's doorstep and in reducing the need for watering, fertilizing, and mowing. Neither promise is automatic.

Nature's beauty is not just in its few showy flowers. More than that, it is a beauty of subtle colors, shapes, and textures that belongs as much to the foliage of grasses and sedges, mosses and ferns, shrubs and trees as to flowers. It is a beauty too of mutual dependencies, those subtle interrelationships between plants, animals, climate, and soil that one talks about in discussing ecosystems.

In the same way, nature's independence of humanity does not reside in the selection of a few choice species. A woodland orchid planted alone in one corner of the flowerbed will no more surely survive than a houseplant left to winter in the snow. Nature's vegetation forms a fragile system. Given the right conditions, it can perpetuate itself perhaps indefinitely without management. But deprived of its accustomed setting and associates it may not continue despite our assistance.

In a sense, these ideas are the meaning of and the justification for a community approach to naturalizing. What distinguishes this approach from the others is the attempt not just to use native plants in the landscape but to use them in a manner which approaches nature's own.

This book is intended to offer basic guidance in realizing the potential beauty and economy of utilizing native plants in the landscape, whether it be a public park, commercial property, or a private yard. It approaches naturalistic landscaping as a process of planning for both human and plant needs, developing a planting plan, and establishing a landscape. Because no single book can hope to be a complete resource on the subject, it liberally recommends other sources for further information.

It must be acknowledged, however, that human understanding is limited. Many questions about nature's systems have not been answered, and therefore every attempt at landscaping in nature's mold is in part an experiment. As with any experiment, it requires study and observation. The landscaper in Maryland faces problems and choices different from those of the landscaper in Illinois. Therefore, visits to local nature preserves and local experts are strongly recommended. Unlike the instantaneous quality of other types of landscapes, this process engages more than just the pocketbook. It rewards thought and curiosity, and it tends to enrich as it proceeds.

Finally, lest it seem that a community approach to landscaping is reserved for the scientist, landscapes based on these principles have been established in settings ranging from public schools and parks to private homes and corporate grounds. While it has as its ideal the restoration of a piece of nature to the human environment, each attempt is a learning experience. Each is different. And each is rewarding in its own way to the expert and the beginner alike.

The book has been designed to guide you through the naturalizing process chronologically. The introductory chapters of Part One explore the rationale for naturalizing and describe the concept of plant communities. The four chapters of Part Two are intended to introduce you to the major types of communities which are native to the Northeast and which you might consider simulating in a landscape. The first three chapters of Part Three describe the planning process involved in designing a naturalistic planting. The last five chapters in that section discuss more specifically the planning and planting information you will need in establishing a given type of community. The concluding chapters in Part Four are meant to illustrate the process from conception to completion, including interactions with neighbors and local officials.

We would like to acknowledge our indebtedness to a number of people for their help in researching, assembling, and writing this book. Thanks are due to Dawn Bedore, Cheryl Haberman, and Lynn Scherbert for their efforts in helping us find the botanical literature on which much of the book is based. Special appreciation is owed to Gloria Barsness, who efficiently and ably typed the bulk of the manuscript. We are deeply indebted to Dr. William Niering of the Connecticut Arboretum for his willing and expert guidance in interpreting the natural vegetation of New England, and to Dr. James Zimmerman of the University of Wisconsin Department of Landscape Architecture for his invaluable assistance with the book's wetland materials. We owe immeasurable gratitude to Dr. Evelyn Howell of the University of Wisconsin Department of Landscape Architecture and Ednah Thomas, Professor Emeritus of English at the University of Wisconsin–Madison, for their guidance in the development and writing of the manuscript. Our gratitude is also due to Renee Graef, without whose suggestions and patience the illustrations would have been impossible. Finally, we would like to express our appreciation to Nancy Diekelmann and Kathleen Schuster, whose support, understanding, and assistance were essential.

We would also like to acknowledge our indebtedness to the work of Jens Jensen and Darrel Morrison, two landscape architects whose foresight in advocating a naturalistic alternative to traditional formal plantings has served as the inspiration for this book.

We owe a last acknowledgment to those working to protect the diversity of species native to North America. Perhaps no provate organization has done more than The Nature Conservancy, whose preservation efforts and philosophy of cooperation among businesses, government, and individuals have been highly successful. Among governmental agencies, none has a greater responsibility than the United States Department of the Interior. Its continuing acquisition and protection of natural areas through the wilderness, wildlife, and parks programs deserves the strongest support. Finally, the University of Wisconsin Arboretum in Madison must be singled out for its pioneering work in restoring and managing native plant communities. It was in the Arboretum's Greene Prairie restoration that the photograph on the jacket of this book was taken.

John Diekelmann
Robert Schuster

part one

Introduction

chapter one

A Natural Alternative

I s it only in remembering childhood that we thrill at the sight of a hillside alive with flowers in spring, the color of a forest in fall, or tracks left in the snow by some unseen wild creature? Or is there something inherent in the natural world that stimulates the eye and excites the mind? While the urban lifestyle has helped us forget our dependencies on nature, many of us continue to feel its emotional appeal.

It is curious, then, that so much of landscaping has become more technological than natural. Few projects are begun without the bulldozer and chain saw. Fewer weekends escape the clamor of motorized mowers and trimmers. And, as though working with inanimate materials and striving for precision, contemporary styles impose an artificial geometry on trees and shrubs, segregate flowers into beds, and dictate level, unchanging expanses of lawn grasses.

Contemporary landscapes are also increasingly expensive. It is estimated that our 40 million lawn mowers consume 200 million gallons of gasoline annually. Sprinkling triples water consumption during the summer and compels an increasing number of cities to develop new pumping facilities and search out new water resources. As much as one-sixth of all commercial fertilizers, manufactured with massive amounts of natural gas, are used to produce not food but greener lawns. At a cost measured more in health than in dollars, nearly 40 percent of all pesticides are applied to lawns and gardens.

For reasons such as these, landscapers have begun experimenting

Fig. 1.1 Large-flowered trillium growing in rich deciduous forest.

Fig. 1.2 Moccasin flower in a dry oak woodland.

Fig. 1.3 Woodland violets in an oak forest.

with more natural alternatives in which plants are allowed to grow, flower, and reproduce with minimal interference. Called *naturalizing*, these experiments have attracted praise and created controversy. On one hand, they have been labeled an invitation to weeds and a euphemism for neglect; on the other, a step toward conservation and a way of restoring beauty to increasingly sterile environments.

Given the variety of these projects, there is inevitably some truth on both sides. It is the purpose of this book, however, to explore the concept as it can be: a method for combining good landscaping practices with plants requiring little maintenance.

An Approach to Naturalizing

A single approach has attracted most of the attention: the *no-mow* concept, in which the mower is simply retired and nature is allowed to take its course. But while this approach saves labor and gasoline, its merits as landscaping need to be weighed.

Where the soil is either wet much of the year or excessively poor and dry, the no-mow approach can initiate an interesting series of natural changes. Within a single growing season, an area left uncut may begin to support a colorful variety of harmless wild plants. A few like Queen Anne's lace and butter-and-eggs are imports to North America and have spread throughout the east. Others like milkweed, evening primrose, and old-field goldenrod are natives which have evolved in areas of natural disturbance where fires or floods have opened and impoverished the land. The natural role of these species, both native and alien, is beneficial. They anchor the soil against erosion and enrich it. And if spared further disturbances, they gradually yield to species better able to withstand competition.

In other areas, especially those enriched with nitrogen fertilizers, the no-mow approach may be less desirable. The first wild species are likely to be plants more closely associated with human than with natural disturbance. With a few familiar exceptions like ragweed, most have been carried here from the agricultural fields of Europe and Asia and can with justification be called weeds.

Here as there, quack grass, Canada thistle, bull thistle, and burdock are as familiar to landscapers as to farmers. Having adapted to routine disturbances, these weeds adjust quickly to changes in their environment, altering growing habits to accommodate mowing, grazing, and tilling. Most of these spread and reproduce rapidly despite efforts to control them. And most are persistent once established. As the familiar sight of abandoned lots and pastures suggests, they can outcompete and gradually eliminate most other nonwoody plants, including imported pests like dandelion.

The no-mow approach must also contend with existing lawn and garden plants. Like weeds, most horticultural species have adapted to cultivation. Many require special handling. Some, like the tulip, become less brilliant, smaller, and less numerous without annual fertilizing and dividing. Others become overly agressive when allowed to grow wild. Throughout the east, popular horticultural species like Kentucky bluegrass, Tartarian and Japanese honeysuckles, barberry, vinca, and multiflora rose have escaped from cultivation to become problem plants in meadows, fields, and woodlots.

Consequently, the no-mow idea is best approached with reservation. In landscapes with problem soils, it can add color and interest while reducing maintenance. But even where it succeeds in producing an attractive, low-maintenance landscape, it may require as many as several decades to achieve the kind of beauty that is possible in returning an area to a more natural state.

A more promising alternative involves planting native, nonweedy species to simulate the wild landscapes growing here thousands of years before the continent was settled. Biologically important and often dramatically beautiful, these landscapes have been destroyed rapidly over the last two centuries and have been forgotten outside the scientific community. Where they remain, however, they harbor the jewels of our native species, including the woodland trilliums, orchids, violets and the grassland lilies, blazing stars, and gentians (Figures 1.1 to 1.6).

These species and their wild companions have evolutionary histories greatly different from either weeds or horticultural species. Living in relatively stable growing environments and thus unable to depend on disturbances for competitive advantage, they have survived because they have developed the ability to exploit certain resources better than their competitors. As a result, most are finely attuned to the land and its resources.

Landscapes of such species are unlike those more familiar to us. In contrast to the relative handful of species found in most abandoned fields and lots, the native grasslands, savannas, forests, and wetlands often support hundreds of species of plants. Unlike our own planted landscapes, flowers and grasses mix in these wild areas with ferns, sedges, mosses, shrubs, and trees. Their combinations are rich and varied and remarkably harmonious over long periods of time (Figure 1.7).

Characteristic of this diversity and order, the native species form intricate layers of plant life in these landscapes. In the forest, a canopy of mature trees shelters lower layers of small trees, shrubs, herbs, and ground-hugging mosses. In the wild grasslands and wetlands, tall grasses, reeds, and sedges overtop layers of smaller light-sensitive or shade-tolerant species. In each case, these layers of plant life reflect an evolutionary process in which the wild species have adapted to and cling to life in specialized niches in the landscape, compounding its variety and beauty (Figure 1.8).

There is also a temporal order in the wild landscape. In the rich hardwood forests of eastern North America, ephemeral species flower before the trees form their leaves. With the shade of summer,

Fig. 1.4 *Prairie lily growing with grasses in a dry grassland.*

Fig. 1.5 *Blazing stars in August in a moist grassland.*

Fig. 1.6   Cream gentians among the lush grasses of a rich prairie.

Fig. 1.7   The intricate mixture of woodland species in the summer deciduous forest.

Fig. 1.8   The multiple layers of wildflowers and grasses in a midwestern prairie.

this floral show gives way to the richly varied foliage of shrubs, ferns, grasses, sedges, and mosses. With fall, as the leaves begin to turn color and drop, late-flowering species produce a second show of color (Figures 1.9 and 1.10).

This seasonal quality is perhaps even more pronounced in the native grasslands, where there are no trees to intercept the sunlight. Flowering begins early in spring and continues uninterrupted through fall in a progression of changing colors and shapes. It has been estimated that in the midwestern prairies, for example, as many as two new species bloom each day from May through October.

Perhaps most important, these wild landscapes are essentially self-sufficient. In their diversity and intimate relationship with the land, they perpetuate themselves without maintenance. Their species require no more water for survival than that provided by summer rains and winter snows. They require no more nutrients than those supplied by the decay of older generations of plants and the soils in which they grow. And they need no artificial protection from the insects and diseases to which the centuries have accustomed them.

Such qualities can be made a part of our own landscapes, but not simply by retiring the lawn mower. Few of the species native to the wild landscapes remain in our urban and agricultural areas. The landscaper who wants to capture their qualities must actively restore the native species to the soil.

Fig. 1.9   A carpet of spring flowers on the floor of a rich maple forest.

Effects of Naturalizing

Naturalizing can effectively eliminate all of the costs associated with routine lawn and garden care. It can also reduce the costs hidden in the production of lawn-care equipment. But its advantages are not limited to economics. Naturalistic plantings of appropriate native plants can also enhance the pleasure we take from our surroundings.

Such plantings do not require the acreage of a public park or a private estate. They can also be established within the limited space of an urban lot. Consider, for example, what can be done in an unused corner of lawn shaded by a single, mature tree. Naturalizing such an area might involve replacing lawn grasses with a variety of moderately shade-tolerant plants native to open woodlands. The selection could include several species of small shrubs, a number of woodland wildflowers, a variety of ferns, and several woodland sedges. Additional variety could be added with small but colorful species of mosses and fungi (Figures 1.11 and 1.12).

Such a planting would do more than free the landscaper from the routine chores of mowing, watering, and fertilizing. It would allow one to look forward to the rich smells of forest soils and the appearance of new seedlings each spring. Its soft, irregular lines would provide a rewarding contrast to the severe geometry that dominates most urban areas. Its foliage would provide privacy. And, with the addition of a path and bench, even this small planting could become a place to escape daily routines and to enjoy instead the songs of birds and the changing patterns of plants. Weeds, a perpetual prob-

Fig. 1.10 *A graceful colony of interrupted ferns in the summer shade of the deciduous forest.*

Fig. 1.11 *A small, unused corner of urban lawn. Note how the straight lines of the fence and building are emphasized by the uniform textures of the lawn.*

Fig. 1.12 The same site planted as a woodland edge. Compare the visual variety of this planting with the previous drawing. Which illustration holds your attention?

lem in formal lawns, would essentially disappear within as little as two years as the native plants became established and the planting matured.

This simple planting would offer all of the qualities which keep a landscape fresh and interesting: a variety of plant materials and colors, a dynamic quality of growth and seasonal change, and a richness of textural pattern. But it would also introduce an element that conventional landscapes do not have: historical and botanical dimension. Aesthetically, it would symbolize the kinds of landscapes native to the continent which greeted our pioneer ancestors. And botanically, it might provide a reservoir of species that are disappearing too rapidly from our lives and land.

Additional Reading

Carson, Rachel, *Silent Spring*, Fawcett Books, Greenwich, Conn., 1962.

Korling, Torkel, *The Prairie: Swell and Swale*, Korling, Dundee, Ill., 1972.

Korling, Torkel, and Robert O. Petty, *Eastern Deciduous Forest*, Korling, Evanston, Ill., 1974.

Leopold, Aldo, *A Sand County Almanac*, Oxford University Press, New York, 1949.

Rudd, Robert L., *Pesticides and the Living Landscape*, University of Wisconsin Press, Madison, 1964.

Thoreau, Henry David, *Walden*, various editions.

Watts, May Theilgaard, *Reading the Landscape of America*, Macmillan, New York, 1957.

chapter two

The Plant Community Model

M ost plants respond differently when left to compete with other plants than when grown under controlled conditions. Certain species of cacti are good examples. In the laboratory, these species thrive under some of the same conditions favorable to sugar maple: rich soils, constant but not excessive moisture, and moderate temperatures. In the wild, however, they are easily outcompeted in such environments and are able to hold their own only in hot, dry, relatively sterile environments like that of the desert.

An example from the area addressed by this book is hairy grama, a delicate grass native to the midwest. Narrow leaves, short stature, and an extensive root system allow it to grow successfully in areas subject to drought during the hot midwestern summers. Where soils of better moisture support larger and more vigorous species, hairy grama is a poor competitor. Consequently, it grows well in the severe sunshine and thin soils of sandy or gravelly midwestern hillsides but rarely appears wild anywhere else in the eastern half of the United States (Figure 2.1).

These differences between plants are seldom reflected in conventional landscapes. Plantings usually are selected more for ornamental value than for their physiology. As a result, many must be nursed along with regular maintenance.

The same approach to planting could produce extensive failures in naturalizing, in which plants are allowed to grow or die with minimal interference. Given the traditional preference for large, showy flowers, it might be tempting to simulate a woodland with such col-

Fig. 2.1 Hairy grama in flower on a dry, sandy hillside.

9

orful natives as big-leaf magnolia from the south, mountain laurel from the east, silky camellia from fertile coastal areas, moccasin flower from acidic forests, showy lady's slipper from wet northern forests, purple clematis from rocky forests, and large-flowered trillium from rich deciduous woods. The results would be striking, but they probably also would be short-lived. It is no accident that this particular combination probably occurs nowhere in the wild. Having evolved in very different settings, several species inevitably would be poorly adapted to any one landscape. Some, far from their normal ranges, could be killed outright by uncustomary weather. Others might languish in competition with better adapted species. And those placed favorably but freed from customary competitors might overpopulate the planting.

Minimizing these problems requires selecting plants first for their fitness for the total planting and only then for color, shape, and texture. The question is how to begin. Picking appropriate plants from the thousands of species native to North America can be a formidable challenge. Even a careful study of guides to the flora of North America cannot guarantee the selection of plants botanically appropriate for a site and compatible with each other. An easier, more reliable approach is to draw upon the concept of native *plant communities.*

Plant Communities

The land provides a multitude of habitats for plants. On the largest scale, precipitation patterns, averages and extremes of temperatures, the length of growing seasons, and the hours of sunlight in a day combine to divide the continent into natural regions of vegetation. However alike Des Moines, Iowa, and Wheeling, West Virginia, may be on any given summer day, whether sharing heat and sunshine or rain and fog, the climates of the two cities are different and so, too, are the types of vegetation characteristic of their regions (Figures 2.2 and 2.3).

Plant habitat also varies within regions. The shape of the land and the character of its soils can modify habitat over a range of miles or within as little as a few yards. In the northern hemisphere, south slopes receive sunlight more directly than those facing north and therefore have longer, warmer, and often drier growing seasons. Sheltered from sun and wind, ravines are generally cooler and more moist than exposed ridges and flats. Local depressions can become pockets of frost during the spring and early fall, their temperatures falling as much as 20 degrees below those of surrounding areas. Coarse sands drain more quickly than fine-textured clays and are therefore more prone to drought. Soils derived from rocks like marble and limestone tend to be less acidic and more fertile than those derived from rocks like granite and quartzite.

Plants growing wild tend to group themselves in accordance with

Fig. 2.2 The level plains topography of western Iowa and northern Missouri.

Fig. 2.3 The mountainous slopes of the Allegheny Mountains in northern West Virginia and western Pennsylvania.

these environmental differences. Those with similar needs for light, warmth, moisture, shelter, and nutrients appear together where there is appropriate habitat. Whether these groupings form forests or meadows, cover hundreds of square miles or only a few square feet, they nevertheless reflect the climate, soils, and topography available to them (Figures 2.4 and 2.5).

Plants also shape their own environments. Forest trees, for example, create *microclimates* that are cooler and more humid in summer than those of nearby grasslands. The leaves of maples decom-

Fig. 2.4 *The sheltered environment of an outcropping of rocks here supports a stand of pines, while the unsheltered slope supports a dry stand of grasses.*

Fig. 2.5 *In this northern landscape bordering Lake Michigan, a conifer forest stops abruptly at the edge of a swale. Standing water supports a northern marsh.*

pose to form richer soils than do the needles of pines. Thus, plants sharing a given place at a given time in the wild exhibit adaptations to each other as well as to the land.

The deeply shaded forests, dominated by beech and maple, that grow in Indiana and Ohio illustrate this point. While a few shade-intolerant plants may survive in scattered patches of sunlight, most of the species native to these forests have evolved more reliable means for survival. Dutchman's-breeches and other spring ephemerals flower and produce seed early, before the trees form their leaves and close out the light needed for photosynthesis. Other species, like maidenhair fern, have developed the ability to carry out photosynthesis in reduced light and so remain green all summer. The parasitic beechdrops have eliminated the need for photosynthesis altogether and live off the roots of the beech tree (Figures 2.6 to 2.8).

Able to exploit the resources available to them in a given environment and to survive the competition of other species also adapted to it, these wild species in effect form functional units of vegetation to which botanists give the name *communities.*

Implicit in the concept of plant communities is the idea that similar environments give rise to similar groups of plants and, conversely, that the presence of certain species can be used as an indicator of environmental conditions. But while the concept expresses the basic organization that is characteristic of wild vegetation, communities themselves are neither fixed nor static.

No two communities, however similar, are ever identical. Two midwestern forests dominated by oaks and hickories will predictably have populations of plants that include white oak, shagbark hickory, gray dogwood, and false Solomon's-seal, but one may also support yellow lady's slipper or poison ivy while the other does not. Black oak or trembling aspen may be abundant in one and relatively rare in the second.

Contributing to such differences is the fact that communities change with environment. In a forest community growing on a north slope, the size, numbers, and reproductive success a given species achieves may change as the habitat becomes more exposed toward the crest of the hill. Individuals of the species may grow larger at the foot of the slope, where there is more shelter. The species' population may decrease with rising elevation. And at some point on the slope, the species may be unable to reproduce itself. These points are different for each species. As a result, communities often change gradually along environmental gradients. Because of the variety of factors that affect habitat, no two points in a given community are identical, much less two points in different communities (Figure 2.9).

A second consequence of this complexity of wild vegetation is that boundaries between communities are seldom clearly identifiable. Rather, as two communities meet they often blend gradually into one another much as the colors of the spectrum do. Exceptions occur only where habitat changes abruptly (Figure 2.10).

Also contributing to differences between communities is the fact that they change over time and reflect their own unique histories. Natural disturbances like those created in a forest by the death of an aged tree are common. With the fall of a tree, the upper forest layers are opened and there is an increase in the amount of light reaching the ground. A few light-tolerant species may respond by growing in size and number. Others less tolerant may suffer.

Fig. 2.6 Dutchman's-breeches brightens the spring forest with its characteristic flowers in early May.

Fig. 2.7 The foliage of maidenhair fern graces the forest floor at the height of summer.

Fig. 2.8   Nonchlorophyllic beechdrops resemble a small dormant shrub.

Fig. 2.9   A representation of a single forest community. Note that in this example tree size is largest and the forest is densest at the bottom of the slope.

Smaller trees often grow rapidly when released from heavy shade and form brushy circles at the base of fallen trees. New species, their seeds brought in by animals or wind, may also take root. Often, however, a younger tree eventually fills the gap created by the death of an older tree, and the community slowly reassumes something like its original structure (Figure 2.11).

More dramatic events initiate a process known as *plant succession*, a sequence of long-term changes in the composition of vegetation accompanying major changes in environment. An example of succession follows the abandonment of pasture lands. In New England, a variety of weedy grasses often dominates the land for several years. Gradually, however, trees and shrubs begin to invade the grassland. Over perhaps the next hundred years, trees, often pines, take root and create a forest community. Where the environment allows, the maturing forest of pines becomes increasingly shady and begins to favor more shade-tolerant species like hemlock and sugar maple. Over the course of several hundred years, the soils and species of the community change, and the natural stand of pines may be replaced by one of hemlock and maple. Such sequences can be initiated by a variety of events, including lumbering, fires, and flooding. Importantly, they can be changed by fresh disturbances, and reflect the seed sources that are available. They also vary from region to region and from one habitat to another. In some areas, grasslands may persist for centuries, as they have in the midwest. In others, maples may never invade a community of pines or oaks. (Figure 2.12).

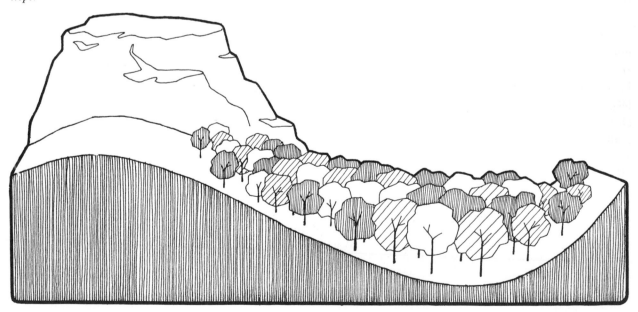

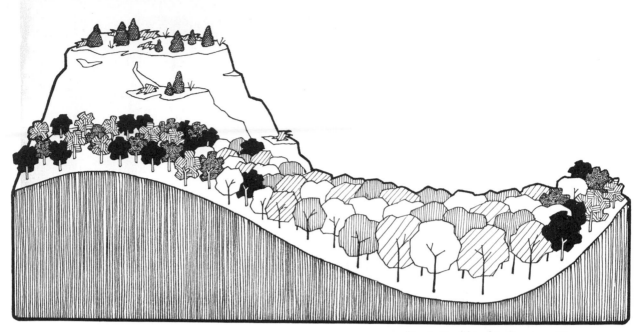

Fig. 2.10 *Two forest communities blend gradually along a gradual slope. Note that on the cliff, where environment changes abruptly from the slopes below, a third community begins and ends distinctly.*

In all of their complexity, communities mirror their environments on a local as well as a regional scale. Climatic changes over centuries are reflected in their composition just as are fleeting disturbances created by man and nature. Plant communities are therefore a dynamic and orderly element of landscapes. In reflecting the geology, climate, and history of the land, they give each region its own unique natural character.

Fig. 2.11 *A dense growth of maples fills a temporary opening in a dark northern maple–hemlock forest.*

Fig. 2.12   Young maples, tolerant of the moderate shade, dominate the undergrowth of this pine forest. Compare this pattern of growth with that in the preceding photo.

Using Communities as a Model for Landscaping

If it were possible to build within a relatively undisturbed natural community, no landscape would be more ideally undemanding or more expressive of the land and its history. Fortunately, given the increasing rarity of such sites, the option is not available to most of us. We can, however, take advantage of such natural areas by using them as models for plantings.

One of the keys to naturalizing is the selection of plants able to grow and reproduce without compromising the vitality of their companions. Plant communities, in which the compatibility of species has been tested for centuries, offer perhaps the best guide. It is not necessary to duplicate the inventory of a community's species, a feat that would be impractical if not impossible. Rather, it is possible to begin by identifying *dominant* species, that is, those which shape their environment by virtue of sheer size or numbers. In woodlands these are the trees and major shrubs; in grasslands, the major grasses. Planting these species creates a habitat within which the need for the routine care of appropriate species is minimized. Given nearby seed sources, other appropriate species may even begin to establish themselves within the planting.

Because even closely related examples of a community are never identical, the landscaper retains some choice. It is possible to create an appropriate planting and at the same time to design for maximum color and effect. It is also possible to eliminate undesirable nondominants like poison ivy.

Selecting an appropriate community as a model, however, is fundamental. It is sensible to begin by considering local communities already adapted to a region's climate. But because environments also vary within regions, not all local communities are equally appropriate. Choosing one that is appropriate may involve looking at those growing on topography and soils similar to those of the site to be planted. This is especially critical in transitional areas between regions, where minor differences in slope or soil can be a major factor in survival. In less marginal areas, estimating the amount of moisture available to plants may be enough. While moisture conditions range from extremely dry to extremely wet, native communities are often classified as dry (xeric), moist (mesic), and wet (hydric). Communities of intermediate preferences are often called dry-mesic or wet-mesic.

In a growing number of urban and rural areas, the issue of pollution invariably complicates these considerations. In some cases, pollutants have radically altered the environment. As a general rule, the acres of pavement and number of heat sources prevalent in most cities have made urban environments warmer and drier than their rural counterparts. The selection of landscaping models for urban areas should reflect these conditions. It may be advisable to choose a more xeric community as a guide than might otherwise be suggested by climate and topography.

A more difficult problem is raised by pollutants like ozone, sulfur dioxide, peroxyacetyl nitrate (PAN), and nitrogen oxide. Relatively little is known about the effects these industrial pollutants have on wild populations of plants. Where standards have been established, the threat posed by a pollutant may be minimal. But standards are incomplete, and their enforcement is often inadequate.

Plants vary greatly in their sensitivity to pollutants. Even individuals within a single species may vary in susceptibility. This, combined with our relatively limited knowledge, makes it difficult to generalize about the success a planting will have in a polluted habitat. The landscaper might prudently plant a wide variety of species from a community and note which do well and which do not. It can also be helpful to find local communities growing successfully near major sources of pollution.

While it may not make sense to plant species that we know will not survive, there is another side to the pollution question. Pollutants affect people as well as plants. For that reason, it may be worth considering the value some plants have as indicators of pollution. Spiderwort, butterfly weed, and some lichens are extremely sensitive to some forms of pollution. Rather than rejecting them for less sensitive plants, it may make sense to use them in the landscape much as coal miners used the canary.

Using living communities of plants as models can help to ensure that landscapes will be in relative harmony with their surroundings. It can also provide design ideas whose appeal can be seen and judged before planting begins. In the following chapters, major communities that can be used as models in the northeastern United

States and southeastern Canada will be discussed, as will the process of translating them into a landscape. But using communities in this way requires more than reading. It also requires repeated visits to local natural areas and the use of all of the senses. Consequently, the reader should use the rest of this book only as a stepping-stone toward gaining a fuller and richer appreciation for the native communities of plants that are part of our natural heritage.

Additional Reading

Braun, E. Lucy, *Deciduous Forests of Eastern North America*, Hafner, New York, 1967.

Curtis, John T., *Vegetation of Wisconsin: An Ordination of Plant Communities*, University of Wisconsin Press, Madison, 1971.

Daubenmire, Rexford, *Plants and Environment: A Textbook of Autecology*, Wiley, New York, 1974.

Ibrahim, Joseph Hindawi, *Air Pollution Injury to Vegetation*, Air Pollution Control Administration Publication No. AP-71, U.S. Government Printing Office, Washington, D.C., 1970.

Whittaker, Robert H., *Communities and Ecosystems*, Macmillan, New York, 1975.

part two

Gathering Ideas—
Plant Communities
in the Northeast

chapter three

The Central Hardwoods Region

The climate of the geographic middle of eastern North America is moist. Annual precipitation ranges from an average of 35 inches near Lake Michigan to more than 50 inches in eastern Kentucky. Because this moisture is distributed evenly throughout the year, drought is a rare climatic event (Figure 3.1).

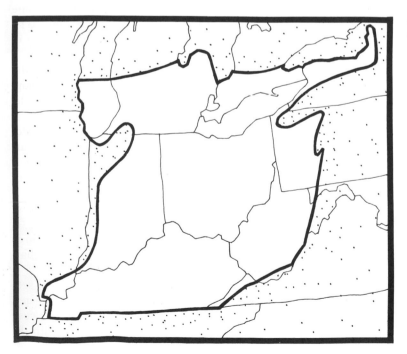

Fig. 3.1   The Central Hardwoods Region.

DURHAM AGRICULTURAL COLLEGE LIBRARY BOOK

fertile plains alternate with low hills capped by resistant sandstones and thin, acid soils. Wetlands are prominent only along the courses of major rivers like the Ohio. And while precipitation is adequate, extensive areas of porous limestone form broad flats of xeric habitat.

The last of these provinces, the Central Lowlands, extends over much of Indiana, Ohio, southern Michigan, and lower Ontario, and lies within the domain of the last glacial ice sheets. The land, deeply covered by glacial debris, is largely level. Wetlands formed by slowly moving streams are common. The soils, largely glacial in origin, are deep and fertile (Figure 3.5).

Forest Communities

The forest communities native to this region are richly varied. Most representative are those which, in concert with the climate, thrive in moist settings. Yet within the region's physical diversity, xeric and wetland forests both find suitable habitat. Given a continental climate, many of these forests are deciduous. But predominantly evergreen communities are also native, and their potential habitat has expanded following settlement.

Mesic Forests Mesic forest communities require abundant, regular, but not excessive moisture. Within these parameters, however, the mesic forests growing here are diverse. Perhaps the richest and most distinctive is the *mixed mesophytic* community, unique among North American forests in that its canopy is not dominated by a single or even several species of trees. Rather, as many as twenty species share dominance in a mixture typical of tropical forests.

This is a forest of deep summer shade cast largely by deciduous species like the maples, basswoods, buckeyes, beech, and tulip tree and enhanced by a prominent understory of small trees like flowering dogwood, ironwood, and musclewood. Shade plays a major role in the forest's composition and appearance. Beneath its dense upper layers, the forest is often open and parklike. Young trees are often few in number and limited primarily to shade-tolerant canopy species. Oaks, intolerant of deep shade, reproduce poorly. In addition, while shrubs are diverse and often showy, most, like the rhododendrons, azalea, witch hazel, and alternate-leaf dogwood, appear in significant numbers only where the canopy is less dense (Figures 3.6 to 3.9).

Fig. 3.6   Dark shade and relative openness are typical of the mixed mesophytic forest in summer.

Fig. 3.7   Small trees form a continuous layer below the canopy, adding to the shade of the forest floor.

Fig. 3.8   The showy blooms of flowering dogwood are conspicuous in the understory in spring.

Fig. 3.9 *A second understory species, witch hazel, blooms in the fall.*

The mixed forest's herbaceous layers are also distinctive and are among the most colorful of any in North America. On the forest's moist, fertile soils, organic materials decompose rapidly, producing a rich humus and allowing little accumulation of leaves. Such conditions favor a characteristic population of herbs like bloodroot, Dutchman's-breeches, trout lily, and anemone. In spring, their showy blooms often carpet the ground in gardenlike profusion. In summer, flowers give way to the lush foilage of ferns and other shade-tolerant herbs, producing an intricate, complex mosaic of textures and shapes unrivaled by other deciduous forests (Figures 3.10 and 3.11).

This mixed forest community is demanding in its habitat, favoring sheltered slopes and rich, moist, drained soils nearly neutral in pH. Such environments are most common in the Appalachian Plateaus, where the community once covered most of the lower mountain slopes and many of those less mountainous. Favorable sites are more limited in the region's other provinces, where they include ravines, deep valleys, and lower north-facing slopes.

Variations from these ideal conditions give rise to other mesic forests, similar in their requirements for moisture but often less diverse and sometimes quite different in population. Lower, wetter valleys

Fig. 3.10 *The variety of spring-flowering herbs like Dutchman's-breeches and spring beauty is characteristic of the rich deciduous forests.*

Fig. 3.11 *In the shade of summer, lush foliage replaces spring flowers on the forest floor.*

Fig. 3.12   Hemlocks and rhododendron give a conspicuous evergreen quality to moist acid ravines.

Fig. 3.13   Hemlocks also form a narrow border along moist, thin-soiled cliff edges.

favor a *beech* forest. Its herbaceous layers are less continuous and less varied than those of the mixed forest, perhaps because the leaves of the beech decompose slowly and create a thick, moderately acidic leaf litter. Sandstone gorges, cooler and usually more acidic than sites preferred by the mixed forest, favor a *hemlock* community in which the herbs of the mixed forest grow poorly if at all. The bedrock, as well as the highly acidic conditions that develop under hemlocks, gives rise instead to a patchy ground cover of wood sorrel, round-leaved violet, and partridgeberry. Where the year-round shade cast by the hemlocks is not too intense, great rhododendron and mountain laurel may also produce dense, colorful shrub thickets. With rising elevation, species like beech, basswood, and buckeye decline in importance, while maple and yellow birch increase. Elevations above 2000 feet, therefore, give rise to a *sugar maple* community. Because maple leaves decompose rapidly to form a rich humus, many of the mixed forest herbs also dominate the maple forest, though often in fewer numbers (Figures 3.12 to 3.14).

Fig. 3.14   The thin ground cover under hemlocks offers a sharp contrast to the deciduous forest.

One last mesic forest deserves special mention. Occurring virtually nowhere south of the glacial border, the *beech–maple* community is the most common mesic forest of the Central Lowlands. Its canopy is dominated by beech and sugar maple. While southern species like yellow buckeye and white basswood are conspicuously absent, northern species like American basswood, northern bush

Fig. 3.15 The oak–hickory forest is characterized by gnarly trees and a shrubby undergrowth.

Fig. 3.16 The dark foliage of mountain laurel distinguishes the chestnut oak forest.

honeysuckle, and wild sarsaparilla play an increasing role northward. Despite these differences, the community resembles the mixed forest in its shade, herbs, and requirements for shelter and moist, fertile soils.

Xeric Forests   Before settlement, forest communities tolerant of relatively dry conditions were less prominent than mesic forests in this region. Xeric habitat was primarily the upper slopes and ridge tops of the Appalachians, the sand and gravel ridges of the Lowlands, and the hills and dry limestone bedrock of the Interior Low Plateau. But human impact has increased xeric habitat, hastening erosion and increasing evaporation by opening up forested lands.

The *chestnut oak* and *pitch pine* forests, two xeric communities widespread in the middle Atlantic states, also grow here. The oak community develops on steep, dry slopes and upper ridges; the more xeric pine forest on sandy soils formed over sandstone. Both are most common in the rugged eastern plateaus, but also occur on favorable sites to the west. An early successional community, the pine forest may also develop on disturbed sites. Both communities, as will be discussed in the following chapter, are characterized by a dense, low shrub layer of evergreen heath species like blueberry and huckleberry. Where this layer is more open, a patchy ground cover of bracken fern, sweet fern, and evergreen herbs like wintergreen may be prominent.

A xeric *oak–hickory* community often associated with the midwest is more common on the less acidic limestone, gravel, and sand topography of the western provinces. It is distinct from the chestnut oak and pine forests in the virtual absence of heath shrubs, whose place is taken by species like gray dogwood and hazelnut. Herbaceous heaths are also infrequent and, as will be discussed later, are replaced by herbs like false Solomon's-seal and Virginia creeper (Figures 3.15 and 3.16).

These xeric communities provide a dramatic contrast to the region's lush mesic forests. Growing on thinner, poorer, and drier soils, their trees are often comparatively small and their canopies less dense, allowing more light to reach the lower layers. There is less variety of herb species than in the mesic forests, but increased light and less competition from tree species permit the development of a more pronounced shrub layer. As a result, shrub thickets often dominate the xeric forests visually.

Hydric Forests   Areas in which the soil is saturated or inundated with water are relatively uncommon south of the glacial border. Wetland forests are most often limited to narrow strips along major rivers. On the glacial topography of the Central Lowlands, however, such forests often cover large areas. Two major types are most common (Figures 3.17 and 3.18).

The *floodplain* community, growing along the margins of major rivers, is one adapted to periodic flooding. Its species are those able to tolerate broad fluctuations in moisture and annual deposits of silt. Many of them also require moderately fertile soils, a condition amply met by the nutrients carried from the uplands by runoff. American elm, silver maple, and cottonwood are the major tree species. To the south, sycamore, sweet gum, and pin oak add diversity. Few shrubs, with the exception of red elderberry, are able to tolerate the floodplain habitat. Vines, however, are prominent and include Virginia creeper, poison ivy, wild grape, and clematis. Ground cover is often patchy, although it may include prominent masses of jewelweed and nettle.

In contrast, the *hardwood swamp* forest occurs in areas where water saturates but does not cover the soil. In this community, organic materials usually collect on the surface of the ground and decompose slowly to form an acidic, infertile humus. The dominant species is the red maple, which often forms dense stands whose shade excludes most undergrowth. Black ash, pin oak, and swamp white oak are other common canopy species, often growing on low mounds less saturated than the other swamp soils. The community grades into shrub communities of alder, willow, and chokeberry.

A *conifer swamp* community dominated by tamarack and black spruce occurs in the Appalachians and north of the glacial border in low, cold, peaty areas. Because it is rare here and more typical further north, it will be discussed in the later chapter devoted to the Northern Conifer–Hardwoods Region.

Savanna and Open Communities

Given the role of forests in this region, communities in which trees are either widely scattered or absent may seem out of place. Yet they occur and, largely unshaded, provide a summer floral show missing in the forests.

Savannas, in which trees either grow as isolated individuals or in scattered groves, are most common on sites too dry or organically poor to support forests. One, the *pine* savanna, grows on acidic, sandy soils too thin and dry to maintain a pitch pine forest. In it, stunted pines and oaks are widely spaced, as are many of the shrubs of the pine forest. Between them, bracken fern, sweet fern, and grassland species form open areas of relatively short vegetation. Among the grassland flora are a variety of midwestern prairie plants such as little bluestem grass, Indian grass, butterfly weed, wild indigo, and a variety of asters and goldenrods. The grasses often appear as individual clumps rather than as a continuous sod and may be separated by bare soil or patches of mosses and lichens (Figure 3.19).

A second savanna community, the *cedar glade*, occurs most often where thin, nonacidic soils cover a limestone bedrock, and is easily recognized by its patchwork of red cedars often rooted in lines

Fig. 3.17   *Along quiet streams, mesic forests grow to the water's edge. The light trunk of sycamore offers a hint of floodplain conditions.*

Fig. 3.18   *Wet forest species like bee balm add a brilliant color to forested depressions in the landscape.*

Fig. 3.19 The open, shrubby pine savanna grows on poor, sandy soils.

Fig. 3.20 Scattered red cedars form cedar glades on thin limestone soils.

formed by cracks in the bedrock. On extreme sites, mosses and lichens may be the only ground cover. But where soils are deeper, a flora of grasses and other herbs typical of the dry prairie gives the community a grassland appearance (Figure 3.20).

The plants of both communities flower abundantly from April through October. Many are small and delicate, with blooms that are inconspicuous when compared with most garden flowers. Nevertheless, their variety and diminutive beauty are rewarding, especially in their barrens settings.

Given time and the development of deeper soils, both communities may slowly develop into open forest. Where environment allows, oaks gradually take root and shade out the grassland species. With increasing shade, woodland herbs of either the pine and chestnut oak forests or the oak-hickory forest gradually become established, transforming the community to one more recognizable as forest.

Treeless, grassland communities also occur regularly throughout the region. As in the midwest, a *dry prairie* community of short- to medium-size grasses may develop on limestone topography and dry, south-facing hillsides. Where moisture is more abundant, a *mesic prairie* community may appear, characterized by a lush growth of chest-high grasses like big bluestem and Indian grass and a variety of large wildflowers like rosinweed and compass plant (Figures 3.21 and 3.22).

The reason for the existence of grasslands in this region has been much debated. One theory is that they developed during a period in which the climate was far drier than it is now. More difficult to answer is why they persist in the face of the moist, modern climate. One explanation is that a long history of annual fires, either natural or set by native Americans to improve hunting, has favored grasses over trees. Another is that the thick prairie sod may prevent trees and shrubs from taking root. A last explanation suggests that prairie soils do not contain the organisms trees require for growth and, therefore, that a change from grassland to forest occurs extremely slowly.

Whatever the reason for their existence, these grassland communities provide a brilliant show of flowers throughout the spring, summer, and fall. The diverse blooms of species like blazing star, coneflower, and black-eyed Susan nestle amid the graceful foliage of the grasses, at times dominating the prairie visually, at others, nearly hidden. The grasses themselves, unlike lawn grasses, turn color in fall and ornament the landscape more subtly but no less beautifully than do the leaves of the deciduous forest.

In wetter locations, especially small depressions in the level topography of the Central Lowlands, *wet prairies* harbor many of the same species. Here, however, species more tolerant of wet soils are most prominent. Turk's-cap lily, Michigan lily, iris, cardinal flower, ironweed, and Joe-Pye weed are colorful examples. Switch grass and bluejoint grass often replace the more xeric little bluestem. In these areas, standing water is usually present only during spring thaws, and the soil is merely damp the rest of the growing season (Figure 3.23).

Where water lies close to the soil's surface or covers it, grassland gives way to open wetland. Two prominent wetland communities found throughout much of the northeast are the *sedge meadow* and *marsh*. The former requires a water level no more than 18 inches below the surface and tolerates shallow standing water. It may sup-

Fig. 3.21 *Short grasses and colorful forbs like blazing star and aster characterize the dry prairie.*

Fig. 3.22 *Mesic prairies support a taller and more luxuriant vegetation.*

Fig. 3.23 *Wet prairie species like sweet black-eyed Susan mix here with cattails at the edge of a marsh.*

Fig. 3.24   *Marsh marigold and the hummocks of hummock sedge* (Carex stricta) *are prominent in this sedge meadow.*

Fig. 3.25   *Marshland aquatics occur in zones related to water depth.*

port wet grassland species like bluejoint grass and iris, but it is dominated by the prominent hummocks of a single species of sedge *(Carex stricta)* growing to a height of perhaps 2 feet. Marshlands, in contrast, are truly aquatic, occurring where water stands permanently with a depth of as much as 3 feet. They support a varied population of plants ranging from emergents, like cattail, in the shallows to floaters, like water lily, and submergents in deeper water. The soils of both communities are highly organic. Trees are relatively uncommon because of the water level (Figures 3.24 and 3.25).

Naturalizing in the Central Hardwoods Region

Settlement has had a major impact on the most characteristic vegetation of this region, the mesic forests. Rich and varied, these forests are also fragile biotic systems sensitive to erosion and drying winds. Clearing has destroyed many of them, and their return is painfully slow, requiring many generations without disturbance.

Incorporating mesic species into the landscape is difficult. It demands a sheltered, moist site and a deep, fertile layer of humus capable of buffering seasonal fluctuations in moisture. Where mature trees like sugar maple exist to provide this environment, some semblance of mesic forest can perhaps be created, beginning with tolerant herbs like large-flowered trillium, hepatica, and mayapple. Where they do not, more practical alternatives are the region's other native communities.

Savanna and nonmesic forest plantings can be created with appropriate herbs, shrubs, and mature trees in a few growing seasons. Attention should, however, be given to soil pH. While many of the xeric species flourish on acid soils, others like the cedars require alkaline conditions for optimal growth.

Grasslands can perhaps be established most quickly and offer both openness and color. In this region, however, they require periodic mowing, clipping, or fire to keep them free of invading trees and shrubs.

Additional Reading

Introductory

Hunt, Charles B., *Physiography of the United States*, W. H. Freeman, San Francisco, 1967.
McCormick, Jack, *The Life of the Forest*, McGraw-Hill, New York, 1966.
Platt, Rutherford, *The Great American Forest*, Prentice-Hall, Englewood Cliffs, N.J., 1965.

Detailed

Braun E. Lucy, *Deciduous Forests of Eastern North America*, Hafner, New York, 1967.
Braun, E. Lucy, "An Ecological Transect of Black Mountain, Kentucky," *Ecological Monographs* 10:193–241, 1940.
Braun, E. Lucy, "Forests of the Cumberland Mountains," *Ecological Monographs* 12:413–447, 1942.
Braun, E. Lucy, "The Vegetation of Pine Mountain, Kentucky," *American Midland Naturalist* 16:517–565, 1935.
Bryant, William S., "The Big Clifty Prairie, A Remnant Outlier of the Prairie Peninsula, Grayson County, Kentucky," *Transactions of the Kentucky Academy of Science* 38:21–25, 1977.
Forsyth, Jane L., "A Geologist Looks at the Natural Vegetation Map of Ohio," *Ohio Journal of Science* 70:180–191, 1970.
Jones, Clyde H., "Studies in Ohio Floristics—III: Vegetation of Ohio Prairies," *Bulletin of the Torrey Botanical Club* 71:536–548, 1944.
McInteer, B. B., "A Change from Grassland to Forest Vegetation in the 'Big Barrens' of Kentucky," *American Midland Naturalist* 35:276–282, 1946.
Niering, W. A., *The Life of the Marsh*, McGraw-Hill, New York, 1949.
Williams, Arthur B., "The Composition and Dynamics of a Beech-Maple Climax Community," *Ecological Monographs* 6:319–408, 1936.
Wistendahl, Warren A., "Buffalo Beats, a Relict Prairie Within a Southeastern Ohio Forest," *Bulletin of the Torrey Botanical Club* 102:178–186, 1975.

chapter four

The Eastern Oak Region

L ike the Central Hardwoods Region, the middle Atlantic states
receive abundant rainfall. Annual precipitation averages more
than 40 inches in most areas. But while the natural vegetation in
this region's moist climate is predominantly deciduous forest, rich
forests of maple, beech, basswood, and buckeye are relatively rare.
Instead, most forests are dominated by oaks (Figure 4.1).

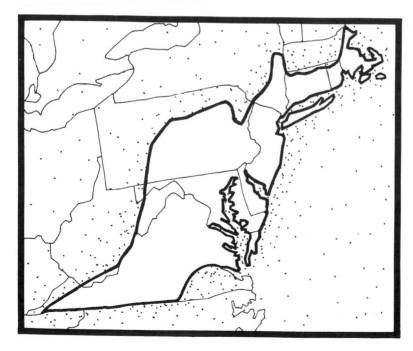

Fig. 4.1   The Eastern Oak Region.

Fig. 4.2 The major geographic
divisions of the region.

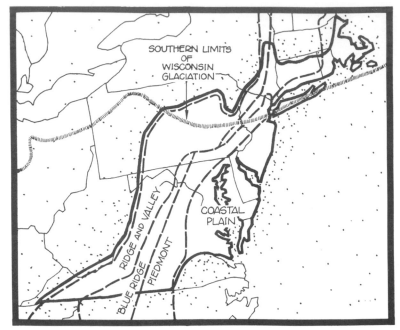

One explanation for the vegetational differences between these two regions lies in the distinction between precipitation totals and effectiveness. Periods of drought are more common here than immediately to the west. And southward, in Virginia at least, the growing season is both longer and warmer, increasing the amount of moisture lost to evaporation. Thus, many of the species of the mixed mesophytic forest, sensitive even to brief periods of moisture shortage, may not be well suited to the eastern states.

A second possible explanation is one related to soils and geography. A distinct border known as the Appalachian Front divides the two regions, and the landscape from here to the east differs markedly from that to the west (Figure 4.2).

The westernmost geographic province of this region, known as the Ridge and Valley, parallels the Appalachian Plateaus and, like them, is underlain by sedimentary rock. But in contrast, severe folding of these strata has produced a series of steep ridges and narrow valleys. Limestone and shale, more erodible than the other strata, form the valley floors and yield relatively fertile soils. More characteristic of the province, however, are the ridges. Steep and capped by resistant sandstones and conglomerates, they are covered with thin, rocky, acidic soils and offer a habitat unsuitable to the rich mesic forests (Figure 4.3).

To the east of the Ridge and Valley lies the Blue Ridge, a narrow mountainous formation of granite and greenstone. Like the western ridges, its slopes are steep, and its underlying rock breaks down

Fig. 4.3 The steep-sided parallel ridges of the Ridge and Valley.

slowly to form thin, infertile soils. Thus, despite its greater elevations, much of the Blue Ridge offers an environment similar to the slopes of the Ridge and Valley (Figure 4.4).

East of the Blue Ridge is the Piedmont, perhaps the least rugged of all of the eastern highlands. Much of its landscape is level to gently rolling, offering appreciable shelter only in its river valleys. Underlain by shale and in places by red sandstone, its soils are in many areas relatively infertile. In Virginia, where the climate is moderate and winter snows less common, year-round rains have washed soluble minerals like calcium out of the topsoil in a weathering process called *leaching*, leaving it even less fertile.

Bordering the ocean from New Jersey south is the Coastal Plain, an area of low relief whose soils have been deposited by runoff from the highlands. Much of the coastal plain lies close to the water table, and areas of wetlands, broken only by low sand hills, are extensive. In its moderate climate, most soils are strongly leached and acidic.

Finally, from New Jersey north into New England the land has been shaped by glaciation and is relatively youthful. Glacial moraines form low hills divided by lakes and slowly moving streams. Glacial outwash has created level, sandy plains on Long Island and Cape Cod. Over much of the area, the soils, carved from the igneous bedrock of southern New England, are thin, rocky, and relatively acidic (Figure 4.5).

Within this landscape, limited areas of moist, fertile soils combined with climatic and historical factors have given rise to a region dominated by oak forests. Human impact in what has come to be the most heavily populated region of eastern North America has also favored oaks. Because most oak species resprout from estab-

lished roots, they recover from fire and cutting more effectively than many mesic forest species.

It should also be mentioned that before the accidental introduction of the chestnut blight fungus from Asia in 1904, the American chestnut was perhaps the most common tree of these forests. By 1940, it had virtually disappeared and now remains a part of the landscape only as a shrub resprouting from the base of decaying parent trees. Its place has in large part been taken by a variety of oaks and hickories.

Forest Communities

Oak forests differ dramatically from those of maple, basswood, and beech. Found most often on drier and less fertile soils, their trees are usually shorter and their canopies more open. More sunlight reaches the lower forest layers, creating an environment that is warmer and drier during the summer. The shrub layer is often more continuous; and here in the east at least, the natural acidity of the soils gives rise to shrub thickets of acid-loving heaths like azalea, laurel, and rhododendron. But perhaps the greatest difference is seen in the ground layers. Oak leaves, like pine needles, decompose slowly and produce a heavy litter as well as a humus that is more acidic than that formed under maples and basswoods. In this environment, the species of forest herbs are different, their variety is diminished, and the plants themselves are often more widely spaced.

Mesic Forests   The *mixed mesophytic* forest common in the Appalachian Plateaus is rare in the eastern states. Dependent on moisture and fertile soils, it is found primarily in major valleys, ravines, and the sheltered topography of north-facing slopes. Where it does occur, it is without two of the most characteristic trees of the Appalachian mountains and plateaus. Yellow buckeye grows nowhere east of the Appalachian Front in these states, and white basswood is found only in the valleys of the Virginia Ridge and Valley.

More typical of moist habitat throughout much of the region is the *mesic oak* forest, whose major species include red and white oak, tulip tree, hickory, and only occasionally sugar maple and beech. This is a community which shares many of the characteristics of the mixed forest. Its trees grow tall and form a closed canopy, casting a deep shade. Below a prominent layer of small trees like flowering dogwood, ironwood, and musclewood, the forest is relatively open. Where shade is less intense, shrubs may be prominent; but rarely are they extensive enough to impede walking. The ground layers include a large variety of ferns including the luxuriant cinnamon fern and New York fern (Figures 4.6 and 4.7).

Beyond these structural similarities, however, this forest is easily distinguished from the mixed forest. Because oaks, hickories, and tulip trees reproduce poorly in their own shade, young trees are less common here than in communities of maples and basswoods. While witch hazel, hazelnut, and mapleleaf viburnum grow where the soils are only moderately acidic, mountain laurel and rhododendron

Fig. 4.6   Tall trees and an understory of dogwood characterize the mesic oak forest.

Fig. 4.7   Ground pine grows abundantly in the ground layer of the mesic forest.

Fig. 4.8   The waxy blooms of pyrola are characteristic of the heath herbs.

add a more prominent note of deep green foliage that contrasts sharply with the foliage of the ferns. Most distinctive is the absence of many of the mixed forest's spring flowers, notably spring beauty, Dutchman's-breeches, and trout lily. Much more characteristic of the acidic conditions are the heath species also found in the xeric oak and pine woods: pipsissewa, wintergreen, and pyrola, plants which bloom in early summer and produce small, waxy flowers. The variety of heath species gives an evergreen quality to the forest that is largely missing from the mixed community (Figures 4.8 and 4.9).

Xeric Forests   The *mixed oak* forest, growing on gentle slopes and moderately dry soils, may be the most familiar community in the region. Sharing characteristics of the mesic oak forest and the region's truly xeric communities, its canopy is predominantly oak. Red, white, black, scarlet, and chestnut oaks form a partly open canopy over a layer of dogwood and ironwood. Perhaps most characteristic is the shrub layer. Growing to a height of 15 feet, mountain laurel often forms a nearly impenetrable barrier visually and physically. While the deep green foliage and colorful flowers of the heaths are only suggested in the mesic oak forest, here laurel and the occasional azaleas and rhododendrons dominate the forest, virtually excluding ferns and other herbs over large areas (Figures 4.10 and 4.11).

Fig. 4.9   Spotted wintergreen is a common heath herb in the oak forests.

Fig. 4.10   Mountain laurel forms a dense shrub layer in the mixed oak forest.

Growing in the drier habitat of ridge tops and upper, south-facing slopes is the more xeric *chestnut oak* community. Its trees, primarily the chestnut oak and a few scarlet oaks, black oaks, and pitch pines, are short and widely spaced. Occasionally open-grown and often windswept, the oaks take on a gnarly character. Understory trees are most often merely younger individuals of the canopy species. The dogwoods are notably absent. The shrub layer is more open than in the mixed oak forest. The tall heaths are often replaced by smaller ones like huckleberry and lowbush blueberry and a few nonheaths like bear oak. With increased sunlight, the herbaceous layer is prominent although sparse. Hay-scented fern occasionally forms extensive beds, while bracken fern, moccasin flower, Pennsylvania sedge, and little bluestem occur as scattered individuals (Figures 4.12 and 4.13).

Similar, but growing almost exclusively on sandy soils, is the *pitch pine* forest. Most common on the drained sands of the Coastal Plain and on the outwash plains north of New Jersey, this is an open, often savannalike forest of southern pines and xeric oaks. Blueberry, huckleberry, bear oak, blackjack oak, and other small shrubs form an occasionally dense shrub layer. Many of the ground layer plants found in the chestnut oak community also grow here, although they may cover as little as 10 percent of the ground's surface (Figures 4.14 to 4.16).

Where pine communities are undisturbed for enough time to allow the organic content of the soil to build up, they may slowly be succeeded by xeric oaks. But while succession is theoretically possible, it rarely runs its course. Hot and dry during late summer, the pine forest is susceptible to fire; and unlike many pines, the pitch pine resprouts following fire, quickly reclaiming its place in the forest.

Hydric Forests Most common on the Coastal Plain and the glacial topography of southern New England, *swamp* forests in the east are dominated by red maple and occasionally by Atlantic white cedar. Enriched by southern coastal species like bog asphodel, they are often highly colorful. Where shade is not intense, swamp azalea, sweet pepperbush, great rhododendron, swamp pink, and the luxuriant cinnamon, royal, and chain ferns produce an especially lush and beautiful understory.

More familiar, perhaps, is the *floodplain* forest found along major streams. Like that of the Central Hardwoods Region, it includes sycamore, American elm, silver maple, river birch, and cottonwood. Shrubs like arrowwood, spicebush, and sweet pepperbush form often impassable thickets along the banks, while skunk cabbage, marsh marigold, cardinal flower, and jewelweed grow where water saturates the soil.

The *bog* forest occurs northward and in the region's higher elevations. A relic of the close of the last ice age, it will be discussed later in association with the northern landscape.

Fig. 4.11 *Brilliant mountain laurel flowers and dark foliage make the mixed oak forest one of the most colorful in the east.*

Fig. 4.12 *Thin soils and sparse undergrowth characterize the chestnut oak forest.*

Fig. 4.13 *The chestnut oak ground layer is thin and scattered.*

Fig. 4.14   Mixed pines and oaks form an open canopy in the pitch pine forest of the New Jersey pine barrens.

Fig. 4.15   Low shrubs dominate the lower layers of the pitch pine forest.

Fig. 4.16   Bracken fern and blueberry are common in the lower pine forest layers.

Savanna and Open Communities

Unforested areas are relatively rare here, as they are in the central states. Nevertheless, they can be found throughout the region, especially on dry, thin soils.

The *cedar glade* and the *pine savanna* already described both occur here. The cedar community is especially common on limestone outcroppings in the Ridge and Valley area to the west. The pine community grades into oak and pine forests on the Coastal Plain and the upper slopes of the western ridges. Both are successional stages leading to reforestation in the abandoned fields of the rocky New England uplands.

Grasslands, although more common now than before settlement, are probably the least studied of all of the eastern communities. One grassland community is widespread on the dry, organically poor, sandy soils of southern Connecticut and Long Island. Evaporation and drainage in these areas are severe, and trees and shrubs germinate poorly. Left unshaded, these plains are dominated by little bluestem, a small- to medium-size grass familiar in the dry prairies of the midwest. Where the soil is extremely dry, the grasses are widely spaced and separated by open ground. But where moisture is more adequate, a more complex community of bluestem, sedges, and wildflowers develops. Here, violets, milkweeds, goldenrods, bush clover, yellow wild indigo, and the brilliant butterfly weed provide abundant color throughout the summer.

Similar communities exist from Cape Cod south to the pine barrens of New Jersey and west onto the Piedmont. Where human
activity is relaxed for several years, they can develop even in urban-
ized settings. In Boston, for example, they can be found in vacant
lots and along rail lines (Figure 4.17).

More mesic grasslands are less common, and their survival may
require human intervention. One notable example is the Big Meadows area of Shenandoah National Park. At an elevation of 3000 feet
and growing in the midst of forest, Big Meadows might be expected
to support trees. However, fires set by native Americans to improve
hunting created an open grassland, maintained today by the Park
Service with periodic mowing and burning (Figure 4.18).

Species found at Big Meadows include big bluestem, Indian grass,
wild onion, blazing star, goldenrod, hay-scented fern, blueberry,
and scattered pines. It is not precisely a prairie, lacking many of the
most typical prairie species, but it resembles prairie in its tall
grasses, layers of flowers, and summer-long flowering season. It
resembles prairie, too, in its response to fire; its flowers and grasses
grow and reproduce better following spring burning.

A similar but more xeric grassland has been created at the Connecticut Arboretum in an abandoned field, following several years
of burning to control the invasion of woody plants. Little bluestem
dominates much of the field, along with blueberry and hay-scented
fern. Yellow wild indigo and a variety of other grassland flowers
have introduced themselves successfully (Figure 4.19).

A wet grassland similar to the wet prairie can be found along
streams and in damp, heavy soils. Among its species are Joe-Pye
weed, ironweed, black-eyed Susan, gentian, cardinal flower, aster,
and goldenrod. It grades into a sedge meadow community where
water stands at or slightly above the surface (Figure 4.20).

*Fig. 4.17   Little bluestem is able to
survive in the poor soils of a railroad
right-of-way.*

*Fig. 4.18   In early summer, the mesic
grassland of Big Meadows is carpeted
with wild onion.*

Fig. 4.19 Hay-scented fern and little bluestem characterize the experimental grassland at the Connecticut Arboretum in New London.

Fig. 4.20 A streamside wet grassland supports the tall, colorful Joe-Pye weed and ironweed.

Naturalizing in the Eastern Oak Region

From experiments like that at the Connecticut Arboretum, it appears that open communities can be established within the forested landscape of the east. Grassland species native to the region are varied and surprisingly common. Although the study of these communities has been neglected, experiences at Big Meadows suggest that if they are given periodic mowing or burning, their long-term survival seems assured.

It is equally certain that without such maintenance, the eastern forests will slowly reclaim the land they have lost. On the glacial landscape to the north, vacant fields are being reclaimed by red cedars, gray birch, pitch pine, and white pine. Cedar, pitch pine, and Virginia pine are playing the same role on the Piedmont; dry oaks and pines on the Coastal Plain.

Plantings of the herbs of the mixed mesophytic forest are probably less favored here than in the central states because of the region's geography and climate, but abundant heath species offer an attractive alternative for woodland plantings. Models are widespread and highly varied.

Additional Reading

Introductory

Hunt, Charles B., *Physiography of the United States*, W. H. Freeman, San Francisco, 1967.

Jorgensen, Neil, *A Sierra Club Naturalist's Guide to Southern New England*, Sierra Club Books, San Francisco, 1978.

Robichaud, Beryl, and Murray F. Buell, *Vegetation of New Jersey: A Study of Landscape Diversity*, Rutgers University Press, New Brunswick, N.J., 1973.

Detailed

Bard, Gily E., "Secondary Succession on the Piedmont of New Jersey," *Ecological Monographs* 22:195–215, 1952.

Braun, E. Lucy, *Deciduous Forests of Eastern North America*, Hafner, New York, 1967.

Britton, Wilton Everett, "Vegetation of the North Haven Sand Plains," *Bulletin of the Torrey Botanical Club* 30:571–619, 1903.

Cain, Stanley A., Mary Nelson, and Walter McLean, "*Andropogon Hemsteadi*: A Long Island Grassland Vegetation Type," *American Midland Naturalist* 18:334–350, 1937.

Davidson, Donald W., and Murray F. Buell, "Shrub and Herb Continua of Upland Forests of Northern New Jersey," *American Midland Naturalist* 77:371–389, 1967.

Greller, Andrew M., "A Classification of Mature Forests on Long Island, New York," *Bulletin of the Torrey Botanical Club* 104:376–382, 1977.

Little, Silas, and Robert T. Escheman, "Nineteen-Year Changes in the Composition of a Stand of *Pinus taeda* in Eastern Maryland," *Bulletin of the Torrey Botanical Club* 103:57–66, 1976.

Niering, William A., "The Past and Present Vegetation of Highpoint State Park, New Jersey," *Ecological Monographs* 23:127–148, 1953.

Olmsted, Charles E., "Vegetation of Certain Sand Plains of Connecticut," *Botanical Gazette* 99:209–300, 1937.

Wales, Bruce A., "Vegetational Analysis of North and South Edges of a Mature Oak-Hickory Forest," *Ecological Monographs* 42:451–471, 1972.

chapter five

The Midwestern Prairie–Oak Region

Figuratively and in a sense literally, the Rocky Mountains cast a shadow over the great plains. Presenting a natural barrier to storms moving eastward from the Pacific Ocean, and stripping them of moisture, the Rockies create a rain shadow on their lee side that is too arid to support large areas of forest.

The upper midwest lies on the fringe of this shadow. Its annual precipitation averages less than 35 inches, and drought is common. Within this climate, the extensive forest of the eastern states reaches its western borders, and isolated islands of forest alternate with a mixture of savanna and grassland (Figure 5.1).

The region's geography complements its climate. Lying entirely within the Central Lowlands, much of it was glaciated during the last ice age. North of the glacial border, much of the land has been left level by glacial deposits as much as 200 feet deep. Its plains are broken by few valleys that might offer shelter to forests. Low hills formed by glacial drumlins, eskers, and moraines, scattered across the landscape, are its major elevations. Glacial debris has, however, provided soils that are deep and fertile (Figures 5.2 and 5.3).

Although glaciated during earlier ice ages, the landscape south of the limit reached by the last glaciers has had longer to develop. Streams cut more deeply and regularly into its surface, and the land is more rolling. Wetlands and lakes common to the north are less prominent.

A major exception to the general topography of the region is the Driftless Area of southwestern Wisconsin. An ancient landscape

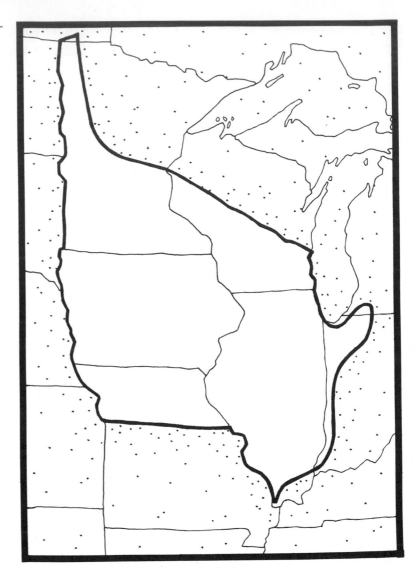

Fig. 5.1 The Midwestern Prairie–Oak Region.

untouched by glaciation, it is dissected by deep ravines and broad valleys. Its upper slopes often are covered only with a thin mantle of soil, in places too shallow to hide the bedrock. Heavier, deeper soils line the valley bottoms. Areas of slowly moving or standing water are uncommon (Figure 5.4).

The midwest, consequently, is a transitional region between the rich deciduous forests to the east and the arid grasslands to the west. Many deciduous species of trees reach the limits of their range within these states. Beech grows only in a narrow band along the western shores of Lake Michigan. Sugar maple reaches its western limits in Iowa and Minnesota; basswood and the oaks in eastern

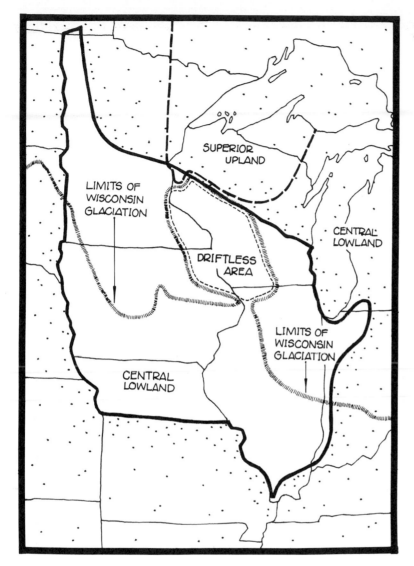

Fig. 5.2 The major geographic divisions of the region.

Nebraska. Within this area, grasslands begin to play the dominant role that forests do in the east, growing naturally on all types of topography. The mixture of communities that results is both rich and varied.

Open Communities

Before the settlement of the midwest in the early nineteenth century, the predominant vegetation was prairie rather than the forests easterners knew. Settlers faced a great sea of grasses, which may have contributed to their reluctance to move westward. It was a

Fig. 5.3 *The rare prairie landscape today suggests the appearance of much of the glaciated portion of the region prior to 1800.*

Fig. 5.4 *The forested slopes of the Driftless Area offer a contrast to the plains. Note the steep slopes of the ridges in the background.*

common belief as little as a century and a half ago that land which did not support trees was too poor to farm.

Today, the rich corn fields of the midwest tell us something different. The deep, black prairie soil is depleted far more slowly than forest soil, and while erosion has carried away perhaps half of it, the soil remains fertile.

That these qualities were not appreciated only six generations ago tells us how unusual natural grasslands are in the world. They were almost entirely foreign to the Europeans who first explored the interior of the continent. Unfortunately, they remain foreign today as well. So complete has been the change from grassland to farm that few midwesterners know what a prairie is. The term is used to describe weedy, abandoned pasturelands which share no species with prairies and the flat topography of the plains themselves. Few virgin prairies remain, but their brilliant flowers and graceful grasses form communities of unmistakable beauty and variety.

Mesic Prairies Growing on level or gently rolling terrain with deep, rich, and moist but well-drained soils, the *mesic prairie* was perhaps the most representative plant community of the midwest less than two centuries ago. In it, trees and shrubs play a minor role. Grasses, covering more than half of the ground's surface, are its true dominants. Most characteristic are the tall grasses like big bluestem and Indian grass, whose seed stalks may reach head height by late summer. Midsize grasses like little bluestem and northern dropseed are less common, usually growing between dense stands of the taller species.

The microclimate of the mesic prairie contrasts sharply with that of the forest. Shade is important in it only relatively close to the ground under the foliage of the grasses. High humidity is often limited to these lower layers as well. As little as two feet off the ground, the hot summer sun and prairie winds reduce moisture well below that found in most forests.

But perhaps its greatest difference from the forest is that its dominant species die back every fall and must begin growth from the ground up each spring. This fact gives the mesic prairie a dramatically different visual quality with each season.

During the spring, the mesic prairie is a sea of flowers. Because most of its grasses are warm season species, reserving their most vigorous growth for the summer months, they are relatively short and inconspicuous in April and May. Small, spring-flowering nongrasses (called *forbs*, not herbs as in the forest) consequently seem to dominate. Among them, shooting star, puccoon, violets, and lousewort produce a carpet of color rivaling that of the mixed mesophytic forest in spring (Figures 5.5 to 5.6)

Summer is the season in which most mesic species bloom. In the forests, 70 percent of the plants flower during the spring; in the mesic prairie, 50 percent from June to August. Coneflowers, blazing stars, rattlesnake master, black-eyed Susan, compass plant, and prairie dock enliven the landscape with a show of colors the forest cannot equal. Flowering species change continually, with as many as two new species coming into bloom each day. In places, blooms may be so conspicuous that they overshadow the foliage of the

Fig. 5.5 *The mesic prairie in early May is a carpet of shooting stars, puccoon, violet, and lousewort.*

Fig. 5.6 *Spring forbs like shooting star overtop the grasses.*

Fig. 5.7   A prominent colony of bedstraw and a few taller forbs like spiderwort and phlox overshadow the still-short early summer grasses.

Fig. 5.8   By midsummer, both the grasses and forbs are taller. Here the prominence of finely textured grasses gives the prairie a quiet, graceful quality.

Fig. 5.9   The coarse leaves of the prairie dock and a mixture of tall sunflowers give the prairie a busy quality that contrasts sharply with the preceding photograph.

Fig. 5.10   A single aster nestles in a sea of late summer grasses.

grasses. This is especially true of species like bedstraw and coreopsis, which form dense, prominent colonies. Elsewhere, flowers may add only a highlight of color to the greens of the grasses. Many of the summer forbs are taller than those of spring, and this, combined with the growth of the grasses, gives the community a sense of great luxuriance (Figures 5.7 to 5.9).

By late summer, the grasses begin to form seedstalks. Late summer forbs like the asters, goldenrods, and sunflowers nestle among them, occasionally hidden from view. In contrast to the brilliant colors of summer, the prairie of late August and September is delicately subdued. The subtle pastels of the grasses blend softly, and even the relatively small flowers of the asters and gentians stand out prominently (Figure 5.10).

By November, the flowering season is over, but the quiet colors of late summer remain. The fall colors of the grasses rival the leaves of the deciduous forest, turning gold, yellow, and deep bronze. Against these colors, the dark shapes of the dried stalks and leaves of many forbs catch the eye. Many of the prairie plants remain standing through the winter, ornamenting the snow as effectively as do the evergreen species of the forest (Figure 5.11).

Xeric Prairies   Found on dry sands and on steep slopes with thin, often stony soils, the *dry prairie* is less luxuriant than the mesic community and has a higher proportion of diminutive species. Indian grass and big bluestem may both grow here, but often as widely scattered individual plants. The smaller grasses like little bluestem, side oats grama, and northern dropseed are more typical. On the driest sites, growth of all species may be restrained, and plants may be separated by patches of bare soil.

Fig. 5.11   The seed heads of little bluestem sparkle in the sun throughout the fall and winter.

Fig. 5.12   The dry prairie pasqueflower blooms early in April just as the grasses break their dormancy.

Fig. 5.13   Distinct clumps of short grasses are typical of the dry prairie.

Fig. 5.14   Dwarf blazing star, asters, and scattered grasses give a rock-garden quality to the late summer dry limestone prairie.

Such a description is deceptive. Like all prairies, the dry community is highly colorful. Because its soils dry out and warm up quickly in spring, the dry prairie blooms earlier than most other plant communities. The showy pasqueflower may flower even before the grasses break their winter dormancy. Prairie smoke, bird's-foot violet, pussytoes, and prairie buttercup follow shortly after. Butterfly weed is prominent in early summer along with phlox and puccoon. Blazing star and coreopsis bloom in midsummer. With fall, the asters, gentians, and goldenrods stand out more prominently than among the tall grasses of the mesic prairie. Even on the rocky soil of limestone hillsides, the community resembles a rock garden, rivaling the mountain meadows in its brilliance (Figures 5.12 to 5.14).

Hydric Prairies   Growing where the water table is high but where soils are not saturated or inundated during the summer, the *wet prairie* like the others is highly colorful. Its dominant plants are

Fig. 5.15 *The dense vegetation of the midsummer wet prairie includes Turk's-cap lily, bergamot, and black-eyed Susan and rivals the mesic prairie for color.*

Fig. 5.16 *Ohio goldenrod and lesser fringed gentian abound in late summer in the moist, alkaline environment of the fen.*

tall grasses, including big bluestem, switch grass, cordgrass, and bluejoint grass. Because the community's soils are wet and slow to warm up in spring, there is little early blooming. Given an abundance of moisture, a number of species not found in the other prairie communities grow here. Among them are such showy plants as Turk's-cap lily, swamp milkweed, and, on the wettest sites, blue flag iris. A number of woodland species can also grow, including wild geranium, wood anemone, wild leek, and trout lily. As in the eastern grasslands, ferns and shrubs may mix with prairie species where there is a continual supply of moisture or where topography provides some shelter (Figure 5.15).

On the wettest soils, where the water table is level with the ground's surface, the wet prairie grades into a sedge meadow community similar to that described in earlier chapters. Cordgrass and bluejoint grass grow in both, as do Joe-Pye weed, Canada anemone, and meadow rue. But distinguishing between the two communities are the prominent hummocks of sedges which give the meadow the appearance of a landscape dotted with islands.

Under highly specialized conditions, a last hydric grassland occurs here and eastward into New York and Ontario: the *fen*. Prairielike and sharing many of the wet prairie grasses and forbs, it is distinctive in at least two respects. Unlike the prairie and more like the meadow, the fen has a deep peaty soil. Critically for its existence, it is also supplied by highly alkaline water welling up from underground. As a consequence, it supports a number of species, including grass-of-Parnassus, not found in the wet prairie (Figure 5.16).

Savanna Communities

Communities of scattered trees and a grassy ground cover were a prominent part of the midwestern landscape prior to the nineteenth century. The *cedar glade* community is still common on the steep upper slopes and limestone cliffs of the Driftless Area and on the limestone gravels of glacial hills. It also grows on well-drained sandy plains. Its ground layer species are primarily those of the dry prairie. On slopes and cliffs, white birch may join the cedars, its bark standing out brightly against the dark foliage of the cedars (Figure 5.17).

More common before settlement, however, was the *oak opening*, a savanna whose trees are primarily bur, black, and white oaks. A century ago, the community ranged across the moisture spectrum, growing on wet, mesic, and dry sites. It has been suggested that, like the prairies, the openings were maintained by fire. The bur oak and to a lesser degree the other oaks are relatively fire-resistant. The thick, corky bark of the bur would have protected it against the fires common on the prairie during the hot, dry midwestern summers, while less resistant species would have been killed. Supporting the fire theory, the oak openings have largely disappeared from the landscape with the control of fires, and have been transformed into forests (Figures 5.18 and 5.19).

Fig. 5.17   The scattered trees of the cedar glades dot sandy outwash plains and limestone hillsides.

Fig. 5.18 The scattered groves of bur oaks are typical of the oak opening. Note the absence of shrubs beneath these trees.

Fig. 5.19 The trees may be denser where the savanna is protected from fire. Here, shrubs and woodland herbs blend with the prairie flora.

The openings that remain are a mixture of woodland and grassland species distributed in accord with the community's pattern of alternating sunlight and shade. The trees may grow as scattered groves or as orchards of individual trees. Unlike cedars, the oaks form distinctive crowns and are open beneath, preserving more of the sense of open prairie. The gnarled, open-grown oaks are rugged and picturesque, especially in winter when their branches are bare.

While prairie forbs and grasses dominate the ground layer, woodland plants may also be prominent. In light shade, oak forest species like gray dogwood, hazelnut, and Virginia creeper mix with prairie

Fig. 5.20   Here a mesic basswood forest grows at the bottom of a north slope. Shrubs are inconspicuous in the shade of the basswoods, but there is a continuous bed of trout lilies.

Fig. 5.21   A mass of mayapples and anemones carpets the floor of this maple–basswood forest.

species like the bluestems, leadplant, puccoon, and bird's-foot violet. In sunlight, wild geranium, columbine, and false Solomon's-seal may grow alongside prairie clovers, lupines, and goldenrods.

Forest Communities

As suggested earlier, a number of the major deciduous trees approach the limits of their ranges before reaching the arid western plains. In contrast, many of the forest herbs range widely through much of the midwest.

On sheltered north slopes and in ravines, a mesic *maple–basswood* forest community contains many of the herbs found in the mixed mesophytic forests of the Appalachians. Trout lilies, bloodroot, hepatica, Dutchman's-breeches, toothwort, and others grow on the most fertile sites beneath a canopy of American basswood, sugar maple, red and white oak, and, along the shores of Lake Michigan, beech. Best developed on the protected slopes of the Driftless Area, this community also occurs in the glaciated sections of the region, but it is common nowhere. As if suggesting its tenuous place in this region, the height of the canopy gradually decreases from east to west, reaching only 50 to 60 feet in northwestern Minnesota (Figures 5.20 and 5.21).

More widespread is the more xeric *oak–hickory* community found most often on south and west slopes and on the thin sand or gravel soils of hilltops and ridges. In a sense, its name is misleading. North of the line reached by the last ice sheets, the trees are predominantly a mix of bur, black, white, and red oaks with only occasional shagbark hickories. Southward, however, southern species like mockernut hickory and pignut hickory are major canopy species.

Fig. 5.22 *Dry oak forests are typical of gentle southwest slopes in the Driftless Area. Woody undergrowth is abundant.*

Like the eastern oak forests, this is one of moderate shade and prominent shrubs. Rather than heath shrubs, however, nonheaths like gray dogwood, hazelnut, bittersweet, gooseberry, and red and black raspberry form a sometimes impenetrable, often prickly lower layer. Herbaceous heaths are also uncommon. More numerous are such familiar species as false Solomon's-seal, hog peanut, Pennsylvania sedge, and enchanter's nightshade (Figures 5.22 and 5.23).

The two wetland forests of this region, the *floodplain* and *hardwood swamp* communities, resemble those of the central states. In the floodplain forest, river birch, cottonwood, swamp white oak, silver maple, and American elm are the major canopy species, while vines like wild grape, Virginia creeper, and poison ivy are common. Sycamore and southern species like pin oak, sour gum, and sweet gum are rare in the northern and western parts of the region (Figure 5.24).

Naturalizing in the Midwestern Prairie–Oak Region

For the landscaper who prefers unshaded park or yard, the midwest offers perhaps the greatest selection of native communities of any region in eastern North America. Like the forests to the east, these prairie communities range across the moisture scale. Their variety and beauty make them an attractive alternative to lawn.

Fig. 5.23 *Sedge and false Solomon's-seal are prominent in the understory of the oak forest. Note the absence of heath species common in the eastern oak forests.*

Fig. 5.24 *Floodplain forests are inundated in early spring. Here the river bluffs of the Mississippi rise abruptly in the background.*

Interest in them has also led to a thriving prairie nursery business, making both seeds and plants readily available.

Here, too, savannas offer choice and practicality. Savanna communities lend themselves to a variety of sites, from xeric hilltops to moist bottoms. But even in the midwest's dry climate, they, like the prairies, do require some annual cutting to keep them open and unforested.

Unlike the regions to the east, in the midwest it is the forest communities that may offer limited choice. Forests with a rich spring flora are relatively uncommon and, given the climate, often difficult to establish. The xeric forests, on the other hand, lack the beautiful eastern heaths. Xeric oak-hickory communities can, however be established throughout much of the region with good results. And lacking some of the eastern flora, they compensate with the bur oak, a gnarled, rugged, highly picturesque species that is rare in the east.

Additional Reading

Introductory

Hunt, Charles B., *Physiography of the United States*, W. H. Freeman, San Francisco, 1967.

Thomson, Betty Flanders, *The Shaping of America's Heartland*, Houghton-Mifflin, Boston, 1977.

Detailed

Aikman, J. M., and A. W. Smelser, "The Structure and Environment of Forest Communities in Central Iowa," *Ecology* 19:141–150, 1938.

Bliss, L. C., and George W. Cox, "Plant Community and Soil Variation within a Northern Indiana Prairie," *American Midland Naturalist* 72:115–128, 1964.

Braun, E. Lucy, *Deciduous Forests of Eastern North America*, Hafner, New York, 1967.

Bray, J. Roger, "Climax Forest Herbs in Prairie," *American Midland Naturalist* 58:434–440, 1957.

Bray, J. Roger, "The Composition of Savanna Vegetation in Wisconsin," *Ecology* 41:721–732, 1960.

Bushey, Charles L., and Robbin C. Moran, "Vascular Flora of Shaw Prairie, Lake County, Illinois," *Transactions of the Illinois State Academy of Science* 71:427–435, 1978.

Curtis, John T., *The Vegetation of Wisconsin: An Ordination of Plant Communities*, University of Wisconsin Press, Madison, 1971.

Drew, William B., "Floristic Composition of Grazed and Ungrazed Prairie Vegetation in North–Central Missouri," *Ecology* 28:26–41, 1947.

Glenn-Lewin, David C., "The Vegetation of Stinson Prairie, Kossuth County, Iowa," *Proceedings of the Iowa Academy of Science* 83:88–93, 1976.

Kucera, C. L., and John H. Ehrenreich, "Some Effects of Annual Burning on Central Missouri Prairie," *Ecology* 43:334–336, 1962.

Old, Sylvia M., "Microclimate, Fire, and Plant Production in an Illinois Prairie," *Ecological Monographs* 39:355–384, 1969.

Peet, Robert K., and Orie L. Loucks, "A Gradient Analysis of Southern Wisconsin Forests," *Ecology* 58:485–499, 1977.

Sorensen, Paul D., "The Williams Prairie: A Prairie Relict in Johnson County," *Proceedings of the Iowa Academy of Science* 69:45–53, 1962.

Woodard, John, "Factors Influencing the Distribution of Tree Vegetation in Champaign County, Illinois," *Ecology* 6:150–156, 1925.

DURHAM AGRICULTURAL
COLLEGE LIBRARY BOOK

chapter six

The Northern Conifer-Hardwoods Region

C limatic patterns change appreciably from one end of this elongated region to the other. Eastward, precipitation averages as much as 40 inches per year in parts of the New England upland. To the west, it declines to as little as 20 inches in northwestern Minnesota. But while parallel changes to the south result in a transition from forest to grassland, here forests are the dominant natural vegetation across the region (Figure 6.1).

Fig. 6.1   The Northern Conifer–Hardwoods Region.

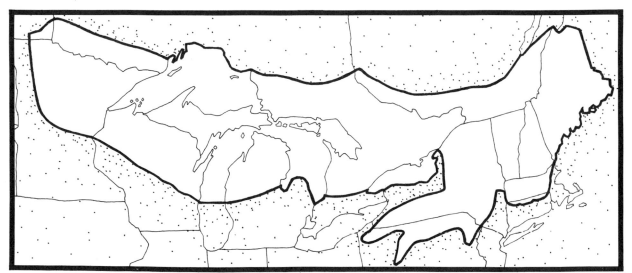

DURHAM AGRICULTURAL
COLLEGE LIBRARY BOOK

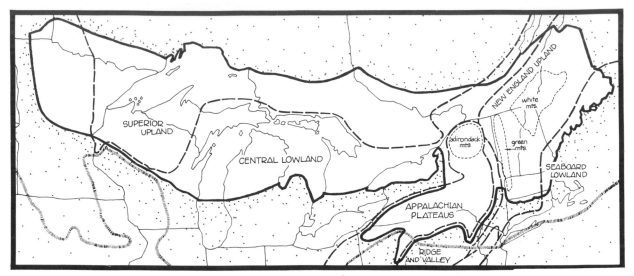

Fig. 6.2 The major geographic divisions of the region.

At least a part of the explanation is related not to precipitation itself, but rather to temperature. Within this region, temperatures average as much as 20 degrees below those to the south. Summers are shorter and often cooler; winters long and frequently bitterly cold. As a result, relatively little of the precipitation that falls is lost to evaporation. The climate even in the northwest, therefore, is generally moist and favorable to trees.

In this northern climate, evergreen trees like pine, hemlock, and spruce are conspicuous, and so too are smaller evergreen species like trailing arbutus, bearberry, leatherleaf, and Labrador tea. Nevertheless, pure or even predominantly evergreen forests are an exception. More characteristic are forests of mixed coniferous and deciduous species. Sugar maple, beech, American basswood, and red oak dominate many of the northern forests in mixture with hemlock and pine. Ground layers are also mixed. Patches of southern forest herbs like squirrel corn, Dutchman's-breeches, and white trout lily alternate with areas of Canada mayflower, Clintonia, and wintergreen.

Here as elsewhere, the landscape of the region affects the distribution of plant life. In a sense, the entire region can be regarded as a single, glacial province. With the exception of the southernmost tip in Pennsylvania, all of it was buried in glacial ice during the last ice age. Glacial deposits still fill ancient valleys and drainageways, blocking the flow of water and creating innumerable lakes and wetlands. In scattered locations, glacial outwash and the beaches of glacial lakes form dry sand plains and low sand hills. In other areas, glacial debris has created steep gravel hills or flats of fine glacial soils (Figures 6.2 and 6.3).

Yet several geographic divisions stand out. Perhaps the most

Fig. 6.4 The more rugged, mountainous terrain is found in the Superior Upland and in the eastern highlands.

prominent of these lie in the east, where the upper extent of the Appalachians creates a broad formation of highlands, encompassing the Adirondack Mountains in northern New York and the White Mountains and Green Mountains in New England. The elevation in these areas is sufficient to bring the cold northern climate far south of its customary latitudes. On their upper slopes, temperatures shape vegetation more than soil and topography do, favoring boreal forests of spruce and fir.

West of the Appalachians, much of the region lies in the Central Lowlands, and mountainous areas are few. Only the Superior

Fig. 6.5 *Flat plains are characteristic of the Central Lowlands division of the region.*

Upland provides areas of appreciable elevation: the Porcupine and Huron Mountains. But even here, elevations are not sufficient to affect climate significantly (Figures 6.4 and 6.5).

Much more influential are the Great Lakes. Moderating winter temperatures, they also provide the moisture for the deep winter snows favorable to boreal communities. Complementing these winter effects, the lakes also cool the summer landscape as far as 20 miles inland, providing an environment suitable for northern species.

While climate favors the growth of forest in this region, the combined influence of climate and topography ensures a mixture of northern and southern elements. Severe climate northward, as well as the effects of elevation to the east and the Great Lakes to the west, creates a habitat for spruce and fir. More moderate climate southward, as well as the lower mountain valleys, provides an environment for deciduous species. Between these extremes, mixed forests of conifers and hardwoods cover much of the region.

Forest Communities

The cool northern climate and the abundant precipitation of the highlands to the east favor mesic forests over those better suited to xeric and hydric environments. Nevertheless, all of these forest communities are well represented. Widespread wetlands, lending themselves poorly to agriculture, have remained relatively unimpaired following settlement. Drier communities, suited to the recolonization of lands that have been burned or cut over, have perhaps benefited from settlement, probably covering more land now than a century ago.

Mesic Forests The most widespread forest of this region is one of sugar maple, beech, yellow birch, American basswood, and hemlock. Growing best on deep, loamy soils, this *mixed hemlock–hardwood* community can develop wherever the topography is not extreme. It is limited primarily by excessive moisture and by the severe exposure of higher altitudes.

In general, this is an open forest in the lower layers. The deep shade cast by the canopy species confines understory trees and shrubs to openings created by the loss of mature canopy trees. In such areas, however, a multitude of shrubs struggle for advantage, including witch hazel, alternate-leaf dogwood, round-leaved dogwood, hazelnut, mountain maple, striped maple, and rhododendron (eastward) (Figures 6.6 and 6.7).

As further south, the leaves of the hardwoods decompose relatively quickly in this community, improving the texture and nutrient content of the soil. Thus, while acidic soils are common in the north, areas long dominated by hardwoods often have a rich humus nearly neutral in pH. Here, many of the spring ephemerals and other early blooming herbs of the rich southern forests create a sea of color before the canopy leafs out. Toothwort, bloodroot, Dutchman's-breeches, bishop's cap, large-flowered trillium, wild ginger, squirrel corn, and white trout lily form a ground layer as colorful as that in the mixed mesophytic forest of the central states. A luxuriant growth of ferns dominates the ground in summer, among them maidenhair, Goldie's fern, silvery spleenwort, sensitive fern, and rattlesnake fern (Figure 6.8).

In contrast, where aging pines or hemlocks are prevalent, the soil is more often covered with a thick layer of needles and is usually

Fig. 6.6 The dense shade in a mixed forest of hemlock and hardwoods keeps the lower forest layers open.

Fig. 6.7 The openness of the forest and the hemlock are both more apparent in the fall and winter after the deciduous species have lost their leaves.

Fig. 6.8 Lush undergrowth is
characteristic of areas dominated by
hardwoods.

strongly acidic. In these areas, northern species like mayflower, twisted-stalk, bluebead lily, starflower, club mosses, wood sorrel, partridgeberry, bunchberry, painted trillium, and crested fern predominate. Their numbers are relatively low in comparison with the herbs of the southern mesic forests, and individual plants are often spaced widely (Figure 6.9).

Given the heavy shade cast by the canopy, changes in these forests over time require openings in the canopy. Few tree species are able to invade and establish themselves without disturbances created by wind, fire, or humankind. Changes over distance, on the other hand, are notable. Across the length of the region, a number of the dominant species reach the limits of their range. Beech, for example, grows nowhere west of extreme eastern Wisconsin. Hemlock and yellow birch reach their limits near the Wisconsin-Minnesota border. As a consequence, the western forests are fewer in tree species than those to the east and are more clearly dominated by two species: basswood and sugar maple. To the east, maple decreases in number relative to beech. Red spruce, mountain laurel, and rhododendron also become prominent.

A second mesic forest, the *boreal* community, occurs on sites where the local climate is significantly cooler than that of surrounding areas. Generally limited to the northern half of the region, such sites include the shores of the Great Lakes and the slopes of the eastern highlands above 3500 feet.

The dominant trees of this community include white spruce (increasing to the north and west), red spruce (increasing to the east), balsam fir, yellow birch, white birch, and smaller numbers of hemlock, maple, and beech. The forest is typically dark and undergrowth is sparse. Openings, however, are common throughout the

Fig. 6.9 Under groves of hemlocks, the ground layer is sparse and open.

Fig. 6.10 *On deep, moist soils, the boreal forest is dense and sometimes impassable.*

Fig. 6.11 *On thinner and drier rocky soils, the boreal forest is open, cool, and inviting.*

forest, and in these beaked hazelnut, hobblebush (eastward), mountain holly (eastward), and saplings of the hardwoods form thickets (Figures 6.10 and 6.11).

The ground layer resembles those of hemlock-dominated forests. Mosses are prominent, as are mayflower, wood sorrel, and spinulose wood fern. Bluebead lily, naked miterwort, blueberry, wild sarsaparilla, and twinflower are common but less numerous. Absent are the southern forest herbs like Dutchman's-breeches and trout lily (Figure 6.12).

Xeric Forests Perhaps more typically associated with the north are the *pine forest* communities which once formed the foundation for a major lumbering industry. Their habitat is primarily dry, sterile, sandy soils, where jack pine may be the dominant species in the west and white pine in the east. A richer community of red and white pines, white birch, red oak, and red maple may also develop on more moist and fertile soils of sand and loam.

The young pine forest is often a dense growth of young, even-age trees and numerous shrubs. But as the forest matures, the pines lose their lower branches and competition thins out the trees, leaving a forest that is relatively light and parklike (Figures 6.13 and 6.14).

In this developing forest, colonies of bracken fern or, eastward, hay-scented fern may cover large areas. Elsewhere, shrubs may be

Fig. 6.12 *The boreal ground layer is diverse where light and moisture permit.*

Fig. 6.13 *The pine forest is often open, littered with needles, and carpeted with bracken fern.*

Fig. 6.14 *In suitable environments, hardwoods like maple form a dense understory of small trees and shrubs below a canopy of pines.*

Fig. 6.15 *Round-leaved dogwood adds its modest flowers and beautiful foliage to the rich pine forest.*

more prominent. Flowering shrubs like shadbush, hazelnut, and mountain laurel (eastward) add a show of color to the tall shrub layer. Blueberry, partridgeberry, and bearberry form a berry-laden lower layer (Figure 6.15).

Underfoot, mats of mosses and needles form a spongy carpet in which the delicate, waxy blooms of pipsissewa and wintergreen mix with the more showy moccasin flower, fringed polygala, painted trillium, and bluebead lily. Bunchberry, clubmosses, and mayflower often form a continuous ground cover (Figures 6.16 and 6.17).

Despite the acidic nature and slow decomposition of pine needles, the quality of the soil in these forests improves slowly over time, as does the general moisture and humidity of the community. As the forest ages, therefore, changes in its composition occur. In the dry jack pine forest, white pines, birch, red maple, and red oak may eventually replace the shade-intolerant jack pine given a favorable environment. In the richer white pine forest, sugar maple, beech, and hemlock often develop as a dense thicket beneath a towering canopy of aged pine. Here, the graceful cinnamon and royal ferns may form large colonies. The age of the pines and the undergrowth of mesic species foreshadow the development of a mixed forest of hemlocks and hardwoods on favorable sites and in the absence of disturbance.

Hydric Forests

Floodplain forests, which develop in areas subject to annual siltation, are relatively uncommon here. But where water is essentially motionless, the *conifer swamp* forest (the bog forest) develops in the peat at the water's edge.

This is a dark evergreen forest of black spruce, tamarack, balsam fir, white pine, jack pine (westward), and white cedar (especially where runoff from the uplands is only moderately acidic). Its understory is dominated by heath shrubs and herbs like Labrador tea, leatherleaf, bog laurel, blueberries, cranberries, and wintergreen. Boreal herbs like bunchberry and bluebead lily are also prominent. Although most of its species are small-flowered and most blooming occurs in the spring when the community is relatively inaccessible, the community is nevertheless appealing in its variety of native orchids and numerous berry-producing shrubs (Figures 6.18 and 6.19).

Savanna and Open Communities

Areas of infertile, sandy soils occur throughout the north. They tend to be droughty, and fires have until recently been routine events, burning off accumulations of organic materials and perpetuating the sterility of the soil. In such habitat, the *pine barren* community of scattered pines, scrub oaks, and aspens has become a fixture of the landscape.

Unlike the southern oak savannas in which the trees preserve a relatively unobstructed view of the land, this northern savanna is more often closed. The low-branching character of the open-grown pines and the shrubby Hill's and black oaks form visual barriers, giving the barrens an atmosphere of privacy and enclosure.

Fig. 6.16   Mosses and heath species like pipsissewa are characteristic of the pine ground layer.

Fig. 6.17   Bunchberry, a relative of the dogwoods, carpets the pine forest floor with its familiar leaves and berries.

Fig. 6.18   The conifer swamp is often dense and spongy underfoot.

Fig. 6.19 *Thick-leaved heaths like Labrador tea dominate the swamp shrub layer.*

Sheltered by the pines in winter, warming early in spring, and hot and dry in summer, the openings between trees are grassy and bear a resemblance to the dry prairies to the south. Enhancing that resemblance are a number of prairie species, including the big and little bluestem grasses, puccoon, lupine, wild indigo, butterfly weed, wild strawberry, aster, and goldenrod. The blooms of these plants give the community a flowering season that continues from early spring through fall (Figure 6.20).

But distinguishing this from the prairies and marking it as a northern community are species like the low blueberries, sweet fern, bracken fern, and hay-scented fern (eastward). These species form distinctive, often circular colonies in both sun and light shade, lending a hint of parklike formality to the community.

This is a community that normally requires periodic catastrophe to perpetuate itself. Protected from cutting or fire, it often fills in gradually with young trees, eventually developing into a dry pine or aspen forest (Figure 6.21).

Relatively unstudied is a second savanna community that develops where fire has destroyed the mixed hemlock–hardwoods forest. Its trees can include any that have escaped burning, including understory species like shadbush. The ground layer includes a large proportion of forest herbs like the club mosses, bunchberry, and wintergreen, while bracken fern and hay-scented fern may form extensive colonies. These woodland species may persist, because the abundant moisture of these sites compensates for the absence of shade. While such savannas seem likely to return to forest with time, examples burned over as many as 70 years ago remain open and parklike in Allegheny National Forest (Figure 6.22).

Fig. 6.20 *In this western jack pine barren, tall prairie grasses like big bluestem mix with young pines.*

Similarly unstudied and occurring on soils ranging from moist loam to sand is the *bracken grassland*. While the community often develops following fire, trees are slow to invade even when protected from burning. Thus, grassland species like ricegrass, bromegrass, June grass, and poverty grass dominate the community along with blueberry, sweet fern, bracken fern, and sedges. Asters, goldenrods, and a number of woodland herbs like wintergreen may also develop (Figure 6.23).

A variety of explanations have been offered for the resistance of these last two communities to invasion by trees. It has been suggested that they develop in areas subject to late spring frosts,

Fig. 6.21 In this barrens community, young pines protected from fire have grown up. In their shade, sedges and bracken fern have begun to replace the grasses.

Fig. 6.22 This hardwoods savanna in the Allegheny National Forest developed after a forest fire early in the century. Ground layer plants include a mixture of grasses, ferns, and forest herbs.

Fig. 6.23 Bracken grassland resembles the pine barrens but is free of the shade of pines and other tree species. Here, goldenrods, bluestem, and sweet fern mix.

Fig. 6.24 *This bog in northern Minnesota borders on open water and is ringed by a dense conifer swamp.*

Fig. 6.25 *The insectivorous sundew is a common species of many bogs.*

although both do occur in areas not subject to unusually cold temperatures. A second explanation is that some of their species are toxic to tree seedlings. Among them are the common hay-scented fern, sweet fern, bracken fern, and pearly everlasting.

A final open community, the *northern bog*, is both more common and more studied. Bog communities occur primarily north and east of a line that extends from the Minnesota–Canada border to the tip of Lake Michigan and east to the Atlantic. They can be found occasionally further south on glacial or mountain topography.

Bog habitat is a mat of undecomposed plant materials, usually sphagnum moss, that develops over cold, nutrient-poor, highly acidic water. Rainfall in excess of evaporation is usually necessary as well, because the bog mat requires a source of moisture low in calcium. Calcium-rich (alkaline) waters cause peaty bog mats to disintegrate.

The vegetation of the bog environment often reflects zones correlated to the depth of the peat supporting it. On the pioneer mat at the water's edge is a loose network of floating herbs and rhizomatous species which bounces underfoot. As the distance from the water's edge increases, the plant composition becomes much like that of a wet meadow. On a relatively firm peat surface, though possibly still floating on the water, is a zone of heath species including Labrador tea. Here, living sphagnum is a dominant feature of the bog, and tamaracks may occur as scattered individuals. Growing to a height of perhaps 35 feet, the trees are subject to windthrow. Their fallen trunks are conspicuous in the bog community and add to the accumulation of debris on which the community develops (Figure 6.24).

Furthest from the water's edge is a bog forest zone similar to the conifer swamp community. The maximum tree cover is about 60 to 70 percent of the surface area. In its shade, bog shrubs are few and forest ground layer species may appear on hummocks raised above water level.

Occasionally, at the upland edge of the bog, a moat of marsh rather than bog species also develops. Where it occurs, it is supported by relatively neutral or alkaline water draining from the mineral soils of the upland.

Although the environment of the bog may sound unappealing, bogs are of major interest because of the species uniquely suited to them. Chief among these are native orchids and carnivorous species like sundew and pitcher plant (Figures 6.25 and 6.26).

Naturalizing in the Northern Conifer–Hardwoods Region

The forests native to this region offer abundant landscaping models. The dense shade cast by hemlock and spruce creates an open forest that is cool, quiet, and tranquil. The pine forests, though still open below, are less dark. The hardwood forests with their lush undergrowth and abundance of spring flowers offer a dramatic contrast.

The climate of the region makes the establishment of a woodland landscape possible almost anywhere, on a wide variety of sites. Attention should be given, however, to matching plantings to the appropriate soils. Hardwoods are adapted to fertile soils, while the evergreens are best suited to more acidic environments.

The more open communities, including the unique northern bog community, also lend themselves to a variety of sites, but in this region all except the bog require annual clipping or burning of woody species to keep them open and unforested.

Fig. 6.26 Sphagnum moss forms a bed for dwarf cranberry and bogbean in this Michigan bog.

Additional Reading

Introductory

Hunt, Charles B., *Physiography of the United States*, W. H. Freeman, San Francisco, 1967.

Jorgensen, Neil, *A Guide to New England's Landscape*, Pequot Press, Chester, Conn., 1977.

Thomson, Betty Flanders, *The Shaping of America's Heartland*, Houghton-Mifflin, Boston, 1977.

Detailed

Alway, F. J., and P. R. McMiller, "Interrelationships of Soil and Forest Cover on Star Island, Minnesota," *Soil Science* 36:281–294, 1933.

Braun, E. Lucy, *Deciduous Forests of Eastern North America*, Hafner, New York, 1967.

Boelter, D. H., and E. S. Verry, "Peatland and Water in the Northern Lake States," *U.S.D.A. Forest Service General Technical Rep. NC-31* North Central Forest Experimental Station, St. Paul, 1977.

Bray, William L., "The Development of the Vegetation of New York State," *Technical Bulletin No. 29* New York State College of Forestry, Syracuse University, 1930.

Buell, Murray F., and William A. Niering, "Fir-Spruce-Birch Forest in Northern Minnesota," *Ecology* 38:602–610, 1957.

Buell, Murray F., and John E. Cantlon, "A Study of Two Forest Stands in Minnesota With an Interpretation of the Prairie-Forest Margin," *Ecology* 32:294–316, 1951.

Conway, V. M., "The Bogs of Central Minnesota," *Ecological Monographs* 19:173–206, 1967.

Curtis, John T., *The Vegetation of Wisconsin: An Ordination of Plant Communities*, University of Wisconsin Press, Madison, 1971.

Dansereau, P., and F. Segadas-Vianna, "Ecological Study of the Peat Bogs of Eastern North America," *Canadian Journal of Botany* 30:490–520, 1952.

Darlington, Henry Townsend, "Vegetation of the Porcupine Mountains, Northern Michigan," Papers, Michigan Academy of Sciences-Arts and Letters 13:9–65, 1931.

Donahue, William H., "Some Plant Communities in the Anthracite Region of Northeastern Pennsylvania," *American Midland Naturalist* 51:203–231, 1954.

Gates, F. C., "The Bogs of Northern Lower Michigan," *Ecological Monographs* 12:213–254, 1942.

Goff, F. Glenn, and Paul H. Zedler, "Structural Gradient Analysis of Upland Forests in the Western Great Lakes Area," *Ecological Monographs* 38:65–86, 1968.

Hough, A. F., and R. D. Forbes, "The Ecology and Silvics of Forests in the High Plateaus of Pennsylvania," *Ecological Monographs* 13:299–320, 1943.

Maycock, Paul F., "The Spruce-Fir Forests of the Keweenaw Peninsula, Northern Michigan," *Ecology* 42:357–365, 1961.

McIntosh, Robert P., "Forests of the Catskill Mountains, New York," *Ecological Monographs* 42:143–161, 1972.

McIntosh, R. P., and R. T. Hurley, "The Spruce-Fir Forests of the Catskill Mountains," *Ecology* 45:314–326, 1964.

Morey, H. F., "A Comparison of Two Virgin Forests in Northwestern Pennsylvania," *Ecology* 17:43–55, 1936.

Oosting, H. J., and W. D. Billings, "A Comparison of Virgin Spruce-Fir Forest in the Northern and Southern Appalachian System," *Ecology* 32:84–103, 1951.

Stearns, Forest, "The Composition of the Sugar Maple-Hemlock-Yellow Birch Association in Northern Wisconsin," *Ecology* 32:245–265, 1951.

Vogl, Richard J., "The Effects of Fire on the Vegetational Composition of Bracken-Grasslands," *Wisconsin Academy of Science, Arts and Letters* 53:67–82, 1964.

part three

Planning and Establishing the Landscape

chapter seven

Analyzing the Site

Landscapes that begin with little thought given to the selection of plants, their placement, and their ultimate effect rarely succeed. Too often, they are not effective and require more maintenance than they might have otherwise. To minimize mistakes and enhance results, this chapter and the two that follow offer a systematic, three-step approach to planning a naturalized planting (Figure 7.1).

At the heart of each step is the preparation of a scale drawing on graph paper. Figure 7.2 is a three-dimensional example. Easier and more useful is the *plan* drawing, represented in Figure 7.3. While the scale used is arbitrary, it should be at least one-quarter inch to the foot (¼″ = 1′0″) to avoid clutter. The flowing lines crossing the drawings are contours, horizontal slices cut through the landscape at regular intervals. If available on large-scale local maps they can be helpful, but are optional. Important topographic features will be identified during planning.

It may also be helpful to make a checklist of items to investigate or record during planning. The headings in this chapter and those following provide a general outline for a list. The additional readings may suggest other items to include in relation to a specific site and specific concerns.

Site analysis is the first stage. Critical to the creation of a low maintenance landscape, it involves assembling basic information before reaching any decisions.

Fig. 7.1 An attractive house lost in the mass of an overgrown planting.

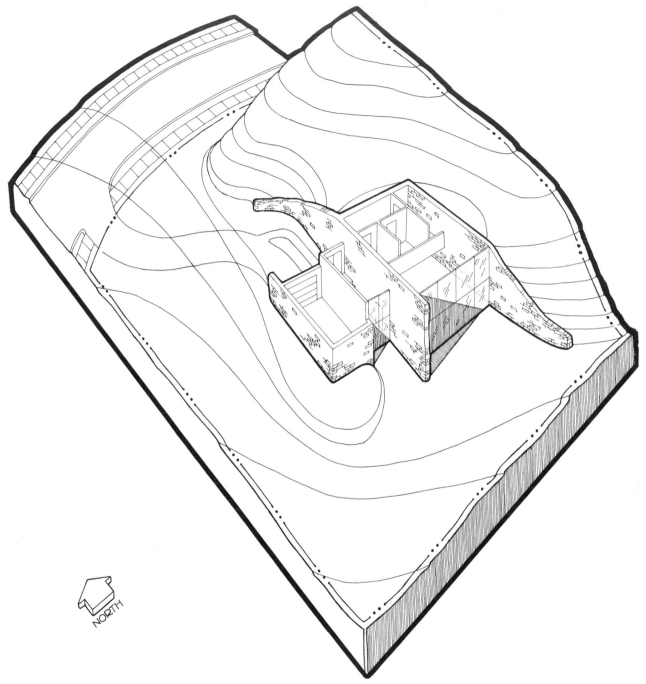

NORTH

Fig. 7.2   Aerial view of hypothetical
site.

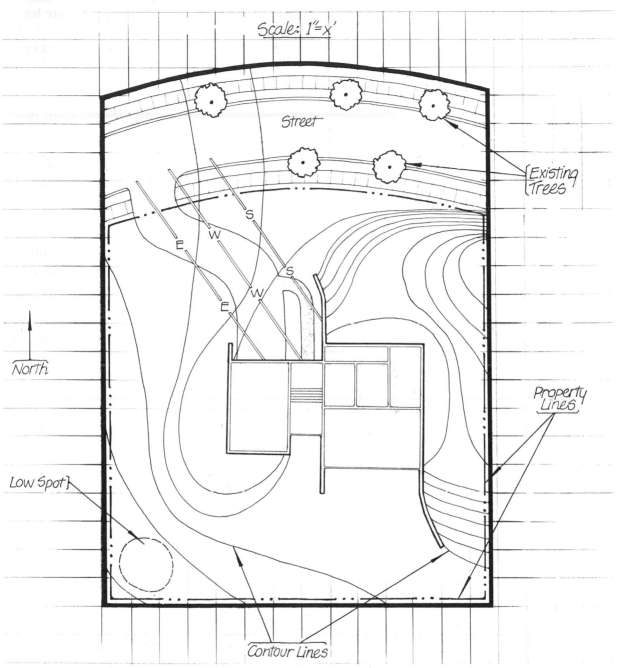

Scale: 1"=x'

Street

Existing
Trees

S

W

E

W

E

S

North

Property
Lines

Low Spot

Contour Lines

Fig. 7.3   Plan view of same site.

Preliminary Data

Basic is a determination of the space to be involved. Property boundaries are the obvious limitations, but equally important are legal easements and planting restrictions. Among the latter are local ordinances governing landscaping near streets and lot lines. Legal descriptions for each of these factors are available from local government offices. The dimensions and locations of the areas affected should be recorded on the first drawing (Figure 7.4).

Structures and paved areas should be added next. On site, they not only limit the space available for planting, they may also dictate planting plans. Windows and doors requiring access, downspouts which saturate the soil following rains, and gutters which collect ice in winter and so threaten trees and shrubs should all be noted. Off-site buildings are important for another reason: their effect on privacy, sunlight, and view. They can be drawn in if scale allows, or they can be noted in the margins (Figures 7.5 and 7.6).

The last preliminary information needed is the location of utility features. Buried lines like those for water, gas, and sewage may conflict with plants that have deep, fibrous roots. Overhead lines like those for electricity and telephones may conflict with tall shrubs and trees. Outdoor water faucets, electrical outlets, meters, air conditioners, and oil-tank fill pipes that require access should also be noted (Figure 7.7).

Environmental Data

The natural environment of a site affects people and plants. Major features of climate, topography, moisture, and soils should be recorded on the drawing. While many of these may be obvious, it can be helpful to observe the kinds of plants already on the site. What they are and whether they are thriving or dying can indicate factors not otherwise apparent and can substantiate other observations.

Climate It is customary to think of climate on a large scale, or regional macroclimate. But climate also reflects local influences. On a smaller scale, or mesoclimate, urban areas are often warmer and drier than the surrounding countryside. Areas bordering major bodies of water have their temperatures moderated in both summer and winter. On the smallest scale, or microclimate, sheltered ravines are cooler and more moist than exposed hillsides; the south sides of buildings are warmer than those facing north (Figure 7.8).

Large-scale patterns of temperature and precipitation shape a region's predominant vegetation, but more local patterns may favor differences. Site analysis should, therefore, compare local with regional figures. Macroclimate data is available through the United States Department of Agriculture; local data through area meteo-

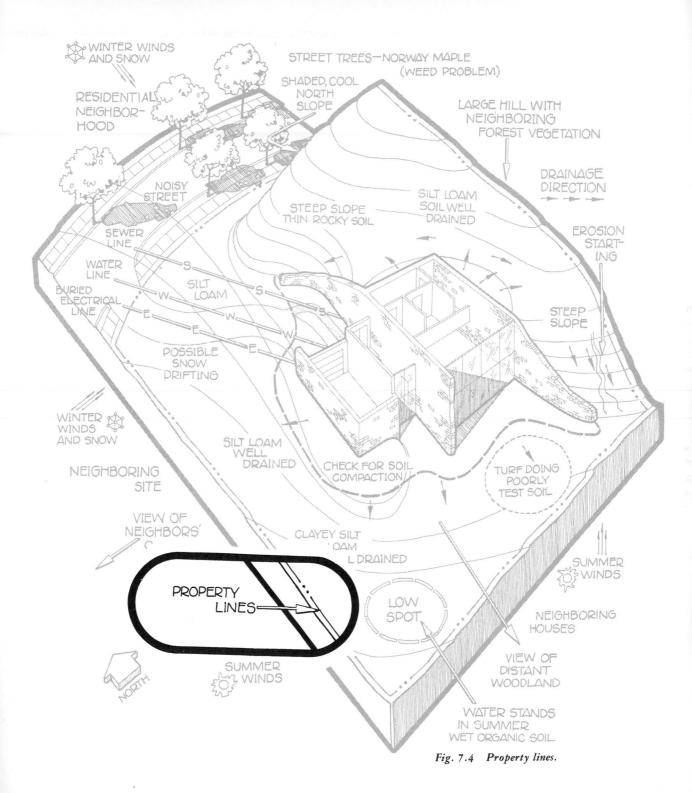

WINTER WINDS AND SNOW

RESIDENTIAL NEIGHBOR-HOOD

STREET TREES—NORWAY MAPLE (WEED PROBLEM)

SHADED, COOL NORTH SLOPE

LARGE HILL WITH NEIGHBORING FOREST VEGETATION

DRAINAGE DIRECTION

NOISY STREET

SILT LOAM SOIL WELL DRAINED

EROSION START-ING

STEEP SLOPE THIN ROCKY SOIL

SEWER LINE

WATER LINE

BURIED ELECTRICAL LINE

SILT LOAM

STEEP SLOPE

POSSIBLE SNOW DRIFTING

WINTER WINDS AND SNOW

NEIGHBORING SITE

SILT LOAM WELL DRAINED

CHECK FOR SOIL COMPACTION

TURF DOING POORLY TEST SOIL

VIEW OF NEIGHBORS'

PROPERTY LINES

CLAYEY SILT 'OAM L DRAINED

LOW SPOT

SUMMER WINDS

NEIGHBORING HOUSES

NORTH

SUMMER WINDS

VIEW OF DISTANT WOODLAND

WATER STANDS IN SUMMER WET ORGANIC SOIL

Fig. 7.4 Property lines.

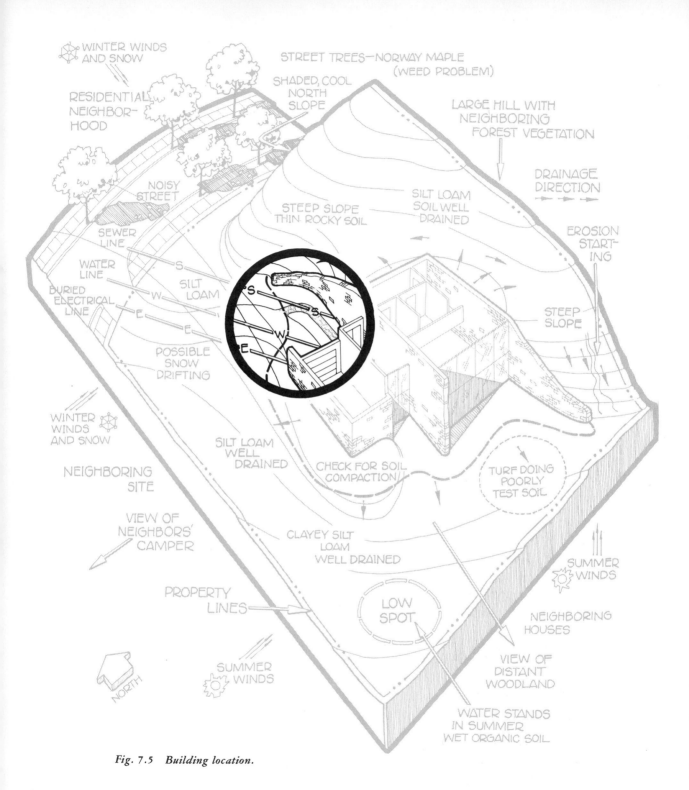

Fig. 7.5 Building location.

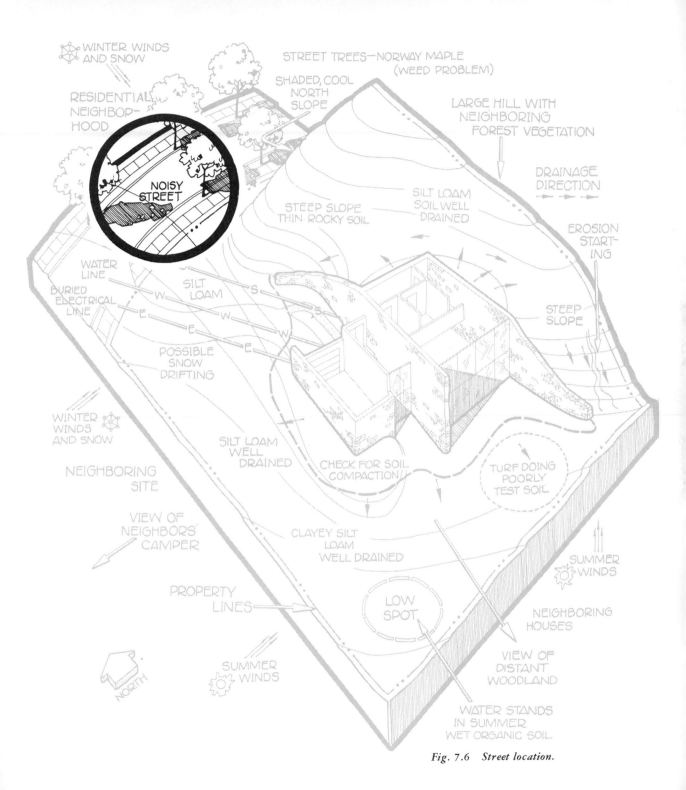

WINTER WINDS AND SNOW

RESIDENTIAL NEIGHBOR-HOOD

STREET TREES—NORWAY MAPLE (WEED PROBLEM)

SHADED, COOL NORTH SLOPE

LARGE HILL WITH NEIGHBORING FOREST VEGETATION

DRAINAGE DIRECTION

NOISY STREET

STEEP SLOPE THIN ROCKY SOIL

SILT LOAM SOIL WELL DRAINED

EROSION STARTING

WATER LINE

SILT LOAM

BURIED ELECTRICAL LINE

STEEP SLOPE

POSSIBLE SNOW DRIFTING

WINTER WINDS AND SNOW

NEIGHBORING SITE

SILT LOAM WELL DRAINED

CHECK FOR SOIL COMPACTION

TURF DOING POORLY TEST SOIL

VIEW OF NEIGHBORS' CAMPER

CLAYEY SILT LOAM WELL DRAINED

SUMMER WINDS

NEIGHBORING HOUSES

PROPERTY LINES

LOW SPOT

VIEW OF DISTANT WOODLAND

NORTH

SUMMER WINDS

WATER STANDS IN SUMMER WET ORGANIC SOIL

Fig. 7.6   Street location.

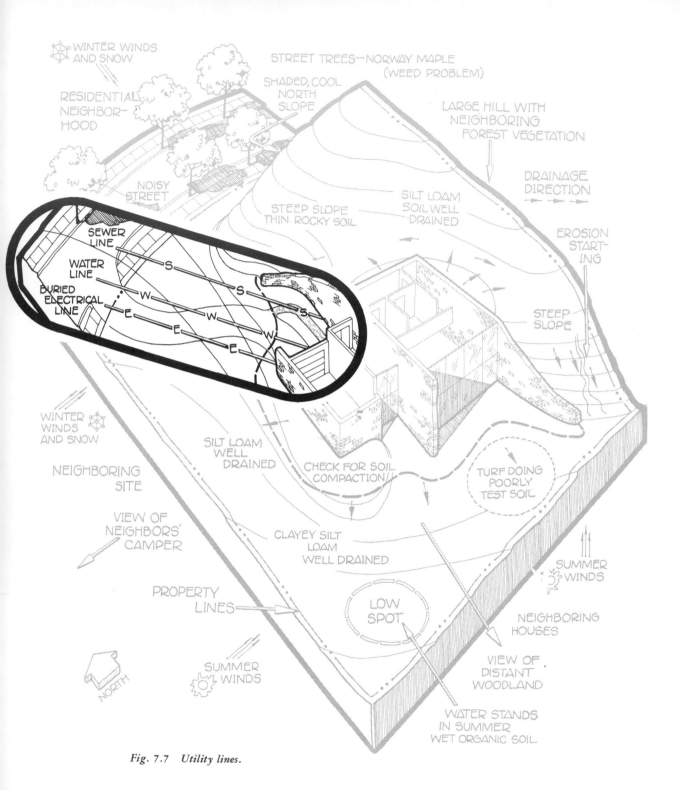

WINTER WINDS AND SNOW

RESIDENTIAL NEIGHBOR- HOOD

NOISY STREET

STREET TREES—NORWAY MAPLE (WEED PROBLEM)

SHADED, COOL NORTH SLOPE

LARGE HILL WITH NEIGHBORING FOREST VEGETATION

DRAINAGE DIRECTION

SILT LOAM SOIL WELL DRAINED

STEEP SLOPE THIN ROCKY SOIL

EROSION START- ING

SEWER LINE

WATER LINE

BURIED ELECTRICAL LINE

STEEP SLOPE

WINTER WINDS AND SNOW

NEIGHBORING SITE

SILT LOAM WELL DRAINED

CHECK FOR SOIL COMPACTION

TURF DOING POORLY TEST SOIL

VIEW OF NEIGHBORS' CAMPER

CLAYEY SILT LOAM WELL DRAINED

SUMMER WINDS

PROPERTY LINES

NEIGHBORING HOUSES

LOW SPOT

NORTH

SUMMER WINDS

VIEW OF DISTANT WOODLAND

WATER STANDS IN SUMMER WET ORGANIC SOIL

Fig. 7.7 Utility lines.

84

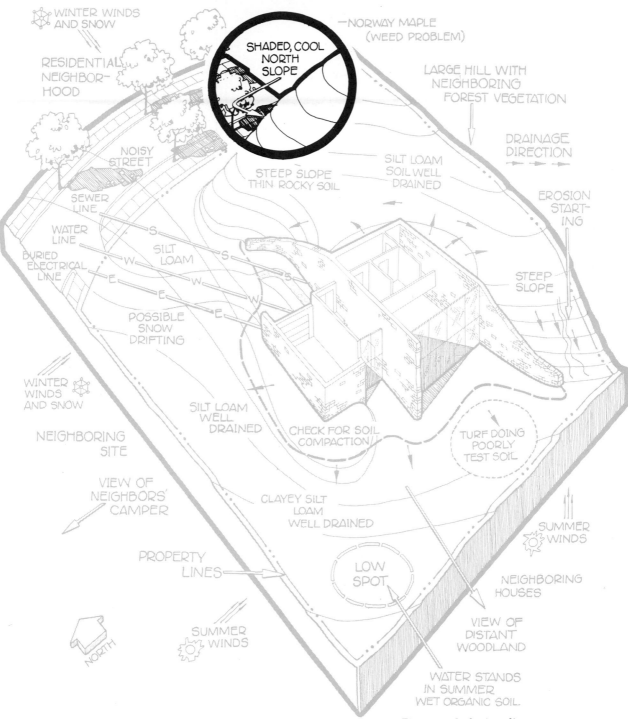

WINTER WINDS AND SNOW

RESIDENTIAL NEIGHBOR-HOOD

NORWAY MAPLE (WEED PROBLEM)

SHADED, COOL NORTH SLOPE

LARGE HILL WITH NEIGHBORING FOREST VEGETATION

DRAINAGE DIRECTION

NOISY STREET

STEEP SLOPE THIN ROCKY SOIL

SILT LOAM SOIL WELL DRAINED

EROSION STARTING

SEWER LINE

WATER LINE

SILT LOAM

BURIED ELECTRICAL LINE

STEEP SLOPE

POSSIBLE SNOW DRIFTING

WINTER WINDS AND SNOW

SILT LOAM WELL DRAINED

NEIGHBORING SITE

CHECK FOR SOIL COMPACTION

TURF DOING POORLY TEST SOIL

VIEW OF NEIGHBORS' CAMPER

CLAYEY SILT LOAM WELL DRAINED

SUMMER WINDS

PROPERTY LINES

LOW SPOT

NEIGHBORING HOUSES

NORTH

SUMMER WINDS

VIEW OF DISTANT WOODLAND

WATER STANDS IN SUMMER WET ORGANIC SOIL.

Fig. 7.8 Cool microclimate.

85

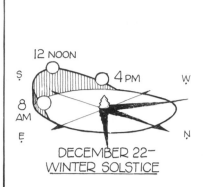
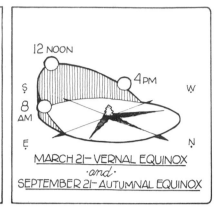

Fig. 7.9 *Seasonal changes in the sun's angle.*

rological services or personal observations. To the extent that local climate resembles regional climate, communities of plants representative of the region are appropriate. Significant differences dictate care in the selection of a model and should be noted, either on the drawing itself or in a separate record.

The hours and angle of sunlight change with the seasons, as suggested in Figure 7.9. Thus, areas shaded much of the day in one season may be sunny in another. Major areas of sun and shade during the growing season should be identified on the drawing for reference during the planting design. In addition, areas warmed by the sun in early spring and cooled by shade in late summer should be noted as potential recreation areas.

Winds in the northeast come predominantly from the southwest in summer and the west and northwest in winter. Their character, however, can be affected locally. Winds passing between buildings usually increase in velocity. Those passing over water will be cooler and more humid than those crossing an expanse of pavement. The direction and season of winds thus affected should be recorded as notes or arrows on the drawing (Figures 7.10 and 7.11).

Finally, less obvious climatic effects such as snowdrift areas and heat radiation from paved surfaces should also be noted.

Topography The lay of the land—its direction of slope, angle, and prominent features—has a major impact on recreation. Steep slopes do not lend themselves to active sports. Gentle south slopes, on the other hand, are unexcelled for warmth during the early spring and late fall. Such factors also affect vegetation. Because cold air sinks during the evening hours, depressions and lower slopes may be natural cold-air drainageways and may favor frost-tolerant plants. Areas of bare rock may support only barrens or cliffside species.

Many of these features will be obvious on a drawing that includes contour lines. For those that do not, significant slopes and their direction should be noted along with other unusual topographic features (Figure 7.12).

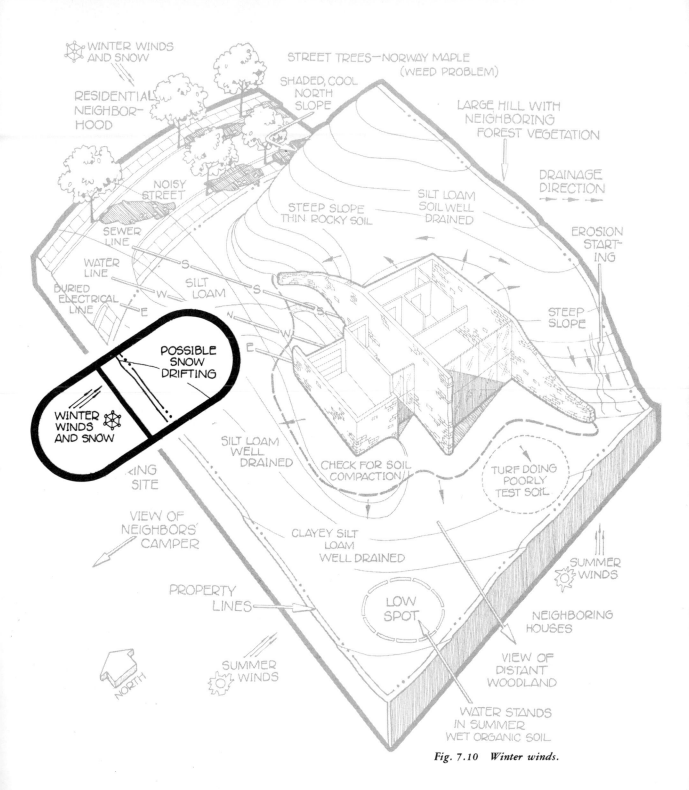

WINTER WINDS AND SNOW

RESIDENTIAL NEIGHBOR-HOOD

STREET TREES—NORWAY MAPLE (WEED PROBLEM)

SHADED, COOL NORTH SLOPE

LARGE HILL WITH NEIGHBORING FOREST VEGETATION

DRAINAGE DIRECTION

NOISY STREET

STEEP SLOPE THIN ROCKY SOIL

SILT LOAM SOIL WELL DRAINED

EROSION START-ING

SEWER LINE

WATER LINE

SILT LOAM

STEEP SLOPE

BURIED ELECTRICAL LINE

POSSIBLE SNOW DRIFTING

WINTER WINDS AND SNOW

SILT LOAM WELL DRAINED

CHECK FOR SOIL COMPACTION

TURF DOING POORLY TEST SOIL

...ING SITE

VIEW OF NEIGHBORS' CAMPER

CLAYEY SILT LOAM WELL DRAINED

SUMMER WINDS

PROPERTY LINES

LOW SPOT

NEIGHBORING HOUSES

NORTH

SUMMER WINDS

VIEW OF DISTANT WOODLAND

WATER STANDS IN SUMMER WET ORGANIC SOIL

Fig. 7.10   Winter winds.

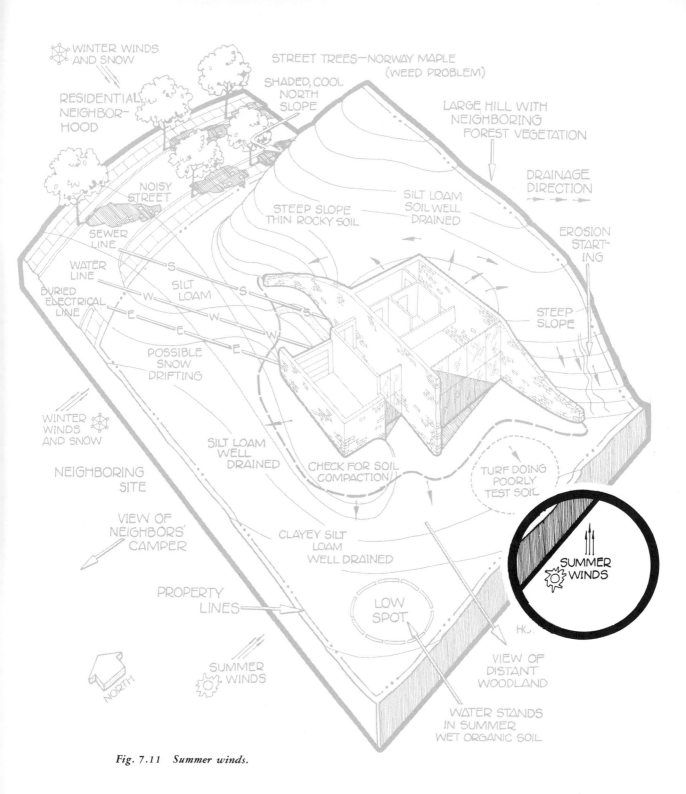

WINTER WINDS AND SNOW

RESIDENTIAL NEIGHBORHOOD

STREET TREES—NORWAY MAPLE (WEED PROBLEM)

SHADED, COOL NORTH SLOPE

LARGE HILL WITH NEIGHBORING FOREST VEGETATION

DRAINAGE DIRECTION

NOISY STREET

STEEP SLOPE THIN ROCKY SOIL

SILT LOAM SOIL WELL DRAINED

EROSION STARTING

SEWER LINE

WATER LINE

BURIED ELECTRICAL LINE

SILT LOAM

STEEP SLOPE

POSSIBLE SNOW DRIFTING

WINTER WINDS AND SNOW

NEIGHBORING SITE

SILT LOAM WELL DRAINED

CHECK FOR SOIL COMPACTION

TURF DOING POORLY TEST SOIL

VIEW OF NEIGHBORS' CAMPER

CLAYEY SILT LOAM WELL DRAINED

PROPERTY LINES

LOW SPOT

SUMMER WINDS

NORTH

SUMMER WINDS

VIEW OF DISTANT WOODLAND

WATER STANDS IN SUMMER WET ORGANIC SOIL

Fig. 7.11 Summer winds.

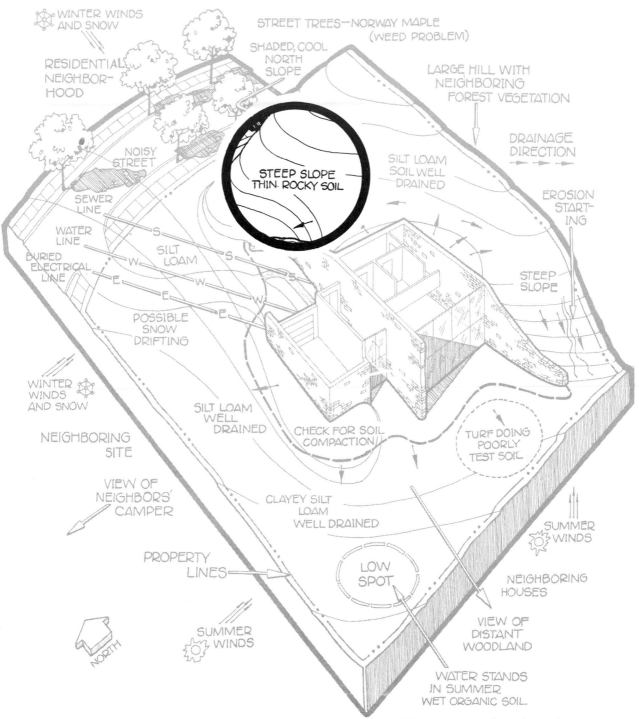

Fig. 7.12 *Steep slope, thin rocky soil.*

89

Moisture Water is an important factor in a plant's environment, so much so that many botanists classify communities along a moisture gradient from very dry to very wet. The moisture level can change dramatically on steep topography. Where the land is flatter, it may be relatively uniform, although differences can be surprising. In much of the Central Lowlands, for example, minor changes in elevation can make the difference between mesic habitat and a wetland.

Existing vegetation can be a major clue to moisture levels. Many lawn grasses prefer moist but not saturated soils and thus can indicate areas that are drier or wetter than average. Topography can also be a clue. Steep upper slopes are usually drier than lower ones. North slopes and shaded areas are usually more moist than those exposed to the sun and wind.

Based on these observations, areas that are xeric (dry) or hydric (wet) should be identified on the drawing.

Drainage areas are a special concern. Periodic extra water may favor some plants over others, but it can also make recreation unpleasant. Severe drainage following a heavy rain can wash out plantings and soil. Drainageways, easily identified during or just after a storm, should be noted, and special note should be made of areas being eroded (Figures 7.13 and 7.14)

Areas of standing water should also be identified. Whether ephemeral or permanent, they may provide the habitat needed for wetland plantings. A conscientious record of when they occur and how long the water lasts can be extremely important in deciding how to use them (Figure 7.15).

Soil Soils, like existing plants, can be used to confirm other environmental observations. For example, an undisturbed area of clay may indicate a natural drainageway where running water has deposited fine particles of soil over many years. But soils are also an important aspect of plant habitat in themselves.

Given the modern use of heavy construction equipment, it is essential to determine the degree to which the site has been disturbed by building. The major problem is soil compaction and is usually most common around buildings themselves. While floodplain species like elm and silver maple have adapted to compacted soils by virtue of their long exposure to annual siltation, the roots of most other species require loose soils in which to breathe.

The condition of a site can be gauged roughly by digging a hole 2 feet deep and filling it with water. After it drains, it should be filled a second time. If it takes an hour or more to drain the second time, special measures may be required to improve the texture of the soil for water-intolerant species. Any areas so affected should be identified on the drawing (Figures 7.16 and 7.17).

Because builders often remove the topsoil from a building site and return only a portion of it, areas that appear to have little or no topsoil should also be identified.

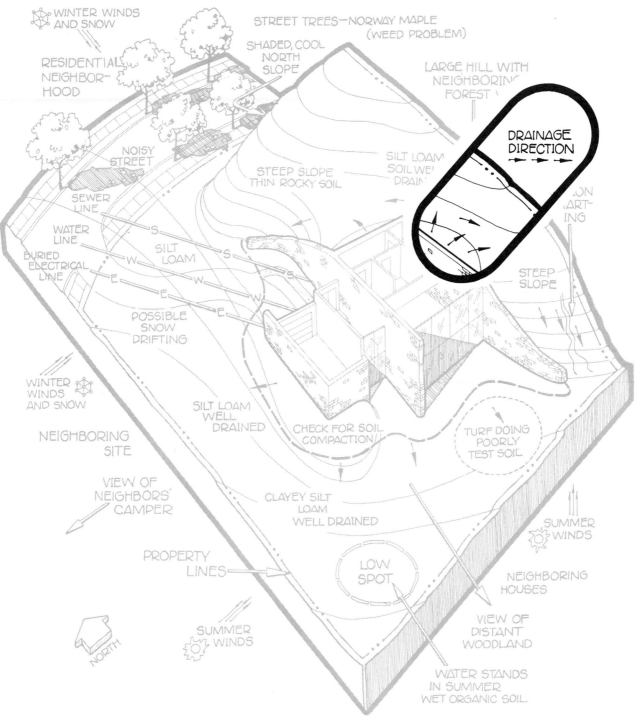

WINTER WINDS
AND SNOW

STREET TREES—NORWAY MAPLE
(WEED PROBLEM)

SHADED, COOL
NORTH
SLOPE

RESIDENTIAL
NEIGHBOR-
HOOD

LARGE HILL WITH
NEIGHBORING
FOREST

DRAINAGE
DIRECTION

NOISY
STREET

SILT LOAM
SOIL WELL
DRAIN

SEWER
LINE

STEEP SLOPE
THIN ROCKY SOIL

WATER
LINE

SILT
LOAM

BURIED
ELECTRICAL
LINE

STEEP
SLOPE

POSSIBLE
SNOW
DRIFTING

WINTER
WINDS
AND SNOW

SILT LOAM
WELL
DRAINED

CHECK FOR SOIL
COMPACTION

TURF DOING
POORLY
TEST SOIL

NEIGHBORING
SITE

VIEW OF
NEIGHBORS'
CAMPER

CLAYEY SILT
LOAM
WELL DRAINED

SUMMER
WINDS

PROPERTY
LINES

NEIGHBORING
HOUSES

LOW
SPOT

VIEW OF
DISTANT
WOODLAND

NORTH

SUMMER
WINDS

WATER STANDS
IN SUMMER
WET ORGANIC SOIL.

Fig. 7.13 *Drainage direction.*

91

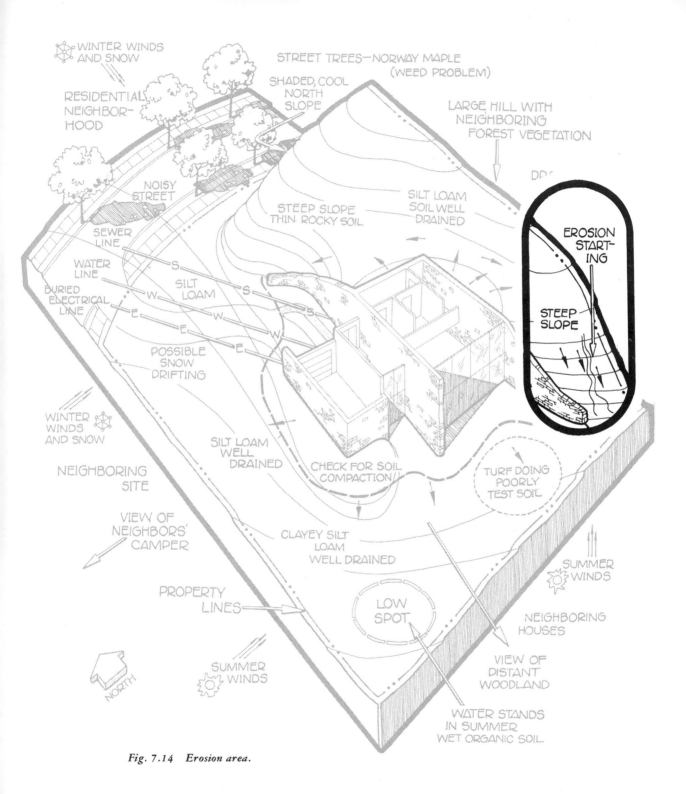

Fig. 7.14 *Erosion area.*

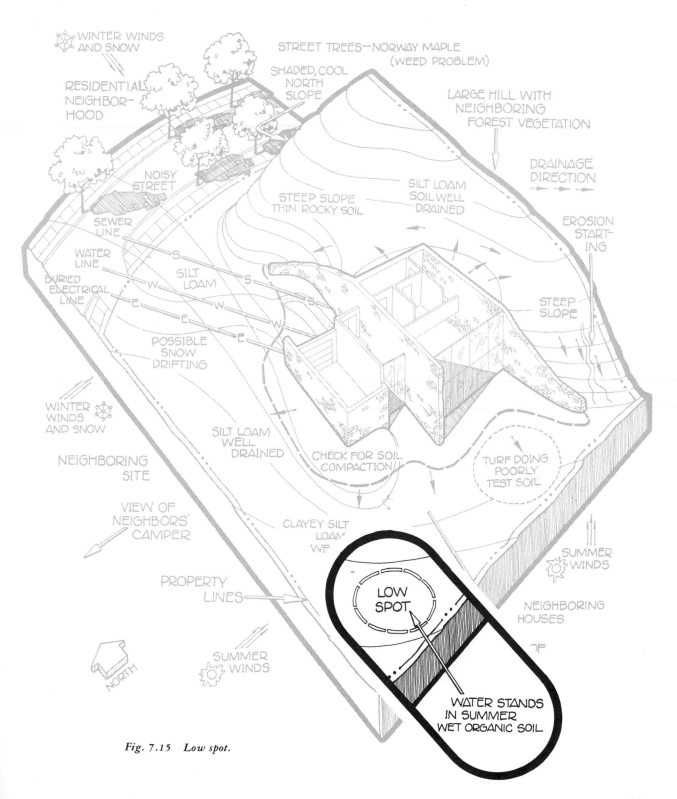

WINTER WINDS AND SNOW

STREET TREES—NORWAY MAPLE (WEED PROBLEM)

RESIDENTIAL NEIGHBOR-HOOD

SHADED, COOL NORTH SLOPE

LARGE HILL WITH NEIGHBORING FOREST VEGETATION

DRAINAGE DIRECTION

NOISY STREET

SILT LOAM SOIL WELL DRAINED

STEEP SLOPE THIN ROCKY SOIL

EROSION STARTING

SEWER LINE

WATER LINE

SILT LOAM

BURIED ELECTRICAL LINE

STEEP SLOPE

POSSIBLE SNOW DRIFTING

WINTER WINDS AND SNOW

SILT LOAM WELL DRAINED

CHECK FOR SOIL COMPACTION

TURF DOING POORLY TEST SOIL

NEIGHBORING SITE

VIEW OF NEIGHBORS' CAMPER

CLAYEY SILT LOAM WF

SUMMER WINDS

NEIGHBORING HOUSES

PROPERTY LINES

OF

LOW SPOT

NORTH

SUMMER WINDS

WATER STANDS IN SUMMER WET ORGANIC SOIL

Fig. 7.15   Low spot.

93

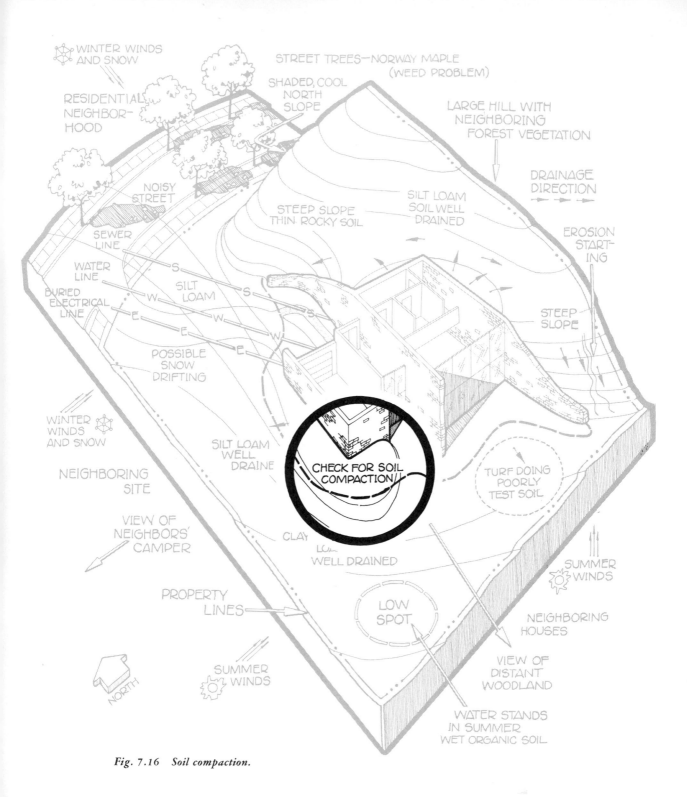

Fig. 7.16 Soil compaction.

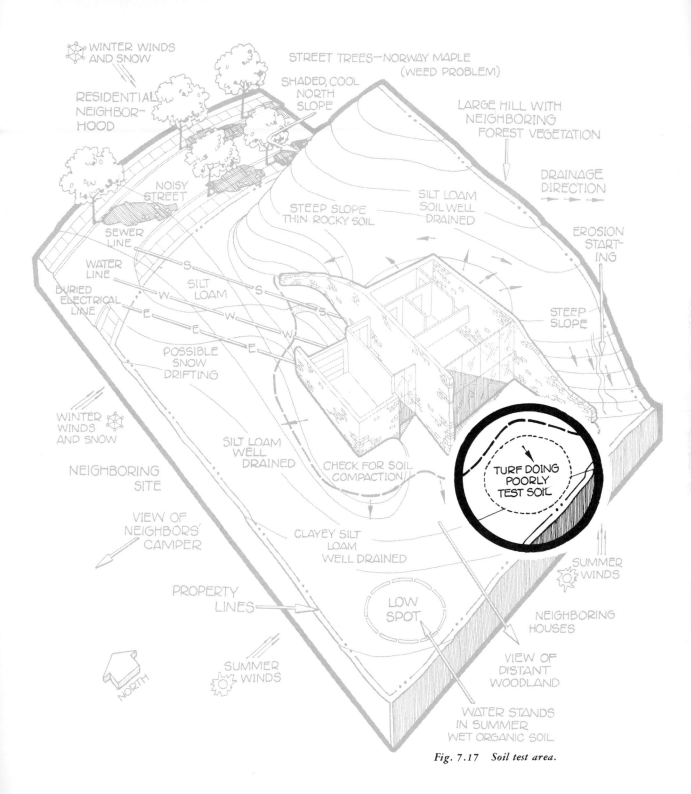

WINTER WINDS AND SNOW

RESIDENTIAL NEIGHBOR- HOOD

STREET TREES—NORWAY MAPLE (WEED PROBLEM)

SHADED, COOL NORTH SLOPE

LARGE HILL WITH NEIGHBORING FOREST VEGETATION

DRAINAGE DIRECTION

NOISY STREET

SILT LOAM SOIL WELL DRAINED

EROSION STARTING

STEEP SLOPE THIN ROCKY SOIL

SEWER LINE

WATER LINE

BURIED ELECTRICAL LINE

SILT LOAM

STEEP SLOPE

POSSIBLE SNOW DRIFTING

WINTER WINDS AND SNOW

SILT LOAM WELL DRAINED

CHECK FOR SOIL COMPACTION

TURF DOING POORLY TEST SOIL

NEIGHBORING SITE

VIEW OF NEIGHBORS' CAMPER

CLAYEY SILT LOAM WELL DRAINED

SUMMER WINDS

PROPERTY LINES

LOW SPOT

NEIGHBORING HOUSES

NORTH

SUMMER WINDS

VIEW OF DISTANT WOODLAND

WATER STANDS IN SUMMER WET ORGANIC SOIL

Fig. 7.17   Soil test area.

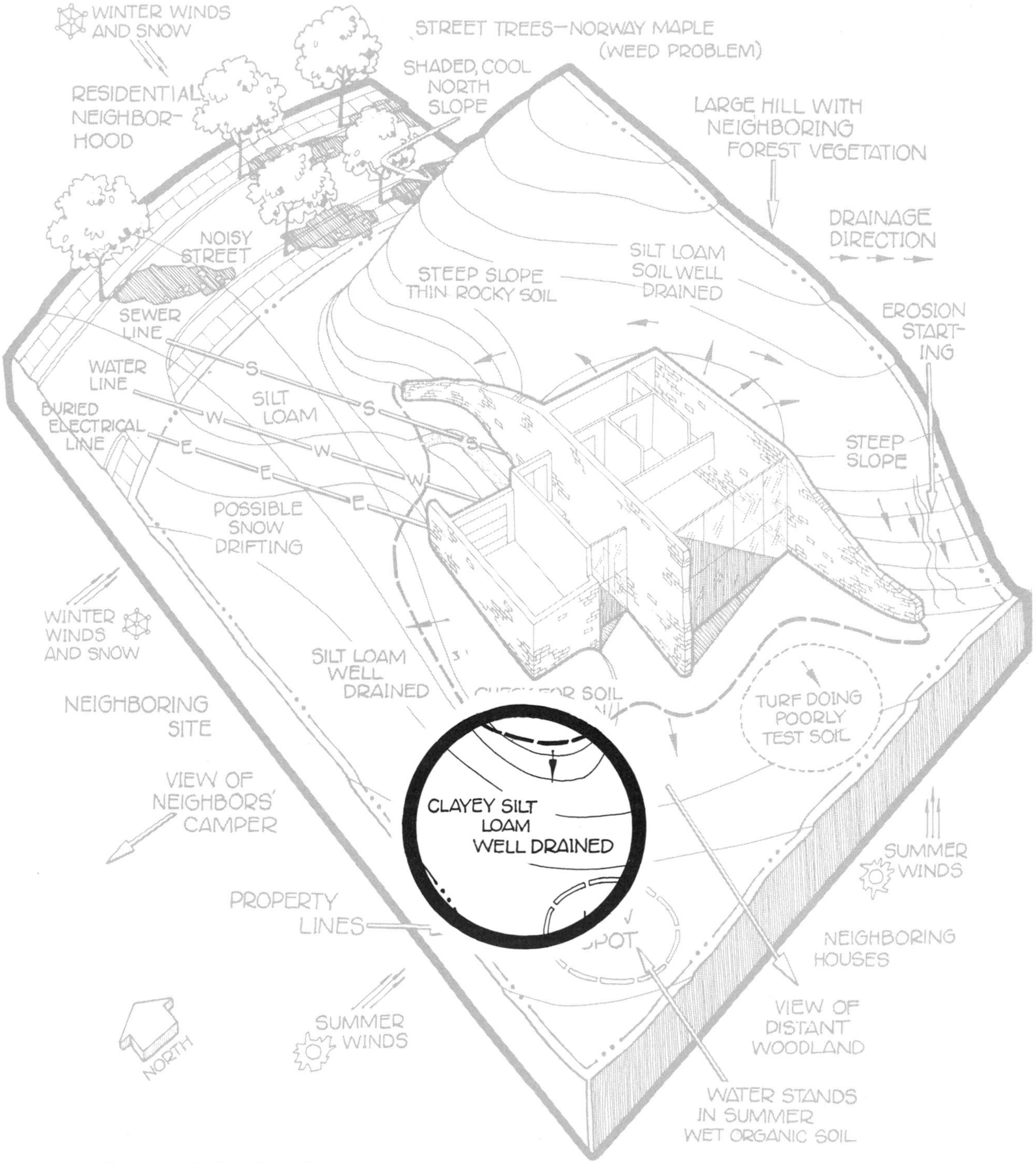

WINTER WINDS AND SNOW
STREET TREES—NORWAY MAPLE (WEED PROBLEM)
SHADED, COOL NORTH SLOPE
RESIDENTIAL NEIGHBOR-HOOD
LARGE HILL WITH NEIGHBORING FOREST VEGETATION
DRAINAGE DIRECTION
NOISY STREET
SILT LOAM SOIL WELL DRAINED
STEEP SLOPE THIN ROCKY SOIL
EROSION START-ING
SEWER LINE
WATER LINE
BURIED ELECTRICAL LINE
SILT LOAM
STEEP SLOPE
POSSIBLE SNOW DRIFTING
WINTER WINDS AND SNOW
SILT LOAM WELL DRAINED
TURF DOING POORLY TEST SOIL
NEIGHBORING SITE
VIEW OF NEIGHBORS' CAMPER
CLAYEY SILT LOAM WELL DRAINED
SUMMER WINDS
PROPERTY LINES
NEIGHBORING HOUSES
NORTH
SUMMER WINDS
VIEW OF DISTANT WOODLAND
WATER STANDS IN SUMMER WET ORGANIC SOIL

Fig. 7.18 Soil test for soil texture.

Areas unaffected by construction should also be appraised for their natural soil characteristics. County agricultural extension offices have records of soil surveys completed in their districts, and these can be helpful in determining the composition, subsurface conditions, depth, and pH of the soil. Some of these surveys also make planting recommendations, but because they tend to draw upon the traditional practice of treating plants as individuals rather than as members of a natural community, their recommendations should be approached with caution.

Where soil surveys are either incomplete or inadequate for planning, two relatively inexpensive options are available. Test kits for determining soil pH are available from most garden supply stores. For a few dollars more, state soils laboratories will test soil samples. Not only are their tests more accurate, they also measure factors that include pH, organic content, phosphorus, potassium, nitrogen, soluble salts, and the percentage of sand, silt, and clay. Soils labs can also determine whether any element of the soil's chemistry is present in sufficient amounts to be toxic. The presence of soluble salts in particular may be an indication of excess fertilization and if high enough may make it desirable to wait a year for rain to wash the salts out of the soil (Figure 7.18).

It is also possible to make a rough appraisal of nonwetland soil texture without testing. The critical factor is the relative proportion of sand, silt, and clay present. Sand grains are the largest soil particles, ranging from $\frac{5}{100}$ to 2 millimeters in diameter. Clay grains are the smallest, measuring less than $\frac{2}{1000}$ millimeter in diameter. Silt grains are intermediate between these. As a general rule, clay is hard and lumpy when dry; and plastic, sticky, and shiny if rubbed between the fingers when wet. Sand feels rough and gritty, and sand grains can be seen without magnification. Silt, again, is intermediate.

Areas with a high or low pH or which are appreciably characterized by sand or clay should be recorded on the drawing.

Miscellaneous Data Completing the site analysis are observations of other, sometimes less tangible factors often related to comfort and privacy. Glare from windows or from cars at night, noise, and pedestrian traffic all affect how a site is used, and should be noted.

The Completed Drawing

Figure 7.19 is an example of a finished drawing. While every site analysis is different, the site analysis drawing should include all of the information about the site that is needed to design a landscape and prepare a planting plan.

It should be noted that while common names have been used to identify plants in these chapters, species are best identified by their

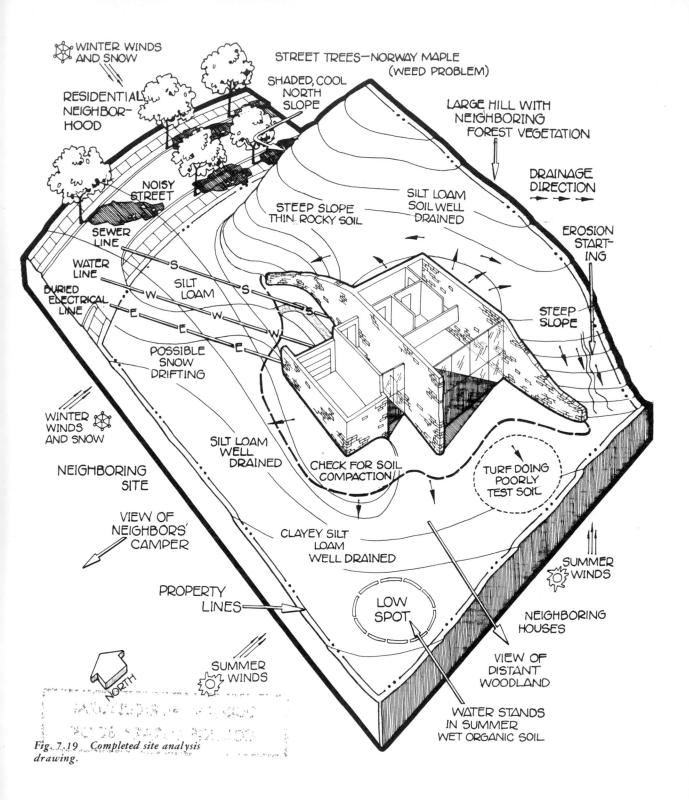

WINTER WINDS AND SNOW

STREET TREES—NORWAY MAPLE (WEED PROBLEM)

RESIDENTIAL NEIGHBORHOOD

SHADED, COOL NORTH SLOPE

LARGE HILL WITH NEIGHBORING FOREST VEGETATION

DRAINAGE DIRECTION

NOISY STREET

SILT LOAM SOIL WELL DRAINED

EROSION STARTING

SEWER LINE

STEEP SLOPE THIN ROCKY SOIL

WATER LINE

SILT LOAM

BURIED ELECTRICAL LINE

STEEP SLOPE

POSSIBLE SNOW DRIFTING

WINTER WINDS AND SNOW

NEIGHBORING SITE

SILT LOAM WELL DRAINED

CHECK FOR SOIL COMPACTION

TURF DOING POORLY TEST SOIL

VIEW OF NEIGHBORS' CAMPER

CLAYEY SILT LOAM WELL DRAINED

SUMMER WINDS

PROPERTY LINES

NEIGHBORING HOUSES

LOW SPOT

VIEW OF DISTANT WOODLAND

NORTH

SUMMER WINDS

WATER STANDS IN SUMMER WET ORGANIC SOIL

Fig. 7.19 Completed site analysis drawing.

scientific (Latin) names. This is because species may have several common names, or two species may share one name. As planning progresses it will become increasingly important to be more specific. For that reason, while the common names will be used in the text, the appendices use both scientific and popular nomenclature. The source for the former is the *Manual of Vascular Plants of the Northeastern United States and Adjacent Canada*, by Henry A. Gleason and Arthur Cronquist.

Additional Reading

Site Analysis

Eckbo, Garrett, *Home Landscape*, McGraw-Hill, New York, 1978.

Lynch, Kevin, *Site Planning*, M.I.T. Press, Cambridge, Mass., 1971.

Ortho Books, *Weather-Wise Gardening*, Chevron Chemical Co., Ortho Division, San Francisco, 1974.

Robinette, Gary, *Plants/People/and Environmental Quality*, U.S. Department of the Interior, National Park Service, Washington, D.C., 1972.

Plant Identification

Brown, Lauren, *Grasses: An Identification Guide*, Houghton-Mifflin, Boston, 1979.

Cobb, Boughton, *A Field Guide to the Ferns*, Houghton-Mifflin, Boston, 1963.

Courtney, Booth, and James Hill Zimmerman, *Wildflowers and Weeds*, Van Nostrand Reinhold Co., New York, 1972.

Gleason, Henry A., and Arthur Cronquist, *Manual of Vascular Plants of Northeastern United States and Adjacent Canada*, Van Nostrand, Princeton, N. J., 1963.

Peterson, Roger Tory, and Margaret McKenny, *A Field Guide to Wildflowers of Northeastern and Northcentral North America*, Houghton-Mifflin, Boston, 1968.

Shuttleworth, Floyd S., and Herbert S. Zim, *Non-Flowering Plants*, Golden, New York, 1967.

Slife, F. W., et al., *Weeds of the North Central States*, Circular 718 of the University of Illinois Agricultural Experiment Station, Urbana, Ill., 1960.

Symonds, George W. D., *The Tree Identification Book*, William Morrow, New York, 1958.

Symonds, George W. D., *The Shrub Identification Book*, William Morrow, New York, 1963.

Wharton, Mary E., and Roger W. Barbour, *Trees and Shrubs of Kentucky*, The University Press of Kentucky, Lexington, 1973.

Wharton, Mary E., and Roger W. Barbour, *The Wildflowers and Ferns of Kentucky*, The University Press of Kentucky, Lexington, 1971.

DURHAM AGRICULTURAL COLLEGE LIBRARY BOOK

PURDUE AGRICULTURAL
COLLEGE LIBRARY BOOK

chapter eight

Planning for Site Use

Site-use planning involves dividing the landscape among recreation, utility, and plantings. Often, the site's environment will weigh as heavily as its space. Where sunlight is limited on the small residential site, for example, it may be necessary to choose between a garden and an area for lounging. Where the site is high and dry, the flora of the mesophytic forest will be inappropriate, but there may be a choice between the flora of the xeric forest and the colorful grasses and forbs of the dry grassland.

The second stage of planning is devoted to making these decisions. Often, it involves choosing between alternative plans, each with its own advantages and disadvantages. It may be helpful, therefore, to sketch initial ideas on transparencies laid over the site analysis drawing. Final decisions are recorded on the second drawing.

Recreation and Utility

One facet of site-use planning is providing for needed activities. Because space rarely is limitless, this requires identifying essential uses and eliminating those that are least important. These choices are basic and should not be rushed. Rather, ideas should be given time to grow and mature.

Assessing Needs Initially, all conceivable uses for the site should be listed in a separate record. Nothing, however mundane, should be omitted at this stage. Clothes-drying is as important for the home site as gardening. Passive activities like bird-watching are no less a part of outdoor life than active ones like basketball. If children will be sharing the landscape, their needs at all stages of growth should be considered along with adult needs.

Once developed, this initial list is refined. When appropriate, items can be combined. When unrealistic for resources, they should be excluded. Because some items can share the same space, given a thoughtful design, this can be a creative step. A space for drying clothes can double as a lounging area if retractable lines are used. When sand rather than grass is used under swings, the area can double as a sandbox.

Two things should be kept in mind during this process. Planning should reflect the priorities of those who will be using the site. A deck or patio may not be necessary even though both are currently popular landscape items. Second, space should be kept as flexible as possible. Areas once paved, for example, are expensive to change later on.

Finally, each item on the revised list should be given a priority and the space needed for each should be noted.

Assessing Space Once the proposed uses for a site are identified, they need to be related to the dimensions of the site itself, its environment, and each other. In naturalizing, one guideline distinguishes this step from traditional approaches: the site should be accepted as it is. It may be possible to fill a low area or to level a hill, but neither is consistent with the philosophy behind naturalizing. Such changes are not only expensive, but, more important, they also destroy the natural character of the land. There can be immense and long-lasting satisfaction in learning to appreciate a site for what it says about the history of the area (Figure 8.1).

Initially, items with related functions should be located near each other. Entertainment areas that utilize indoor facilities are best located near a door. Items with off-site relationships—such as trash pickup and mailboxes—are best located near the street.

Safety and convenience dictate that other items also be given a placement priority. For the family with young children, it may be desirable to provide a backyard pathway so that youngsters do not have to approach the street to meet their friends.

The plan that results from these initial placements should be evaluated in terms of the site's physical environment. Comfort and logic dictate that some activities are more appropriate in some areas than in others. Among the most important environmental considerations are sunlight and warmth. Gardens require sunlight much of the day, and if the garden has a high priority it may outweigh others. Extending a garden's growing season requires locating it away from cold air drainageways as well. Unshaded, pavement heats up during the day and releases its heat slowly at night. Thus, summer sitting

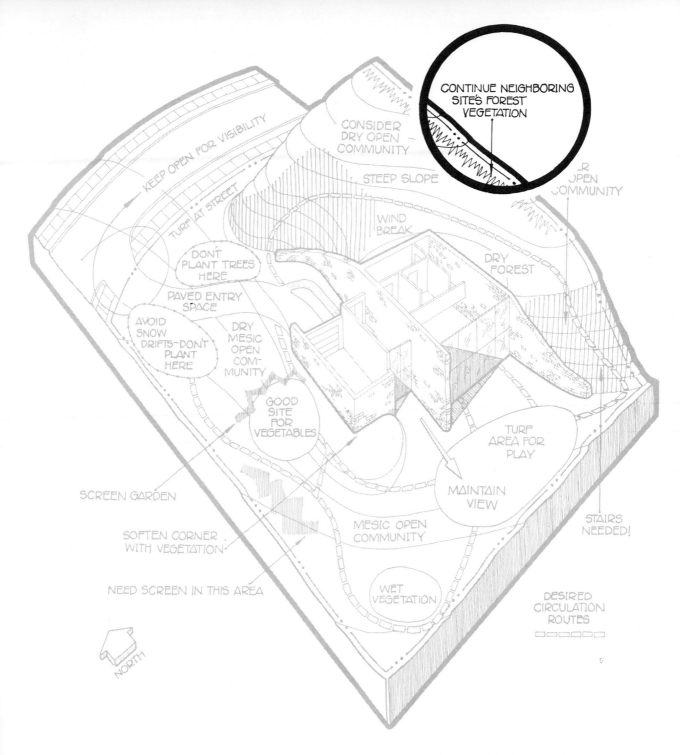

Fig. 8.1 *Neighboring native vegetation.*

Fig. 8.2 *People enjoying south slope.*

areas are best located away from paved areas, but in spring and fall comfort may be enhanced by nearby drives or walks. Sunny south slopes can be used in much the same way (Figure 8.2).

Soil types and drainage areas should also be considered. Drainageways may be unsuitable play areas following rains. Not only will they be wet, they may also be subject to erosion and may collect runoff sediment. Low areas underlain by clay will warm up late in spring, making them poor places for early-season vegetables (Figures 8.3 to 8.6).

Finally, aesthetics should also be weighed. The sound of cars braking for a stop sign, or the view of a neighbor's parked camper, may not detract from active sports, but it can diminish the enjoyment of conversation and a contemplative mood.

Where environmental considerations conflict with convenience and function, the conflict can only be resolved in terms of personal priorities. Choosing between a sitting area close to the back door but with a poor view and one further from the house with a better view is necessarily a subjective judgment but is nonetheless important.

Recording Design Decisions   The most suitable alternatives are recorded either on the second drawing directly or on a transparent overlay. While exact dimensions may change slightly as planning continues, spaces should be roughed in as accurately as possible (Figure 8.7).

Pathways should also be roughed in where needed. Because their exact dimensions and routes will be determined on the final drawing, at this stage they should be kept simple and direct (Figure 8.8).

Finally, before plantings are considered, the proposed plan is given a final evaluation. Undesirable views that require screening

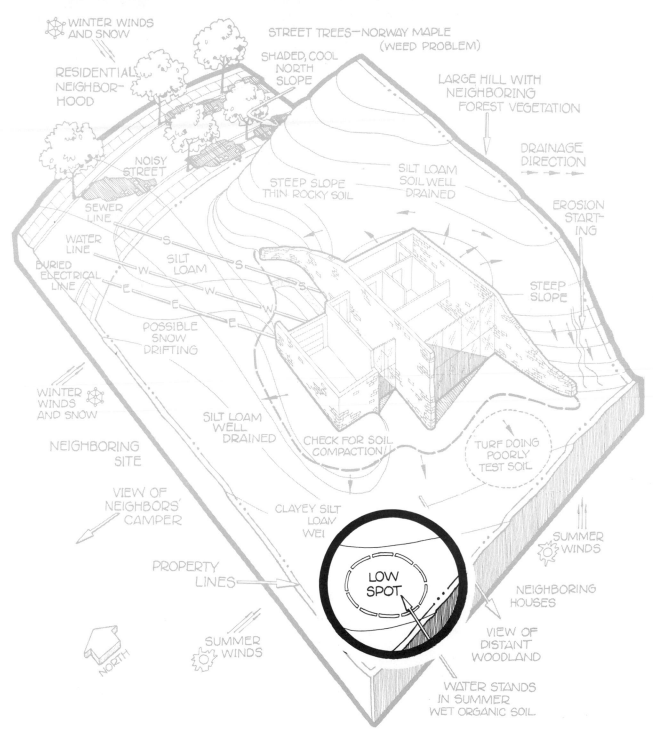

Fig. 8.3 Low spot.

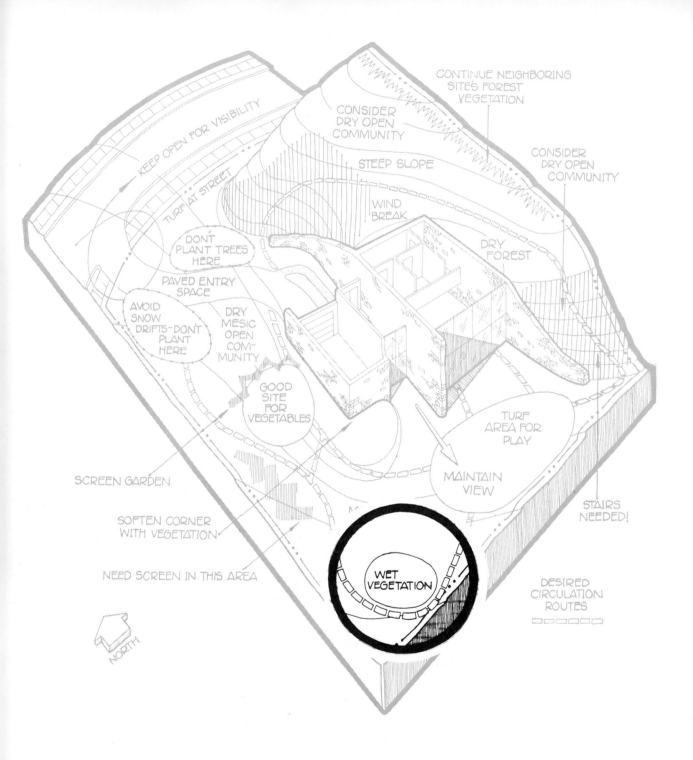

Fig. 8.4   *Wet vegetation.*

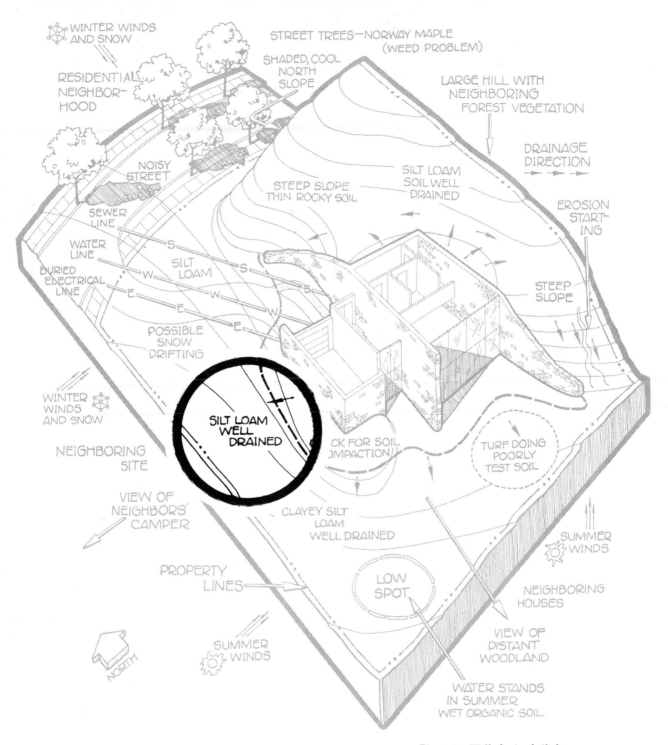

Fig. 8.5 Well-drained silt loam area.

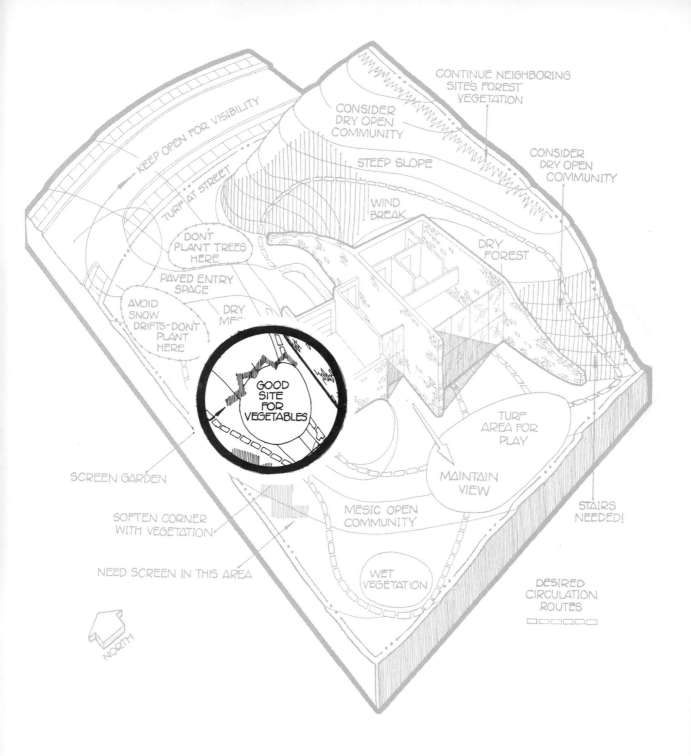

CONTINUE NEIGHBORING
SITE'S FOREST
VEGETATION

CONSIDER
DRY OPEN
COMMUNITY

CONSIDER
DRY OPEN
COMMUNITY

KEEP OPEN FOR VISIBILITY

STEEP SLOPE

WIND
BREAK

TURF AT STREET

DRY
FOREST

DON'T
PLANT TREES
HERE

PAVED ENTRY
SPACE

AVOID
SNOW
DRIFTS—DON'T
PLANT
HERE

DRY
MES...

GOOD
SITE
FOR
VEGETABLES

TURF
AREA FOR
PLAY

SCREEN GARDEN

MAINTAIN
VIEW

STAIRS
NEEDED!

SOFTEN CORNER
WITH VEGETATION

MESIC OPEN
COMMUNITY

NEED SCREEN IN THIS AREA

WET
VEGETATION

DESIRED
CIRCULATION
ROUTES

NORTH

Fig. 8.6   Vegetable garden site.

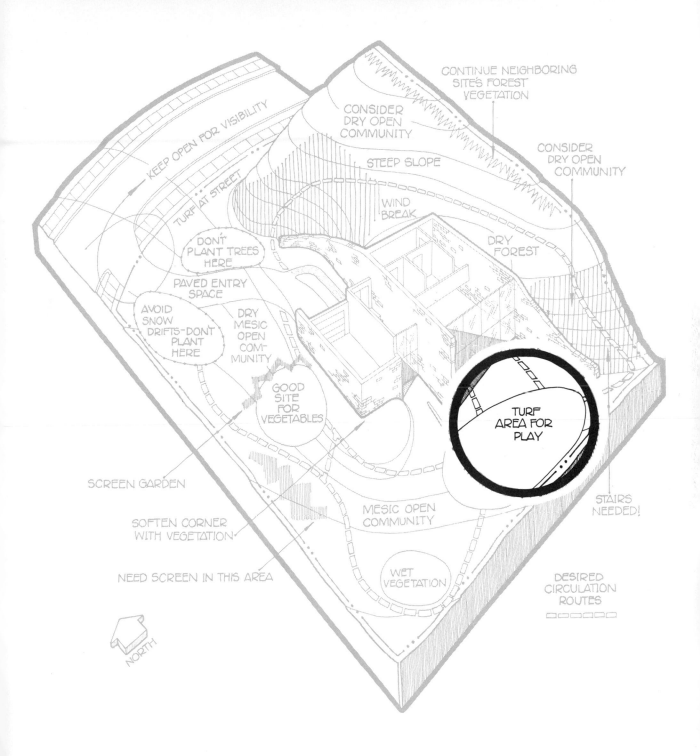

CONTINUE NEIGHBORING SITE'S FOREST VEGETATION

CONSIDER DRY OPEN COMMUNITY

CONSIDER DRY OPEN COMMUNITY

STEEP SLOPE

KEEP OPEN FOR VISIBILITY

TURF AT STREET

WIND BREAK

DRY FOREST

DON'T PLANT TREES HERE

PAVED ENTRY SPACE

AVOID SNOW DRIFTS-DON'T PLANT HERE

DRY MESIC OPEN COMMUNITY

GOOD SITE FOR VEGETABLES

TURF AREA FOR PLAY

SCREEN GARDEN

STAIRS NEEDED!

SOFTEN CORNER WITH VEGETATION

MESIC OPEN COMMUNITY

NEED SCREEN IN THIS AREA

WET VEGETATION

DESIRED CIRCULATION ROUTES
☐☐☐☐☐☐☐

NORTH

Fig. 8.7 Turf area for play.

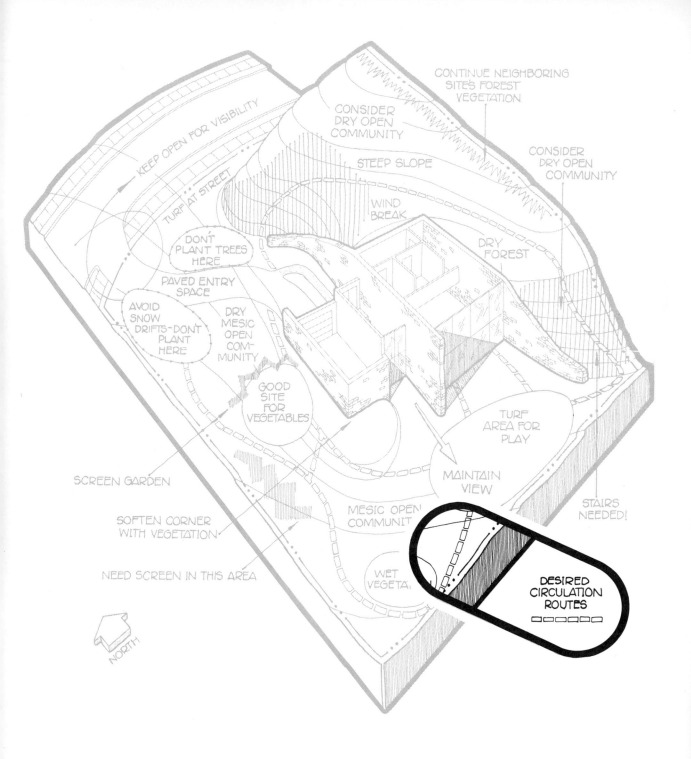

Fig. 8.8 *Desired circulation routes.*

and areas that require shelter from the sun and wind should both be noted on the plan. Conversely, positive features to preserve—such as a good view through a window—should also be recorded (Figures 8.9 and 8.10).

Plantings

Each of the native plant communities introduced earlier has its own unique visual and physical characteristics and its own environmental requirements. Based on these considerations, the desired communities are identified and roughed in on the second drawing. The exact placement of individual plants is reserved for the final drawing.

Functional Considerations

Plant communities can be turned to advantage for physical comfort, visual screening, and energy conservation. Each, however, serves those ends differently. As a general guideline, they can be divided into three major groups: open communities (the grasslands), semishaded communities (the savannas), and shaded communities (the forests). Obviously, these divisions are not clear-cut. The tall-grass prairie, for example, may conceal more of the horizon in late summer than a mature pine wood. Thus, while these divisions can serve as a guide, it is important to get to know the local communities firsthand before selecting any as a model.

Comfort at different seasons of the year is a major landscaping concern. Deciduous forest communities allow the ground to warm early in spring before the leaves form, but shade it and keep it cool in summer. Evergreen communities, on the other hand, block the sun year-round. The grasslands provide little shade at any time of the year, but often warm up quickly in spring.

Screening is a second concern. Woody communities can effectively screen unpleasant views, provide visual privacy, and control unwanted pedestrian traffic. The last of these usually requires only planting the dense shrubbery characteristic of the oak woodlands. Visual screening, however, requires more careful planning.

The critical factor in creating an effective screen is the *sight line*, the line of view between an object and the observer. To be effective, the vegetation used must be tall enough to intercept this line at some point along its length. While this can be a relatively simple consideration on a level site, on uneven topography the height can change with distance from the observer. On a site like that illustrated in Figure 8.11, small shrubs or tall grasses must be placed relatively close to the viewer to be effective. If more distant placement is required, taller shrubs or trees are required.

A second factor in selecting vegetation for screening is its foliage. Fifteen to thiry feet of deciduous trees and shrubs may be needed to maintain an effective screen in winter. Thus, evergreens, which retain their foliage year-round, may be preferable where space is limited (Figures 8.12 and 8.13).

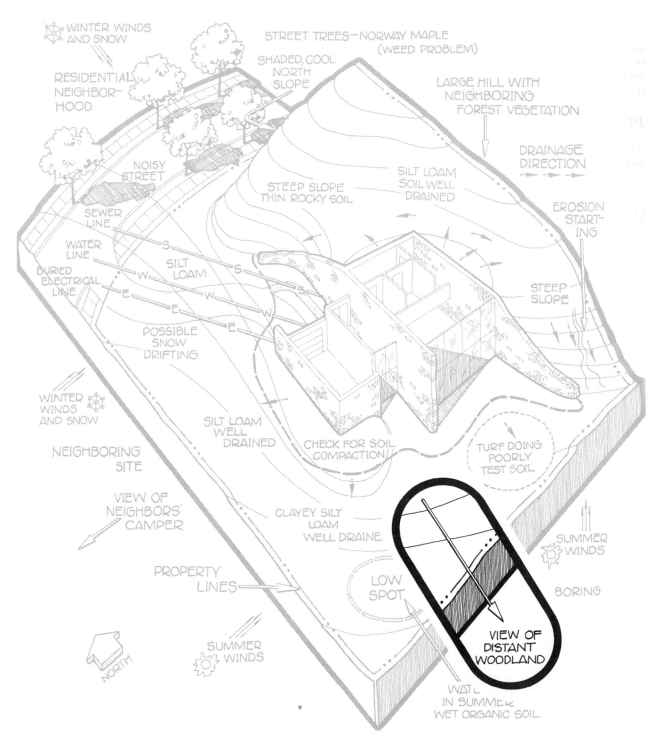

Fig. 8.9 *View of distant woodland.*

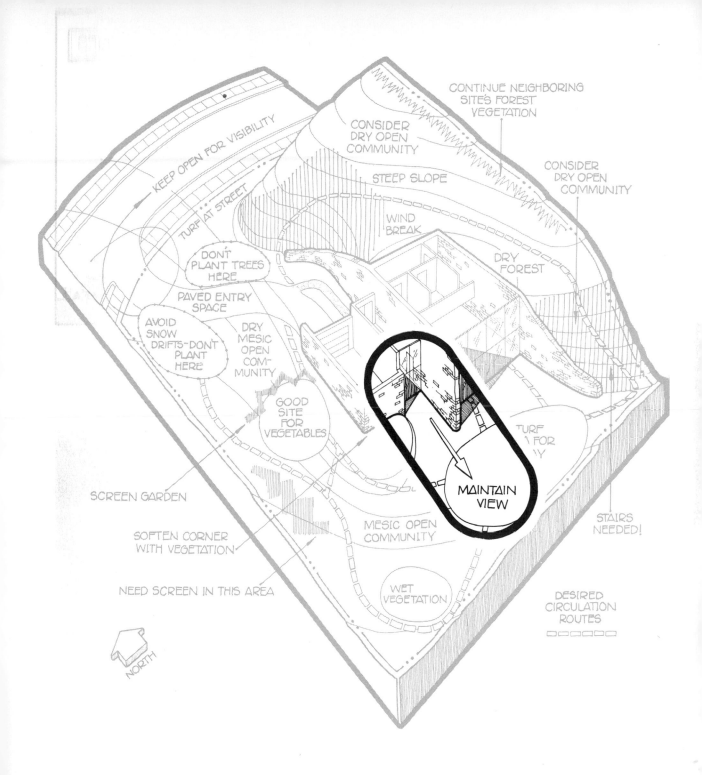

CONTINUE NEIGHBORING SITE'S FOREST VEGETATION

CONSIDER DRY OPEN COMMUNITY

CONSIDER DRY OPEN COMMUNITY

KEEP OPEN FOR VISIBILITY

TURF AT STREET

STEEP SLOPE

WIND BREAK

DRY FOREST

DON'T PLANT TREES HERE

PAVED ENTRY SPACE

AVOID SNOW DRIFTS—DON'T PLANT HERE

DRY MESIC OPEN COMMUNITY

GOOD SITE FOR VEGETABLES

MAINTAIN VIEW

TURF FOR

SCREEN GARDEN

SOFTEN CORNER WITH VEGETATION

MESIC OPEN COMMUNITY

STAIRS NEEDED!

NEED SCREEN IN THIS AREA

WET VEGETATION

DESIRED CIRCULATION ROUTES

NORTH

Fig. 8.10   Maintain view.

113

Fig. 8.11 *Sight-line evaluation technique.*

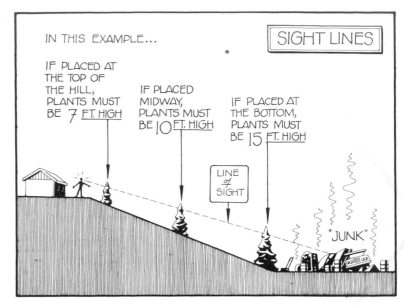

Fig. 8.12 *A single row of deciduous shrubs will not totally screen a view.*

Where the need is to preserve a view rather than to block it, open communities rather than wooded ones may be the obvious choice, although again a mature stand of pines can be used to maintain a lateral view while also providing a psychological sense of privacy. It should also be noted that the height of grassland vegetation changes with the season and the community. A waving mass of big bluestem in late August can be as effective a screen as a planting of mountain laurel, but earlier in the year the same grasses may not block the view of even a young child. The smaller grasses typical of the xeric grasslands have a maximum height of about 3 feet, and thus effectively preserve a view throughout the season.

Finally, vegetation can be used for energy conservation, a benefit rarely discussed despite our heightened awareness of the need for it. As farmers in the plains states well know, windbreaks planted to block prevailing winter winds can be a significant source of insulation. Where space is unlimited, deciduous woodlands can be used, but evergreens are more effective for most practical purposes. There is, however, a caution in planting an evergreen windbreak: it should not form a solid barrier. Where it does, it creates an area of low pressure immediately to the leeward side, pulling winds downward and reducing the length of the area of shelter. It has the same effect on drifting snow. As wind velocity falls, snow tends to settle and accumulate—an especially important concern near driveways and walks (Figure 8.14).

Vegetation can also be used as a natural air-conditioner. Foliage overhanging a roof during the summer has the same cooling effect on buildings that it has on people. But while evergreens continue to shade buildings during the winter, deciduous species allow the sun to warm them after the leaves fall. There is again one caution in using plants for air conditioning. Care should be taken to avoid placing them where they will shade solar collectors at any time of the year.

Despite the variety of ways plants can be used to improve the environment of a landscape, there is one thing they cannot do. Plants do not control sound effectively. Many hundreds of feet of vegetation are required for even nominal sound abatement. Usually, a border of trees and shrubs will not reduce heavy traffic noise to a level below that of normal conversation. On most sites, therefore, effective sound control requires the use of fencing or earth berms.

Fig. 8.13   Coniferous screen.

Fig. 8.14   Snow accumulates behind a row of conifers.

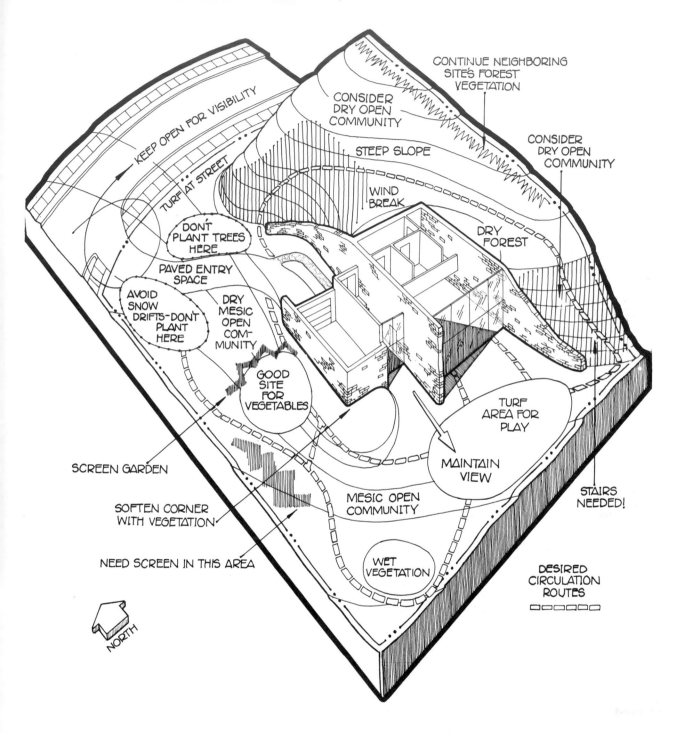

CONTINUE NEIGHBORING SITE'S FOREST VEGETATION

CONSIDER DRY OPEN COMMUNITY

CONSIDER DRY OPEN COMMUNITY

STEEP SLOPE

KEEP OPEN FOR VISIBILITY

TURF AT STREET

WIND BREAK

DRY FOREST

DON'T PLANT TREES HERE

PAVED ENTRY SPACE

AVOID SNOW DRIFTS-DON'T PLANT HERE

DRY MESIC OPEN COMMUNITY

GOOD SITE FOR VEGETABLES

TURF AREA FOR PLAY

SCREEN GARDEN

MAINTAIN VIEW

STAIRS NEEDED!

SOFTEN CORNER WITH VEGETATION

MESIC OPEN COMMUNITY

NEED SCREEN IN THIS AREA

WET VEGETATION

DESIRED CIRCULATION ROUTES

NORTH

Fig. 8.15 The completed use-planning drawing.

116

Environmental Considerations An evaluation of the functional advantages of the various types of plantings possible will give an initial idea of the types of communities to plant and where to locate them. But those decisions must also be related to the environment the site offers.

The communities selected should be appropriate for the region, to minimize maintenance. Although beautiful, the eastern azaleas and laurels are not native to the upper midwest. Keeping them alive during the severe midwestern winters may be difficult. They may also require periodic additions of soil acidifiers. It is far more logical to plant natives already adapted to local climate.

Not all communities native to a region are equally appropriate for a given site in it, however. Even though the mixed mesophytic forest is representative of the central states, it is inappropriate where the soils are strongly acidic or degraded by erosion. The information on the site analysis drawing describes the local habitat and should be used in the selection of local communities of plants.

These basic guidelines do not eliminate all choice. On dry, sandy soils to the north, pine woodlands, pine barrens, and bracken grasslands are all appropriate planting choices. On a moist, fertile site in the central states, choices include the mesic prairie, the oak opening, and the mesic deciduous woodland. It is important to note, however, that while all these choices are appropriate, not all will be equally easy to establish or free of maintenance. Creating a mesic woodland requires some provision for shade as well as an annual renewal of the organic litter layer. If a mature maple or basswood shades the site and there is shelter from wind, maintenance will be minimal and the tree will provide needed litter. On the other hand, if the site is barren of trees, establishing the forest herbs may require either the purchase of mature trees or a wait of several years for saplings to grow.

The following chapters provide more specific information related to the choice of communities.

The Completed Drawing

Careful consideration of personal requirements for the site, planting preferences, and environment will produce a general site plan that identifies the communities to be established, the recreation and utility areas to be created, and the locations for them. All of this information is recorded on the second drawing. Figure 8.15 is an example of a completed site use drawing.

Additional Reading

Robinette, Gary, *Plants/People/and Environmental Quality*, U.S. Dept. of the Interior, National Park Service, Washington, D.C., 1972.
U.S. Department of Agriculture, *Landscape for Living*, The Yearbook of Agriculture, 1972.

chapter nine

Designing
the Planting Plan

T he final phase of planning, planting design, is primarily aesthetic. It involves the choice of species to be planted, their numbers, and their placement, and has one major guideline: the planting
should look natural. The severe geometry of conventional designs is
replaced, therefore, by the more subtle and varied patterns of the
native landscape. At the same time, a variety of aesthetic principles
can be incorporated to heighten the planting's effect. While this may
seem inconsistent, "rules" need not be incompatible with naturalizing. A parallel exists in other arts. Music, for example, is a fundamental, emotional form of expression, but it achieves its effect
through a structure of tonal and rhythmic rules. In the same way,
the aesthetic qualities of vegetation can be employed to enhance the
enjoyment of a landscape. Success requires the development of a
sense of taste and appreciation for the visual aspects of native communities through contact with them.

Although professionals often work with models, the design can be
worked out on the site itself. A variety of objects, including sticks
and strings, can be used to simulate the size and height of plants.
These are moved around and viewed from different angles until the
most satisfactory locations are found. Final decisions are recorded
on the third drawing, which is used as a planting guide.

Elements of Design

Color, line, and texture are among the principal aesthetic elements
nature offers. Lighting, in turn, heightens and adds variety to each

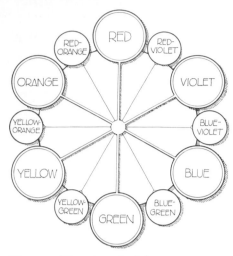

Fig. 9.1   The color wheel.

of these basic elements. The following pages serve as a brief introduction to these design tools and their use.

Color   Color is often less flamboyant and more controlled in nature than in the commercial world. It exists most obviously in flowers but is also found in foliage, buds, stems, bark, and the dried materials of fall and winter. Because much of nature's color is seasonal, planning for it throughout the year requires the use of a variety of species.

Color effect in nature as in art is achieved through six basic elements and the interactions between them. For simplicity, they can be called hue, brilliance, afterimage, saturation, cool-warm contrast, and proportion.

Hue   Red, orange, yellow, green, blue, and violet—the most prominent bands of the rainbow—are chromatic colors at their greatest intensity. These are the major hues and are represented as the larger circles on the color wheel in Figure 9.1. Combinations, along with the occasional inclusion of achromatic colors (white, gray, and black), can be used to give a landscape expressive feelings ranging from extreme liveliness to relative restraint, as illustrated in Color Plates 4, 7, and 47.

Minor hues are those intermediate between the basic six and do not have as strong an impact. They can be used to add variety and richness to a planting. Although countless minor hues occur in nature, only the six most easily recognized have been included on the color wheel, where they are represented as smaller circles.

Brilliance   The basic hues exist in a range of darker shades and lighter tints that represent degrees of brilliance. Contrast in brilliance enhances a plant's basic hue. Dark backgrounds cause lighter colors to seem more intense, while light backgrounds make darker colors seem less intense (see Color Plates 6 and 9). The opposite effect is achieved by reducing contrast. Blue flowers on a brown background or yellow flowers on a white background seem subdued.

In landscaping as in painting, contrast in brilliance can be used to create a dynamic impression of depth. Both light colors against dark and dark colors against light appear closer to the viewer than they are. This can be an especially important factor in selecting plants for use near buildings.

Afterimage   Afterimage is a phenomenon recognized by both artists and psychologists. It occurs when a person of normal color vision stares at a given hue. The eye demands a second color to balance the first and produces an impression of it whether or not the color is present. This second color is the *complement* of the first. The color wheel has been drawn so that opposing hues are complementary pairs.

An example of the effect of afterimage occurs while viewing a landscape of green foliage. The eye perceives the complementary color red, and any red flower or fruit that may be present appears especially vivid. Color Plate 47 is an illustration. Plates 12 and 20 are examples involving other pairs of colors.

Afterimage also affects perception in at least two other ways. If purple prairie clover and butterfly weed are planted near each other in a sea of grasses, the purple of the clover and the orange of the butterfly weed will be tinged with red (the complement to the greens of the grasses) and will appear to vibrate. In contrast, if a group of yellow-green plants is located near a group of blue-green plants of equal brilliance, the afterimages (red-violet and red-orange respectively) mix with the original colors in a way that reduces the vividness of the entire planting. To avoid this negative effect, it may be necessary to select plants whose colors differ in brilliance. The light-dark contrast will reduce the effect of afterimage.

When achromatic colors are located next to chromatic colors of the same brilliance, they lose their achromatic character because of afterimage. Thus, when white flowers are mixed with pink, the white blooms take on a greenish cast because of the afterimage created by the pink blooms. To keep achromatic colors looking pure, the hues of adjacent plantings should be of a different brilliance.

Saturation Hues unmixed with achromatic colors are considered to be saturated. Those mixed with white, gray, or black reflect degrees of desaturation. Contrast in saturation as in brilliance can be used to create an illusion of depth without evoking the effects of afterimage. A pure hue located next to the same hue unsaturated will appear closer to the viewer than the latter. Free of afterimage, this type of contrast has a restful effect (see Color Plates 16 and 39).

Cool-Warm Contrast Psychologically, the colors from yellow to red-violet on the color wheel appear warm, while those from yellow-green to violet appear cool. By itself, this effect can be used to create a landscape that suggests either tranquility or activity (see Color Plates 6, 24, and 38). Contrasts between colors can also be used. Because cool colors appear further away from the viewer than do warm, contrast can be used to suggest depth. The effect is relative, however. A warm color may seem cool when placed next to a warmer color. In addition, when a contrast in brilliance is added, the illusion of depth can either be enhanced or diminished.

Proportion Hues differ in visual intensity. A viewer must see a larger area of a less intense color to get the same impact from it as from a lesser amount of a more intense color. Based on their inherent brilliance, the following proportions of the major hues have essentially the same impact: yellow-3, orange-4, red-6, green-6, blue-8, and violet-9. Because yellow has three times the intensity of violet, it should occupy only one-third the area to produce a balanced, harmonious effect. This effect is relative to the background, however. Yellow set against white will appear less intense than when set against a darker color. Like brilliance, proportion can be used to create an illusion of depth. A small patch of green set against a

Fig. 9.2   An enclosure formed by the vertical lines of tall grasses. (Photo by David Bach.)

Fig. 9.3   A linear pattern acts as a space divider.

brown background appears to withdraw, while a patch of yellow seems to advance. The variety of effects created by proportion are illustrated in Color Plates 11, 12, and 47.

Line   In nature, lines are created primarily by the trunks of trees, their branches, and the stems of shrubs and herbs. They can be used to direct the eye and shape a space. Like woody plants, tall grasses can be used effectively to outline and enclose an area. In addition, their growth as the season progresses creates a dynamic effect by changing the size and feeling of a space.

The arrangement of lines also affects perception. A combination of lines that produces a simpler figure than the sum of the lines would otherwise indicate is seen as an integrated whole. Its harmony can produce a feeling of tranquility. In contrast, more complex patterns can make an area seem busier and smaller (Figures 9.2 and 9.3).

Texture   Texture is the term used to define the visual quality of a surface, and, like lines, plant textures can be used to alter the perception of an area. Fine textures tend to retreat from the viewer, while coarser ones tend to advance. Thus contrasting textures, like colors, can be used to add depth to a planting (see Color Plate 16). This effect also makes an area seem larger, because the eye, having more work to do, requires more time to take it in.

Light   The everchanging direction and character of natural lighting can add to the effect of color, line, and texture. A tree viewed against the light stands out dramatically from its background and makes us feel its closeness more acutely (see Color Plate 42). Green foliage appears yellow-green when viewed against the sun and blue-green when viewed with it (see Color Plate 41). When seen from a dark spot against a dark background, the emerald green of brightly lit grasses is especially striking (see Color Plate 26). Thus, spectacular effects can sometimes be created by designing a planting to take advantage of the shallow angle of the sun in the morning and evening (see Color Plate 21).

Spatial Design

The perception of an area, the feeling it gives, is in large part shaped by the nature of the vegetation that surrounds it. A small space surrounded by trees will feel smaller than if it were surrounded by grasses reaching just above eye level. It will retain a feeling of privacy, yet will feel somewhat expansive, if openings are left between trees or if open-branching species are used.

The design of enclosing vegetation should be as free-form as possible. As suggested earlier, it is desirable to avoid planting screens in straight lines. When limited space makes this impractical, the

Fig. 9.4 *The graceful curves of natural streams can serve as models for a naturalistic planting.*

Fig. 9.5 *Note the nonnatural quality created by the straight lines in this traditional landscape.*

Fig. 9.6 *A curved pathway begins to add a natural quality to the same residence. (John Diekelmann, landscape architect.)*

Fig. 9.7 *Again, note the predominant linear forms.*

sense of linearity can at least be minimized through the use of a variety of species. A planting will feel most natural if its lines resemble the curves of a river or the gentle billows of a cloud. In attempting to achieve this effect, however, there is one caution. Curves that become too regular, like those of a piece of corrugated roofing, will look just as unnatural as a straight line (Figures 9.4 to 9.8).

The horizontal or ground plane of an area is also important in a design. The use of lighting effects or repetition of plant materials to draw the eye along can create a dynamic feeling (see Color Plate 39). Repeated colors (Color Plate 23) and the use of water can also attract the eye. If space allows, a rise in elevation with the hint of something beyond is also effective. To avoid the feeling of contrivance, however, a special feature such as a rock outcropping or an especially colorful grouping of plants should be used as a reward to the eye.

Finally, overhead enclosures can also affect the feeling a space gives. Depending on its height, a canopy can provide a sense of privacy or majesty. It is not necessary to have a solid canopy. To gain some sense of the effects of a canopy, compare the feeling of standing under a lone tree with that of standing in a forest of mature pines (Figures 9.9 and 9.10).

Among the emotional qualities that can be designed into a space are mystery, suspense, surprise, and tranquility. The first two can be created with dark, tunnellike plantings of shrubs and trees. Surprise is a greater challenge, because once a device has been experienced it wears thin. One of the best possibilities is a vivid display of flowers that appears suddenly around a corner. Because they will bloom only for a brief period, the effect is rarely worn out. Tranquility is perhaps the most important emotional attribute a land-

Fig. 9.8 *The curved pathway and naturalistic plantings invite the eye to explore the space. (John Diekelmann, landscape architect.)*

scape can have. Cool, intimate spaces during the summer, sunny areas warmed in winter, and shaded areas with an expansive or dramatic overlook are a few of the designs that can be used to create a relaxed or pensive mood (see Color Plates 7, 21, and 40) (Figure 9.11).

The sequence of spaces can also have an important effect on emotion. If a path is noisy, the tranquility of the area it leads to can be diminished. On the other hand, if it is quiet and easily walked, the destination will feel more relaxing.

The key to a successful landscape design is a diversity of spaces. Areas that complement a range of emotions can be created even within a small landscape with careful planning and the effective use of plants (Figures 9.12 and 9.13).

Plant Placement

Planting patterns are important not only in achieving a natural feeling, but also in taking advantage of plants for function as well as beauty. The following pages offer a number of general guidelines.

Spacing The natural growth patterns of individual species should be used as a guide to planting. Forcing them into other patterns not only destroys the natural effect of a planting, it also increases the need for maintenance. In general, species either grow in clusters or

Fig. 9.9 *An urban site without overhead enclosure.*

Fig. 9.10 *An urban site in which a mature tree forms an overhead enclosure.*

Fig. 9.11 *Tunnel space entry, Great Smoky Mountains National Park.*

Fig. 9.12   Traditional planting.

Fig. 9.13   Possible naturalized planting.

as randomly spaced individuals. Those that are randomly spaced usually reproduce by seed rather than by vegetative means. Because they spread by means of wind or animal dispersal, their density varies from area to area. Distinct clusters, however, are rare. Plants spreading vegetatively as well as by seed often form distinct clumps which are separated by spaces devoid of the same species. The size of these colonies can be relatively uniform or may vary widely.

The geometry of traditional landscapes is especially apparent in the spacing given to trees. Street plantings usually are 40 feet on center. In nature, the spacing of trees varies from community to community and ranges from clumps of birches and oaks to the randomly spaced trees of the savannas (Figures 9.14 and 9.15).

Fig. 9.14   Basswood clumps in mesic forest.

Fig. 9.15   Aggregated group of oaks in savanna.

Masses and Specimens   Plantings of shrub and small tree masses for the sake of screening usually incorporate from one to three species. Repeated masses should be kept relatively alike with only minor variations. The planting patterns should reflect natural growth. Shrubs that spread vegetatively, like sumac and gray dogwood, require minimal planning because they will fill in to form thickets. Nonspreading plants like nannyberry viburnum and witch hazel will remain as planted for generations and should be placed carefully. The key in using them is to make certain that views are blocked from all angles (Figures 9.16 and 9.17).

Fig. 9.16   Edge with island of shrubs.

Fig. 9.17   Edge with contrasts of color and shape.

Specimen plants can be used to emphasize the mass itself or can act as counterpoints. Usually, plants used as specimens should have a distinctive shape year-round, as do bur oaks, pines, musclewood, hawthorns, and prairie crab apple. These species will be set apart from their background because of their shapes, whether planted as part of a mass or apart from it. They can be planted as solitary plants or in groups of from two to five. Larger groups, however, become masses in themselves (Figure 9.18).

Fig. 9.18   White pine specimens occurring as a repetitive spatial element.

Planting on Slopes Retaining a natural look when planting slopes or uneven topography requires special attention. If a hilltop is to be planted in woodland, the trees should trail down the slope to emphasize the roll of the land. Plantings at the base of hills should begin a few feet up the slope to emphasize the rise in terrain. It is important, as well, to avoid planting along contour lines. Plantings that follow the contour will appear unnaturally linear (Figures 9.19 and 9.20).

Fig. 9.19   Linear patterns rising up along contours.

Fig. 9.20   Vegetation beginning upslope.

Planting at Buildings   Two major questions arise in designing plantings near buildings: how to soften the transition from building to landscape, and whether or not to emphasize the character of the building.

Most modern structures are constructed with components that have been manufactured in mass. By necessity, these have straight lines and pronounced edges. The best contemporary architects have recognized this fact and have expressed it honestly in their designs. For most purposes, it probably will not be desirable to hide the character of the well-designed building. Globular plantings, neutral in shape, are often highly effective in such situations (Figures 9.21 and 9.22).

Most buildings can also be classified as either vertical, horizontal, or cubical. Where shape conflicts with the lay of the land, blending the building into its surroundings requires some care. For the tall building on level terrain, horizontal masses of plants of decreasing height can be used to create a gradual transition. Where shape complements terrain, on the other hand, the transition is easier and plantings should reinforce the shape of the building. A planting of grasses or low shrubs can simply and effectively blend a long, low building into a level landscape.

Usually, it is best to use plantings at the corners of a building, although the symmetry that results from planting corners alike should be avoided. An exception to this general rule is a corner with windows or one with an acute angle. These should be left unplanted and treated as part of the terrain. Corners should probably also be left unplanted if an entire facade of the building is to be empha-

Fig. 9.21   *LaFayette Park, Detroit, Mich. (Ludwig Mies van der Rohe, architect.)*

Fig. 9.22   *Residence with matching vegetation forms.*

Fig. 9.23 Residence with vegetation as backdrop.

sized, although low shrubs or grasses can be used if they do not cut into the visual volume of the building (Figure 9.23).

An additional concern when planting near buildings is whether to use deciduous or evergreen species. Because deciduous species lose their leaves in fall, the view of the building they give will change with the seasons, revealing more in winter and less in summer.

Finally, it is basic to naturalizing that plants are allowed to grow to their natural size and shape. Because growth is not repressed, it is especially important to anticipate the ultimate size plantings will achieve and to plan for it (Figures 9.24 to 9.27).

Pathway Design

Pathways are far more important in naturalizing than in the conventional landscape dominated by lawn. They allow access to major plantings and serve as an aesthetic link between plantings. In general, the size of a path should reflect its importance. Major paths should be wider than secondary ones, especially as they approach entries to buildings. Path width, however, should reflect need. Even in a low-traffic area, a 5-foot path may be desirable because it will allow people to walk together and converse.

In the natural setting, paths should be allowed to meander much like a river. When run directly between two points, they take on the artificiality of a street. The route probably should not circle back and forth arbitrarily, however. Usually it is best if a pathway leads fairly regularly toward its destination.

Path edges are a special challenge. The traditional practice of lining paths with logs or fences is predictable and unnatural, and usu-

Fig. 9.24 Insignificant clipped vegetation at base of house.

Fig. 9.25 Residence dwarfed by specimen tree.

Fig. 9.26 The ever-popular evergreens are always appropriate.

Fig. 9.27 For a few years at least.

ally it is unnecessary in all but the most heavily used public areas. A border more in keeping with naturalizing might involve a partial border of local stone, but even this should be used only when it is necessary to protect fragile plants. In most cases, it is best simply to edge a path with vegetation (Figures 9.28 to 9.32).

Topography should also be considered in pathway design. It is best to avoid routing a path directly uphill. Not only does it make walking difficult, it increases the risk of erosion. Where limited space makes such a route necessary, stairs should be used, but must be kept structurally separate from ground level. If not, water will collect along the edges of the steps and will produce erosion.

Fig. 9.28   Stairway at the Clearing. (Jens Jensen, landscape architect.)

Fig. 9.29   Natural rock formation, Door County, Wis.

Fig. 9.30   Residence with flagstone driveway. (John Diekelmann, landscape architect.)

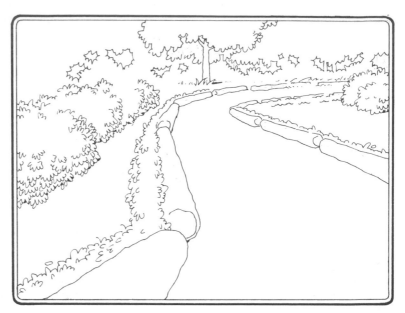

Fig. 9.31 *Path bordered and rigidly directed.*

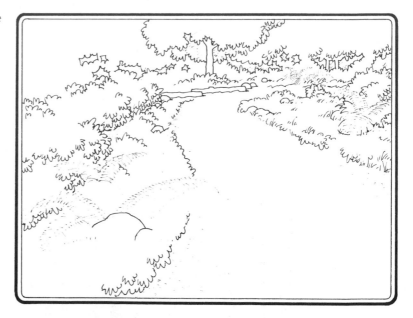

Fig. 9.32 *Path directed, not bordered.*

Design Conflicts

Often, naturalistic designs will require some adjustment to avoid personal conflict with neighbors or aesthetic conflict with their landscapes. In general, it is best to let neighbors know what is planned for a landscape, to devote high maintenance to highly visible areas, to relate a planting as much as possible to the neighborhood, and to screen "objectionable" plantings with more acceptable ones. Shrub masses are acceptably traditional and can be used to screen unconventional grassland plantings. To be most effective, however, they should be purchased in mature sizes or allowed to grow for a couple of seasons before initiating a grassland. Mulching and maintaining a clear demarcation between shrub bed and the mowed turf at the street front will also make the planting more acceptable. The transition from conventional landscapes to natural ones can also be softened. Rather than planting a front yard of tall grasses, it may be desirable to plant colorful forbs mixed with shorter grasses and sedges.

A second kind of conflict that can arise is one between aesthetics and function. For purposes of energy conservation, it may be necessary to block an attractive view to the northwest. In this case, seating can be placed on the view side of the windbreak for use when desired. A parallel situation can be found in Frank Lloyd Wright's design for Falling Water, where the house is located *over* a waterfall. Occupants are required to walk out of the house to view the falls, creating a more active and striking experience. Other apparent conflicts can be turned to advantage with similar creativity (Figure 9.33).

Fig. 9.33   Falling Water. (Frank Lloyd Wright, architect.)

Plant Sources

A major consideration in planting design is the availability of the native plant materials needed in a community approach to naturalizing. There is a concern among some botanists that the integrity of the genetic makeup of local species may be compromised by the introduction of plants from distant areas. While local plants have adapted to their environment over thousands of years, plants of the same species from other areas may have adapted to different conditions. While paper birches in southern Wisconsin grow successfully on exposed southwest slopes, those brought in from northern Wisconsin do poorly in the same areas. It has also been observed that the leaves of musclewood trees brought in from milder climates turn black with the first frost, while the leaves of those indigenous to the north have a beautiful yellow-bronze fall color.

The safest and most ethical answer to this problem is to make every attempt to use plants from populations growing within 50 miles of the site to be planted. Not only will they be more likely to thrive, they may help to insure the preservation of locally adapted species.

If no local nursery carries the plants a design calls for, it may be necessary to propagate them. While this may lengthen the time needed to establish a planting, it can also be rewarding. A number of the references listed in the additional reading contain information on the propagation of both woody and herbaceous native species.

Digging from the Wild It cannot be stressed too strongly that undisturbed native plant communities are becoming rare and that their preservation is a major priority. *Therefore plants should never be removed from a native stand unless it is threatened with immediate destruction.* It should also be noted that in recent years a variety of organizations have devoted great time and effort to the restoration of native vegetation to roadsides, school grounds, parks, and private property. For that reason, it is best never to dig plants from public places and to dig on private property only with the permission of the owner.

Within these guidelines, there distressingly remain many areas where digging may be appropriate, among them housing developments, waste-disposal sites, landfill areas, quarries, and agricultural areas. Where such areas are available, digging has one major advantage in addition to its economic savings. One square foot of wild sod offers a diverse natural grouping of plants that requires years to develop when beginning with seeds or seedlings. Many wild plants, excluding trees and large shrubs, can be transplanted successfully if given adequate water and an appropriate environment. It is especially important to dig as deep as possible (8 to 12 inches) to get as many roots as can be taken.

Nursery Purchases One advantage that nursery stock has over plants dug from the wild is that usually the roots are more compact. This is an especially important advantage with large trees and shrubs. When buying from a nursery, however, it is important to determine whether the nursery grows its own plants or buys from large wholesale nurseries. Locally grown materials are usually from stocks adapted to the local climate. Those purchased are usually brought in from distant sources.

Final Considerations

In designing a landscape it is best to anticipate the time and effort that will be required to establish it. Naturalized landscapes cannot be established as quickly and usually not as simply as a lawn. They do require time to develop and mature. If conditions are right, a grassland planting might require three growing seasons to become well established. A woodland begun from scratch may take up to 30 if it requires planting trees. Thus, it might be desirable to limit the size of the initial planting to dimensions that will be easy to manage, such as the area of a vegetable garden. If too much is attempted at once, the entire project may suffer because of neglect that would have been avoided with a smaller planting.

The time involved can be abbreviated with the use of larger nursery stock, but this can be expensive. The least expensive and, in the long run, the most interesting and educational approach is to begin with smaller materials and to let the planting develop naturally.

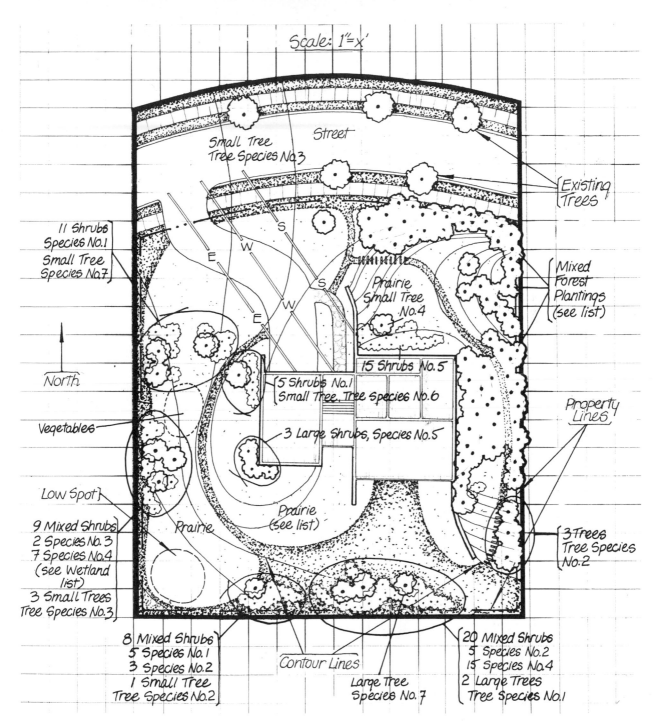

Scale: 1"=x'

Street

Small Tree
Tree Species No.3

Existing
Trees

11 Shrubs
Species No.1
Small Tree
Species No.7

S
W
E
W
E
S

Prairie
Small Tree
No.4

Mixed
Forest
Plantings
(see list)

North

Vegetables

5 Shrubs No.1
Small Tree, Tree Species No.6

15 Shrubs No.5

3 Large Shrubs, Species No.5

Property
Lines

Low Spot

Prairie

9 Mixed Shrubs
2 Species No. 3
7 Species No.4
(see Wetland
list)
3 Small Trees
Tree Species No.3

Prairie
(see list)

3 Trees
Tree Species
No.2

8 Mixed Shrubs
5 Species No.1
3 Species No.2
1 Small Tree
Tree Species No.2

Contour Lines

Large Tree
Species No. 7

20 Mixed Shrubs
5 Species No.2
15 Species No.4
2 Large Trees
Tree Species No.1

Fig. 9.34 Planting plan.

135

NORTH

Fig. 9.35 Aerial view of planting.

The Finished Drawing

Figure 9.34 represents a completed planting plan, and Figure 9.35 is an aerial view of the same planting when matured. Professional landscape architects usually provide more elaborate drawings because theirs are a part of the legal documents for a project. On most private sites, however, the drawings are personal property and serve only as a guide to planting.

Whatever the detail of the drawing, it should include at least an identification of the species to be planted, the numbers of them required, and the locations for planting. This information will not only help to avoid planting mistakes, but will help as well in estimating the cost of the planting.

Because nurseries often categorize plants as evergreens, trees, shrubs, vines, and herbaceous species, it will be helpful to make a separate list of needed plants and to organize it in the same way.

The chapters that follow will cover in greater detail the design, planting techniques, and maintenance of the major types of native communities introduced earlier.

Record Keeping

A useful and enjoyable part of naturalizing is the recording of *phenological* phenomena, the dates that certain events occur. Examples include the arrival of the first robin or the bloom of the first hepatica or pasqueflower. Such information collected for a planting, local natural areas, and roadsides can be a valuable tool in evaluating the environment of a site and an area.

Climatological records can also be useful. A rain gauge, for example, can help in determining whether a new planting requires sprinkling.

An especially rewarding record is a yearly listing of volunteer species, plants that have taken root on their own. As the habitat of a planting matures, appropriate species will begin to establish themselves if there are local sources of seed. They will germinate on small areas of disturbance created by animals many people consider pests: moles, gophers, woodchucks, and others. A record of volunteers can serve as an indication of the health and maturation of a planting.

Additional Reading

Introductory

Eaton, Leonard K., *Landscape Artist in America: The Life and Work of Jens Jensen*, University of Chicago Press, Chicago, 1964.

Grant, John A., and Carol L. Grant, *Garden Design Illustrated*, University of Washington Press, Seattle, 1978.

Haring, Elda, *The Complete Book of Growing Plants from Seed*, Hawthorne, New York, 1967.

Hightshoe, Gary L., *Native Trees for Urban and Rural America*, Iowa State University Research Foundation, Ames, 1978.

Itten, Johannes, *Design and Form*, Van Nostrand Reinhold, New York, 1975.

Morrison, Darrel, *The Native Plant Community Approach to Landscape Design*, University of Wisconsin Extension Bulletin, Madison, expected publication 1981.

Ortho Books, *Do-It-Yourself Garden Construction Know-How*, Chevron Chemical Co., Ortho Division, San Francisco, 1976.

Ortho Books, *The World of Trees*, Chevron Chemical Co., Ortho Division, San Francisco, 1977.

Roberts, Edith Adelaide, and Elsa Rehmann, *American Plants for American Gardens: Plant Ecology—The Study of Plants in Relation to Their Environment*, Macmillan, New York, 1929.

Robinson, Florence Bell, *Planting Design*, McGraw-Hill, New York, 1940.

Soil Conservation Society of America, *Sources of Native Seeds and Plants*, Ankeny, Ia., undated.

Detailed

Fairbrother, Nan, *The Nature of Landscape Design: As an Art Form, A Craft, A Social Necessity*, Knopf, New York, 1974.

Gleason, Henry A., and Arthur Cronquist, *Manual of Vascular Plants of Northeastern United States and Adjacent Canada*, D. Van Nostrand, Princeton, 1963.

Hartmann, Hudson T., and Dale E. Kester, *Plant Propagation: Principles and Practices*, Prentice-Hall, Englewood Cliffs, N.J., 1975.

Itten, Johannes, *The Art of Color*, Van Nostrand Reinhold, New York, 1973.

Schopmeyer, C. S. Tech. Coord., *Seeds of Woody Plants in the United States*, Agriculture Handbook No. 450, Forest Service, U.S. Department of Agriculture, Washington, D.C., 1974.

chapter ten

Open Landscapes

"**O**pen" landscapes are those in which sunlight and the line of sight are unbroken by trees and tall shrubs. For our purposes, they are also those in which feet will stay dry most or all of the year. The models are the native grasslands.

Unshaded, the native communities are dominated by grasses and enlivened throughout the growing season with abundant flowers. Graceful and colorful, they are among the most attractive of the natural communities. As landscapes, they are also among the quickest to establish.

Grassland plantings, however, are also those most affected by local ordinances. The reason is that most planting laws dictate that grasses not exceed a given height, usually 4 to 8 inches. These well-intentioned laws were enacted at a time when energy was abundant and inexpensive and unmowed landscapes signified building neglect. Today, both premises are dated. Energy has become a resource to conserve. And with the growing enjoyment of things natural, unmowed areas often reflect little about the condition of buildings. Still, these older laws continue to interfere with a legitimate interest in landscaping alternatives.

Fortunately, they have slowly begun to change. In at least two states, Maryland and Wisconsin, the courts have affirmed the right to let grasses grow to a natural height. At least one city, Madison, Wisconsin, has also passed an ordinance that attempts to modernize the concept of landscaping. In Madison, the landscaper can obtain a permit to plant native grasses. The ordinance has especially benefited schools with environmental education programs.

Legal and social progress is being made. Where individuals have shown a sincere interest, many cities have begun to make allowances for landscapes of grassland species. Still, the landscaper is strongly advised to consult city officials before proceeding.

Environmental Considerations

Many grassland species are remarkably tolerant of a variety of environments. Witness, for example, the fact that little bluestem occurs in dry to moderately moist habitats from Missouri to Maine. Several factors, however, do shape the native communities, among them light, topography, soil, and moisture gradient.

Light   While a number of grassland species do well in partial shade, most require 6 or more hours of full sunlight a day. Without it, they may be weakened, may fail to produce viable seed, and may gradually be replaced by species better adapted to shade.

Topography   While grasslands occur on virtually all topographic sites, landforms can play a critical role in marginal areas. South and west slopes are most favorable, because their environment is usually warmer and drier than others. East and north slopes are cooler and in moist climates favor the growth of trees.

Soil   In many ways, soil conditions affect grasslands as much as does topography. Many grassland species do well on sand, silt, and clay. Acidity, unless extreme, is not a major factor. In marginal areas, however, well-drained sands will favor the drought-tolerant grasses over trees. Similarly, saturated, poorly drained clays appear to be detrimental to trees and so favor grassland communities.

Moisture Gradient   The amount of moisture available in the soil dictates which grassland species will do best. Soils are conventionally classified as dry (xeric), dry-mesic, mesic, wet-mesic, and wet (hydric). As discussed earlier, each favors a particular population of plants. Thus, determining where a site or parts of it fit on this scale will dictate the selection of species. Wet species may out-compete xeric on moist sites, but may succumb to drought on dry sites.

Regional Considerations

While native grasslands in the northeastern United States and in lower Canada have many qualities in common, there are regional differences. A major one is that of ecotype. While little bluestem occurs throughout, local populations may have unique characteristics. Theoretically, a plant taken beyond its climatic range may not survive even though plants of the same species are native to the area. If it does survive, it may be weakened and prone to disease.

Researchers have also noted that some species growing in old fields have lighter seeds (by a factor of as much as three) and grow taller than the same species growing in prairies. These may reflect ecotypic differences or merely temporary responses to a different environment. Because of these unknowns, obtaining predictable results may require the use of plant stocks from sites that are stable and similar to the area to be planted. If such sites are not available, experimental plots are advisable as a prologue to a full-scale planting.

Habitat preferences also vary with region. In the Central Hardwoods Region, some species found in forest communities elsewhere may grow successfully in grasslands because of the relatively moist climate. Conversely, some species adapted to openings in moist climates may do poorly in drier regions unless sheltered by trees. Examples of the former include shooting star, wild geranium, and trout lily. Examples of the latter are prairie willow and marsh violet.

Finally, the character of grasslands may change from region to region. In the central and midwestern states, they are almost entirely composed of grasses and other nonwoody, flowering species. In the east and north, ferns and heath shrubs like blueberry may be prominent members of the community.

Design Considerations

Grassland communities offer abundant design possibilities, ranging from broad textural and color choices to the physical motion of plants as they are played upon by the wind. It is important, however, to remember that while forbs may appear to play a dominant role at some times of the year, grasses are the natural dominants numerically (Figures 10.1 and 10.2).

Fig. 10.1   Prairie in fall with grasses visually dominant.

Fig. 10.2   Prairie in fall with forbs visually dominant.

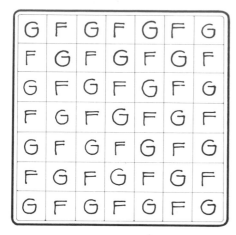

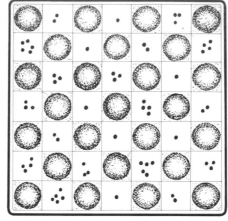

G—GRASS   F—FORB

Fig. 10.3   Stylized plan of prairie planting—half forb, half grasses.

—GRASS   •••—FORB STEMS

Fig. 10.4   Same planting after 5 years. Remember some spring-blooming forbs will not be visible.

Fig. 10.5   Prairie phlox and nodding wild onion among short grasses.

A general rule for achieving the most natural-looking landscape is to plant half nonspreading forbs and half nonspreading grasses. Aggressive species like switch grass, prairie coreopsis, wild strawberry, flowering spurge, whorled milkweed, and the roses and sunflowers should be excluded initially. The grasses will usually increase in coverage 1 to 2 inches per year, while the forbs will add only a few additional stalks. Thus when grasses and forbs are alternated every square foot, the grasses will eventually fill in to produce a natural pattern. Spreading species, which produce vegetatively as well as by seed, can be added once the initial planting is established (Figures 10.3 and 10.4).

The size of the species used will also have a major impact on the appearance of the planting. On small dry sites, for example, it may be desirable to use only short, finely textured species like June grass, side oats grama, little bluestem, northern dropseed, yellow star grass, blue-eyed grass, shooting star, downy gentian, and purple prairie clover. Larger plants like prairie dock and big bluestem, unless used in moderation, will make the site feel smaller and may compromise its open feeling. On the other hand, if it is desirable to plant the landscape so that a major change in character occurs over the growing season, taller species will be needed so that the height of the planting will increase over the summer. The height of such a planting will change gradually, and late in the season the viewer will experience an enclosure of tall, relatively coarse plants (Figures 10.5 and 10.6).

Selecting plants for color is both rewarding and a major challenge, because the range and possible combinations of colors are striking. It is worth remembering that both dried materials and

Fig. 10.6   Tall species included—prairie closes up.

Fig. 10.7   Dried prairie plant patterns.

grasses contribute color. The reproductive patterns of plants also affect design. Northern bedstraw, for example, spreads vegetatively and should be planted in masses to form a bed of white when in bloom. In contrast, prairie lily occurs primarily as isolated individuals and should be scattered throughout a planting (Figures 10.7 and 10.8).

Fig. 10.8   Dried prairie plant patterns.

One method for determining the impact of a plan before planting is to make a series of drawings representing periods of from 2 weeks to a month apart during the growing season. Each plant should be represented as a symbol on the drawings and colored to match its natural color. Forbs can be represented by a daisy (✿) or a circle; grasses by an inverted broomhead (🌾). The symbols should be drawn to approximate scale. The resulting series of drawings will suggest the progression of colors and patterns through the season.

The fact that grassland plants support each other physically should also be weighed. Planted as individuals, taller plants often respond to the absence of competition by growing spindly and become prone to collapse. It is especially important to consider size along the edges of a planting. Tall grasses like big bluestem planted next to a path may impede walking and may end up underfoot.

Pathways

Circulation routes are usually desirable in all but the smallest plantings. The major question in planning for them is their surface. The simplest are those composed of lawn grasses and maintained by mowing. A rationale for their use is that lawn species like Kentucky bluegrass are usually present in planted grasslands despite weeding and logically ought to be put to some positive use. Mowed paths are scaled to the width of the lawn mower, usually double it, for convenience. An objection for some people is that mowed grasses seem inappropriate in a naturalized landscape.

An alternative includes planted surfaces of native species like side oats grama (cut to a height of 6 to 8 inches if necessary), hairy grama, Pennsylvania sedge, and buffalo grass (to the west). Path rush (*Juncus tenuis*) is an alternative on wetter sites. It thrives on trampling, but like the sedge it is limited in availability commercially. Use of the sedge or the rush may require enlisting the help of a local botanist to locate, propagate, and experiment with the species.

Other options include bark chips and stone. Because they decompose, bark chips require replacement every two to three years, an expensive undertaking unless free materials are available. Gravel, more effective from a wear standpoint, tends to scatter under heavy traffic. It also requires the use of an impermeable surface beneath it to inhibit plant growth. Although plastic is often used, its appropriateness, like that of mowing, is open to question. An alternative is to use compacted limestone or granite, surfaces which also lend themselves to wheelchair use (Figure 10.9).

Hard surfaces like flagstone, concrete, and asphalt are economically questionable in all but major pathways. Concrete, however, does lend itself to texturing and can be made to resemble natural rock. Thus, it can be an attractive option for high traffic areas or where expense is unimportant.

Fig. 10.9 Turf grass–gravel path–prairie grass planting. Shorter grasses at path would help soften transition.

Planting Techniques

The major issue in planting is whether to use seeds, seedlings, or a combination of both. The most expensive option is to purchase seedlings from a commercial nursery. Professional plantings using commercial seed are also expensive, although less so. One way to cut costs is to invest personal time in starting seedlings. Most species are easily grown in greenhouses, cold frames, or nursery plots. Least expensive is to seed a site directly with seeds gathered by hand. The randomness of this last approach will also give the planting a more natural feeling, a quality difficult to achieve using seedlings without careful planning.

Again, the choice of species is important. Long-lived plants often prevent other species from occupying their space, a form of "squatter's rights" in the plant world. Fast-spreading species will quickly fill the void of a new planting and so inhibit the establishment of less aggressive species. And helping some species to spread and hold their place is the factor of *allelopathy*, an ability to give off substances toxic to other plants, occasionally even those of the same species. Examples of allelopathic grassland species are sunflowers, pussytoes, and possibly stiff goldenrod, Canada goldenrod, and prairie coreopsis.

These factors can be turned to advantage, however, if the aggressive species is short-lived. Such species, called companion plants, include Canada wild rye and black-eyed Susan. Their rapid development can inhibit the spread of weed species. In addition, they have a showy appearance even within the first season, a valuable public-relations advantage.

Fig. 10.10   Example of first year's planting into mulch. See color plate 50 for appearance 2½ years later. (John Diekelmann, landscape architect.)

Fig. 10.11   Miniplanting—end of first growing season.

Fig. 10.12   Same planting—end of second growing season.

Small-Site Planting   The definition of "small" varies from individual to individual, but for most purposes it means a site less than half an acre in area. Depending on time, energy, and money, it may be desirable to start small to gain experience before attempting a large-scale planting.

Preparation of the small site involves mulching, whether the ground is left intact or turned using a cultivator. The site is covered with at least 10 layers of newsprint, with each group of sheets overlapping at least halfway onto the next. The paper is then soaked thoroughly and covered with woodchips or any other heavy, organic, nontoxic material to hold it in place. Mulch and paper are left in place for at least 2 months if the soil has not been stripped of vegetation. After this time, the paper can be punctured with a sharp shovel and existing vegetation will be dead. A few dandelions may have forced through the mulch, and quack grass rhizomes may have threaded horizontally through the layers of paper, but these are only cosmetic problems if weeded quickly and will not affect the planting. Both newspaper and mulch will decompose over several years, adding organic material to the soil.

Planting initially resembles vegetable gardening. Seeds or seedlings are set out, watered, and weeded by hand. Results are apparent the first season, and weeding continues the second. By the end of the third, the planting usually has filled in. If seed is to be distributed by hand, light seeds should be mixed with an equal volume of wet sand to insure even distribution and should be raked into the soil (without newsprint cover) to ensure positive contact with it.

With proper site preparation, both the seed and seedling approaches yield good results and usually take about the same amount of time to become relatively weed-free (Figures 10.10 to 10.12).

"One-Time" Planting (Large Sites)   Sites of half an acre or more normally require the use of mechanical planters if a grassland is to be established in a single planting. As a matter of economics, seeds are used rather than seedlings. The major question is the seeding rate. At present, the optimum rate is subject to debate. While it depends on seed purity, germination rate, and the number of seeds per ounce, recommendations range from 7 to 20 pounds of seeds per acre. Numerous rates have been tried, all with some success and some failure. If a mixture of grass seeds alone is used, 7 pounds per acre may be sufficient if drilled into the soil, 20 pounds if broadcast by hand. Forbs can then be introduced as seedlings. It has been claimed, however, that a lighter rate of grass seed will yield a planting richer in forbs.

The problems in using bulk figures are numerous. Seeds of a given species can vary widely in weight. And seeds of different species have extremely different weights, ranging from 800 seeds to the ounce (needlegrass) to more than 200,000 (downy gentian). Until additional experiments are conducted, direct seeding using mixtures of seeds will remain somewhat unpredictable.

The recommended planting procedure for the first year is to deep-plow to break up the existing sod, to remove quack grass rhizomes mechanically, to disk as weeds germinate, to plant a cover crop of oats, soybeans, or buckwheat, and to harvest the cover crop.

During the second year, the grassland seeds are planted into the cover crop stubble. In mechanical planting, seeds are inserted into

DURHAM AGRICULTURAL COLLEGE LIBRARY BOOK

Fig. 10.13   Shredder-type mower being used during early stages of prairie planting. (Photo by Darrel Morrison. Darrel Morrison, landscape architect.)

Fig. 10.14   Grass drill. (Photo with permission of James Truax.)

Fig. 10.15 Grasses emerging in drill rows—manufacturing plant. (Photo by Darrel Morrison. Darrel Morrison, landscape architect.)

Fig. 10.16 Forbs emerging in hand-broadcast areas. (Photo by Darrel Morrison. Darrel Morrison, landscape architect.)

place with a device called a "drill." The drill specifically designed for grassland seeds is the Truax drill available from James Truax in Minneapolis. It is drawn behind a tractor and plants in a linear pattern. Rows are spaced every 8 inches. If both grass and forb seeds are to be planted, the rows should form a grid; grasses are planted in one direction and forbs in another.

The resulting rows are both an advantage and a problem. They make it relatively easy to determine if seedlings have become established, but the rows remain prominent for at least 3 years. After three or four seasons, however, the rows usually disappear and the planting begins to look more natural.

In no case should companion plants be mixed in the same rows with other seeds. Their aggressiveness will adversely affect the development of desired plants.

Following planting, weeds are mowed with a shredder-type mower set just above the level of the growing grassland species. Mowing should be repeated each time the weeds are about to bloom or reach 12 inches in height (Figures 10.13 to 10.18).

Incremental Planting (Large Sites) An alternative for large, relatively dry sites is the incremental approach, which involves inserting seeds or seedlings into the existing sod. It may be less satisfactory than the method just described, because weed species like Kentucky bluegrass and red clover may persist for years. On the other hand, plants can be established the first year. If seeds are used, the surface of the sod should be broken mechanically to ensure contact with the soil. The possibility of failure increases with seeds, because of the competition of existing plants. The use of seedlings requires regular sprinkling and protection from small mam-

Fig. 10.17 Planting after two growing seasons. (Photo by Darrell Morrison. Darrell Morrison, landscape architect.)

mals to minimize failure. Competition and disturbance are both reduced if the sod is slit rather than excavated and if planting is done in the fall rather than spring.

Because the sod is left in place, burning becomes the most desirable method of management. Late spring burns will weaken nonnative species and reduce competition.

Planting Wet Sites   Sites where water stands during most of the spring season usually are unplowable and unmulchable except in fall. The soil is usually either peat or damp sand and clay. Less is known about planting these areas than any other. A major danger is that plantings may be washed out or merely floated out. Late-season planting is recommended. Areas subject to flowing water are perhaps more suitable for wetland plantings than grassland.

A second major problem is one properly classified as management. On these sites, reed canary grass, a nonnative, is especially aggressive. Originally planted for erosion control and forage, it tolerates heavy siltation and may be allelopathic. The only known method for controlling it is to remove it physically, probably prohibitive on a large scale. Preventing continued siltation may help, as may mulching.

Planting Steep Slopes   Severe slopes present another special problem. Examples include highway embankments, surface-mining areas, and areas regraded for construction. These severe areas require special preparation techniques aimed at preventing erosion. Combinations of mulching, netting, and staking are recommended. Once the surface has been stabilized, small areas can be hand-planted as in the small-site planting procedures described earlier. A successful approach to larger areas is hydroseeding. Because this requires special equipment and trained operators, local highway departments and soil conservation agencies should be used as resources.

Management

Many problems associated with grassland plantings are more perceived than real. Although most people want a "weed-free" landscape, a planting should be evaluated as a whole. If present, undesired plants should be evaluated to see if they are increasing or decreasing. Often, during the initial stages of a planting, agricultural weeds like lamb's-quarter, foxtail, and velvetleaf will be prominent, but they gradually decline as the planting matures.

Although a planting may seem to be a disaster during the first or second season, experienced landscapers do not give up. Young grassland plants tend to emphasize root rather than stem growth. Thus, while desired seedlings are often invisible in a sea of weeds, a careful search usually reveals large numbers of them. Among the

Fig. 10.18   *Planting after* three *growing seasons. (Darrel Morrison, landscape architect.)*

grasses, native species can be distinguished from weedy by their hairy stems and the fact that they cannot be pulled from the soil with their roots.

If seedlings cannot be detected, it may mean that the seeds used are dormant. Although it is thought that the germination rate decreases with age, seeds have germinated years after a planting. For that reason, it is not advisable to give up for at least 1 year. If at the end of the third season no appreciable number of plants can be found, the planting should then be reevaluated. Failure may be due to seeds that have failed to germinate, or it may reflect the inappropriateness of the site.

Maintenance can be divided into two time periods, short-term (the first 3 years) and long-term (following the third year). Short-term maintenance consists of mowing or, if there is sufficient material, burning. New plantings should be mowed just above the height of the seedlings at about the time that weeds shade more than 50 percent of the ground surface. This procedure protects plants from excessive shading and also sets back the weeds because much of their energy has gone into the production of foliage. Burning is ideal during the second spring following planting. Like mowing, it weakens early-season weeds, but it also warms the soil and can stimulate seedling growth. Woody plants should be pulled early.

During the short-term phase of maintenance, care should be taken to prevent the establishment of several biennial and perennial species which can become serious problems. Among the former are white and yellow sweet clover, wild parsnip, plumeless thistle, and musk thistle. Among the latter are leafy spurge and Canada thistle. The best strategy is to remove these plants physically as soon as they appear. The biennials will be controlled, because their seed source is removed. The perennials will be weakened by continued weeding. Early detection is critical. If large populations of these species are allowed to develop, drastic, large-scale mowing and possibly even chemical treatment may be needed to maintain a planting.

Long-term maintenance is minor and is directed toward not weeds but rather woody plants. While weeds usually decline with time, on all but the least favorable sites woody species gradually increase. Again, either mowing or burning is needed to control the problem and to remove the buildup of litter.

Mowing Periodic mowing is an effective approach to managing a grassland. Early, it can control the development of weeds. Late, it can control shrubs and trees as they germinate. It can be done in either spring or fall. Fall mowing will not compact the soil as much, but it does destroy wildlife food and cover as well as the aesthetics of standing plant materials. If mowing is chosen either because it is more convenient or because burning is forbidden, the resulting thatch should be removed. A thatch buildup can be detrimental to some plants.

1

2

3

4

5

6

7

9

10

11

8

12

MESIC DECIDUOUS WOODLANDS

VISUAL CONTRASTS OF WOODLANDS

21

23

33

36

37

38

34

35

48

49

50

51

52

53

54

Burning Where burning is allowed and can be controlled, it is preferable to mowing. But before beginning a burn, it is important to collect all of the information possible about its effect on the landscape and its flora and fauna. Forest Service publications can be helpful. Second, anyone who might be involved should be notified, including neighbors and the fire department.

The day selected for a burn should be one of relative calm but not perfectly still. A light, steady wind of from 1 to 3 miles per hour is ideal, because it will produce a sustained fire in one direction. Turbulent winds must be avoided, because they produce erratic, unpredictable fires that are difficult to control. Turbulence is at a minimum usually at night and early in the morning.

Preparation involves the creation of a firebreak and the presence of several pieces of equipment, including either a hose or a backpack sprayer, a fire slapper, and rakes. Firebreaks include paved surfaces and mowed areas. They should be cleared of litter and thoroughly wetted before the burn.

The burn itself should be limited to small areas at one time. Because grasses are very flammable and their flames tend to create their own wind, large areas of burn can get out of hand. A second argument for burning small sections of the whole is that animal and insect life are benefited if alternate sections are burned in alternate years, always leaving some sections unburned as refuges. The burn is not completed until all evidence of fire is out (Figures 10.19 and 10.20).

Whether it consists of mowing or burning, the long-term maintenance of a grassland planting of appropriate natives is far less expensive and consumes fewer resources than the management of traditional landscapes.

Additional Reading

Introductory.

Green, H. C., and J. T. Curtis, "The Re-establishment of Prairie in the University of Wisconsin Arboretum," *Wildflower* 29:77–88, 1953.

Moeller, Robert, "Methods of Prairie Development Used at the Aullwood Audubon Center, Dayton, Ohio," *Ohio Journal of Science* 73(5):307–311, 1973.

Nichols, Stan, and Lynn Entine, *Prairie Primer*, University of Wisconsin Extension Bulletin, 1976.

Rock, Harold, *Prairie Propagation Handbook*, Boerner Botanical Gardens, Hales Corners, Wis., 1971.

Smith, J. Robert, and Beatrice S. Smith, *The Prairie Garden: Seventy Native Plants You Can Grow in Town or Country*, University of Wisconsin Press, Madison, 1980.

Detailed

Anderson, R. C., and C. Van Valkenburg, "Response of a Southern Illinois Grassland Community to Burning," *Transactions of the Illinois State Academy of Science, 69(4):399–414, 1977.*

NATURALIZED
LANDSCAPES

Fig. 10.19 *Fire in a savanna. (Photo by Robert Swartz.)*

Fig. 10.20 *"Burning crew" member using fire slapper made from rake handle and used truck mud flap. (Photo by Evelyn Howell.)*

Butler, J. E., *Interrelations of Antecological Characteristics of Prairie Herbs*, unpublished Ph.D. thesis, University of Wisconsin, Madison, 1954.

Christiansen, Paul A., and Roger Q. Landers, *Notes on Prairie Species in Iowa. I. Germination and Establishment of Several Species*, Iowa Academy of Science, 73:51–59, 1966.

Christiansen, Paul A., and Roger Q. Landers, *Notes on Prairie Species in Iowa. II. Establishment by Sod and Seedling Transplants*, Iowa Academy of Science, 76:94–104, 1969.

Cottam, G., and H. Wilson, "Community Dynamics on an Artificial Prairie," *Ecology* 47:88–96, 1966.

Curtis, J. T., *The Vegetation of Wisconsin: An Ordination of Plant Communities*, University of Wisconsin Press, Madison, 1971.

Ehrenreich, John H., and John M. Aikman, "An Ecological Study of the Effect of Certain Management Practices of Native Prairie in Iowa," *Ecological Monographs* 33:113–130, 1963.

Gaylor, Harry P., *Wild Fires: Prevention and Control*, Robert J. Brady Co., Bowie, Md., 1974.

Glenn-Lewis, David C., and Roger Q. Landers Jr., eds., *Fifth Midwest Prairie Conference Proceedings*, Iowa State University, Ames, Iowa, 1978.

Hulbert, Lloyd C., ed., *Third Midwest Prairie Conference Proceedings*, Kansas State University, Manhattan, Kansas, 1973.

Pemble, Richard H., R. L. Stuckey, and L. E. Elfner, *Native Grassland Ecosystems East of the Rocky Mountains in North America: A Preliminary Bibliography, A Supplement to Prairie: A Multiple View*, Mohan K. Wali, ed., University of North Dakota Press, Grand Forks, 1975.

Schramm, Peter, ed., *Proceedings of a Symposium on Prairie and Prairie Restoration*, Knox College, Galesburg, Ill., 1970.

Schwarzmeier, Jerry, *Data on Seed Weight and Germination*, Mimeographed data sheet, University of Wisconsin Arboretum, Madison, undated.

Stuckey, R. L., ed., *Proceedings of the Sixth North American Prairie Conference*, Ohio State University, Columbus, Ohio, in press.

Swan, F., "Post-Fire Response of Four Plant Communities in South-Central New York State," *Ecology* 51:1074–1081, 1970.

Wali, Mohan K., *Prairie: A Multiple View*, University of North Dakota Press, Grand Forks, 1975.

Zimmerman, James H., ed., *Proceedings of the Second Midwest Prairie Conference*, Madison, Wis., 1972.

chapter eleven

Semishaded Landscapes

I n summer, plantings modeled after the native savannas—the openings, glades, and barrens—may be the most comfortable of all landscapes. Open expanses broken by oases of shade, they provide shelter from the sun and allow breezes to circulate freely.

Such plantings also have a second major advantage. They lend themselves to sites of virtually any size. Like their models, they can consist of a single tree in an open landscape or of a series of groves in a landscape covering several acres (Figures 11.1 and 11.2).

Fig. 11.1 A savanna consisting of a single tree—a serviceberry in an Allegheny National Forest "orchard."

Fig. 11.2 Allison Savanna, Minnesota.

Fig. 11.3 Fire burning through oak opening. (Photo by Robert Swartz.)

Fig. 11.4 Oak opening in process of changing to forest.

Environmental Considerations

In a sense, the savanna combines elements of the grassland and the forest. Species which grow in either of those community types can also be found in savannas. But, importantly, from the combination of elements unique qualities also arise, requiring populations of plants with broad tolerances.

Light patterns, for example, are more complex than in either grassland or forest. Light intensity ranges from full sunlight to deep shade. While many species favored at one extreme or the other grow in the savanna, the broad middle ground is filled with species which are tolerant of both sun and shade.

A parallel situation exists in relation to wind. Most species adapted to full sun are also adapted to winds. Many of those adapted to shade are accustomed to the relative shelter of forest. Many of the species found in the savanna, however, tolerate a mixture of these conditions: simultaneous wind and shade.

Many savanna communities also occur naturally in relatively severe environments, those with xeric soils, south and west slopes, or prominent bedrock. Many also are favored by relatively alkaline or relatively acidic soils. With few exceptions, they occur in areas favorable to wildfire. While such conditions are optimal for few species, the relatively tolerant species of the savannas find them more favorable than the more demanding species characteristic of forests do. As a result, savannas were historically able to resist major invasions by trees. It is interesting to note that with the development of modern systems of fire protection, many of the natural savannas have in fact been transformed to woodland (Figures 11.3 and 11.4).

Regional Considerations

Savanna communities are distributed relatively predictably throughout the northeast. Those dominated by pines are found most often at the northern and southern extremes of the area, while the band between these extremes is most characterized by oak savannas. The cedar glades occur throughout, but usually are limited to limestone bluffs and glacial moraines facing south or west.

Design Considerations

Because much of the savanna environment is open and unshaded, many of the design factors that apply to open communities also apply here. In addition, however, because trees and shade are also a major element of the savanna landscape, attention must be given to the design of the canopy layer and the shaded understory layers which grow beneath it.

In both the pine and oak savannas, trees are distributed in randomly spaced groves or clumps. The transition to the open grassland is usually softened by scattered lone trees. In many cases, these

Fig. 11.5   Oak opening tree species
distribution. Note multiple trunks—
possibly the result of resprouting
because of fire—and the distribution of
ground layer species in relation to the
tree canopies.

Fig. 11.6   Oak opening tree
distribution.

patterns are ensured by the history of the community's development. A single tree taking root and growing to maturity produces
seeds which in turn fall to the ground and root near the parent tree.
Thus, the oak and pine savannas are characterized by groups of
trees, often even-aged (Figures 11.5 and 11.6).

Cedars, in contrast, often take root after their seeds have passed
through the digestive tracts of birds. The tree patterns that result
are often highly random, although they do reflect the presence of
perches used by birds. The cedars may grow, therefore, near fence
lines or under the branches of an existing tree (Figures 11.7 and
11.8).

These natural patterns should be followed to give an appropriate

Fig. 11.7   Cedar protected from fire
by rock outcrop.

Fig. 11.8 Cedar growing at the base of tree.

Fig. 11.9 Trees planted in a traditional pattern.

Fig. 11.10 A contrast: the diverse composition of a cedar glade.

visual quality to the savanna planting. Because the pines and cedars of these communities also lend themselves to screening, these patterns can also be used to give more diversity than traditional hedge patterns used for screening (Figures 11.9 and 11.10).

A final concern when planting cedars is their extreme sensitivity to fire. Cedars grow most often in situations where they have been sheltered from wildfire, such as a west-facing cliff. If they are to be used where such natural protection is not available, special precautions may be needed, especially when fire is to be a management tool. Alternatives include leaving the area immediately around them cleared of topsoil or placing flagstone near them to discourage the growth of flammable vegetation. An additional alternative is to plant evergreen or fire-resistant ground-layer plants near their trunks when branching patterns allow. Among such species are the violets, wild strawberry, Pennsylvania sedge, alumroot, and prairie smoke.

The distribution of ground layer plants in natural savannas seems to be related to two factors, light and possibly a chemical interaction with the leaves of the trees.

Light patterns vary from one species of tree to another. Many cedars and some open-grown pines branch to the ground surface, casting a shade so dense that few species can survive in it. Open oaks, on the other hand, often branch so far from the ground that the species found only in sunlight can grow successfully beneath them. However, as the trees grow and as the canopies of individual trees touch and create larger areas of shade, species composition will change with the decrease in sunlight (Figures 11.11 and 11.12).

In some savannas, a prominent change in vegetation occurs at the drip line of the canopy, the circle formed under the outermost tips of a tree's branches. This may be due to shade, but in some cases it may also be related to the allelopathic effects of fallen and decaying leaves. Among the trees which have the ability to inhibit some plants chemically are oaks, hackberries, sycamores, walnuts, and butternuts.

These ground-layer patterns, like those of the trees, should be used as a guide in creating a natural-looking planting and one which is in harmony with its environment. As suggested earlier, however, the quest for natural appearances does not exclude a consideration

Fig. 11.11   Low-branching cedar in an unburned sand prairie.

Fig. 11.12   High-branched black oaks in Hoosier Prairie and Savanna, Indiana.

Fig. 11.13 *Patterns of light and shade in an Allegheny National Forest "orchard."*

of aesthetics. The patterns of sunlight and shade that can be created in a savanna planting can be striking if care is taken in planning for them (Figure 11.13).

Pathway Design

The materials used for paths through savannas are the same as those used in open communities. Unlike paths in open plantings, however, those running through a savanna landscape can take advantage of scattered trees to provide a variety of visual experiences. Among the qualities that can be built into pathways is the contrast between sunlight and shade. Many plants are especially attractive when viewed in sunlight from a spot that is shaded (Figures 11.14 to 11.17).

Planting Techniques

While the open areas of a savanna can be planted using any of the techniques discussed in the last chapter, such techniques require modification when planting beneath existing trees. It is extremely important to avoid any tree's feeder roots, most of which lie in the upper 12 inches of the soil. For that reason, plowing is not recommended as an approach to site preparation. Alternatives include mulching and the use of native plants as temporary ground covers.

Mulching will not damage roots physically, although there is a concern that it may deprive roots of oxygen. If mulching is used, therefore, it may be best, at least on fine-textured, poorly drained soils, to mulch only parts of the ground beneath a tree at any one time. Conservatively, no more than one-sixth of the area enclosed by

Fig. 11.14   Pathway in an oak opening.

Fig. 11.15   Pathway in an oak opening.

the drip line should be mulched in a given year. Six years, therefore, should be allowed to complete a planting (Figure 11.18).

Another method for replacing sod is to encourage native plants to become a ground cover. They, along with leaf litter, will eventually suppress existing grasses. Plants that can be used for this purpose include Virginia creeper, common blue violet, and wild strawberry, species which out-compete bluegrass in shade and can be controlled in native plantings. Once the sod has been killed, they can be removed by hand where desired plantings are to be established.

Where local ordinances allow, burning may offer a third alternative for site preparation. With it, the area beneath the tree is burned

Fig. 11.16   A view of a prairie landscape from a grove of oaks.

Fig. 11.17   A shaded area formed under an open-grown oak.

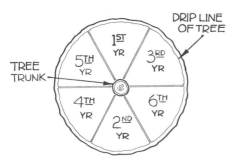

Fig. 11.18   A plan of a possible mulching sequence.

and seeded with desired plants. This technique has at least two disadvantages, however. Fire can damage the trunk of all but the most fire-resistant trees unless extreme care is taken. It is also possible that, on fertile soils, grasses may recover and grow robustly, outcompeting some seedlings.

Where there are no existing trees, site preparation resembles that for establishing a grassland. The concern instead becomes one of species selection—specifically, the selection of tree species which do not spread vegetatively and thus do not form thickets. In addition to the traditional savanna species, hawthorns, crab apples, ironwood, and serviceberry are all appropriate, especially on smaller sites.

Maintenance

Many of the same maintenance concerns of grassland plantings apply to savannas, although the emphases may be different in the shaded portions of the planting. Where shade is appreciable, few of the "weed" species common in early grassland plantings will persist. However, woody species may be especially troublesome. For the sake of the woodland herbs being planted, it is desirable to control the growth of shrubs and young trees sufficiently to prevent the formation of a thicket. While many of these ground-layer species will tolerate some shade, most can be out-competed by a heavy growth of shrubs. The maintenance effort, therefore, should be directed at the control of woody species either with the traditional control in open communities, fire, or with annual clipping.

Additional Reading

Detailed

Bray, J. R., "The Distribution of Savanna Species in Relation to Light Intensity," *Canadian Journal of Botany* 36:671–681, 1958.

Bray, J. R., "The Composition of Savanna Vegetation in Wisconsin," *Ecology* 41:721–732, 1960.

Curtis, J. T., *The Vegetation of Wisconsin: An Ordination of Plant Communities*, University of Wisconsin Press, Madison, 1971.

chapter twelve

Shaded Landscapes

I n nature, most landscapes dominated by shade are those with
mature trees and a nearly continuous canopy of foliage. They
offer shelter from the sun and often from the wind. Psychologically,
at least, they also offer a sense of solitude and privacy. Such landscapes are diverse, complex, colorful, and often striking in the
height and size their trees achieve.

Plantings modeled after the native forests share all of these qualities, but they are among the most time-consuming to create unless
a site is already maturely wooded. Most canopy species and some
understory species require decades to mature. By their nature, such
plantings also require relatively large sites.

Plantings of the native forest herbs can, however, be created on
smaller sites. Smaller species of trees and large shrubs can be used
to create the needed shade even within the often-limited scale of
urban lots. Where the environment is otherwise favorable, such
plantings can also be created without trees in the shade of buildings.

Environmental Considerations

Although forest plantations devoted to lumbering may suggest otherwise, forest communities are environmentally complex. Those
native to the northeast are highly varied even within a given region
or locale. Among the factors which shape them are light, moisture,
wind, slope, soil, and litter layer.

Light Forest communities all share subdued light levels. Their
species are adapted to shade, and many depend on it for survival.

Fig. 12.1   A protected ravine in Indiana.

Fig. 12.2   A north slope maple–basswood forest in southwestern Wisconsin.

Shade is a relative term, however, and the degree of light that penetrates a forest canopy varies widely from one type of community to another. Among the darkest forests are those dominated by evergreens like hemlock and arborvitae. In them, shade is a year-round phenomenon. Forests of deciduous species like maple and basswood may be equally dark in summer but are relatively shadeless in early spring. As a result, they support the ephemeral herbs which require the sun's heat and light in spring. Communities of pines and oaks allow more light to pass through the canopy layer, often resulting in a taller and denser understory flora.

Light levels also vary within communities. While canopy species are relatively long-lived, they do succumb to old age, disease, wind, and countless other factors. Although a community may be dark overall, light levels in the resulting openings may be intense. Frequently, understory growth in such areas is robust and uncharacteristic of the community as a whole.

Moisture   Across the northeast, forests occur on sites that range across most of the moisture scale, from xeric to hydric. Different moisture levels, however, favor different populations of plants. The rich flora of the mesophytic forests of the central states require abundant moisture but do not tolerate saturated soils. Pine and oak forest flora tolerate relatively dry sites and are, therefore, more competitive on them than mesic species like maple and basswood.

Wind   Air movement can have a major effect on a community's species population. Many of the herbs found in mesic forests are competitive there not only because they tolerate low light levels but because they also require the protection that the forest affords them from the drying effect of strong winds. When they occur in regions where precipitation is marginal for them, it is on north slopes or in ravines sheltered from the wind that they are most often found (Figures 12.1 and 12.2).

Slope   The direction and angle of slope affects forest populations in at least two ways. Species intolerant of accumulations of litter may be favored by steep slopes on which winds or runoff carry litter away. Species sensitive to wind and light are favored, at least in regions marginal for them, by north and east slopes, which offer shelter from prevailing storms and the most direct rays of the sun. The more tolerant xeric communities are better adapted to the less sheltered south and west slopes.

Soil   Soil characteristics shape plant populations in numerous ways, some of which are as yet poorly understood. Among the major factors is pH, the degree to which the soil is either acidic or alkaline. Many species are extremely sensitive to pH and tolerate a relatively narrow range on the acid-base scale. Prominent among these, again, are the mesic forest herbs, which do not grow successfully on highly acidic soils.

The organic content of the soil is also a major factor. Not only does a high organic component keep the soil light and well aerated, it also acts like a sponge in storing moisture. Plants sensitive to drought, therefore, do best where organic materials are present in sufficient amounts to buffer periods of limited rainfall and high temperatures.

Litter and Humus Litter, undecomposed leaves and woody materials, and humus, decomposing organic materials, contribute to the development of soil, the protection of ground-layer plants, and the infiltration of rainfall into the soil. The characteristics of litter and humus, however, vary from community to community. Litter tends to accumulate under evergreens and under hardwoods like beech and oak, and so may smother small plants. It accumulates little under mesic species like maple and basswood. Humus, too, can be divided into two major types.

Mull humus is highly decomposed and nutrient-rich, and so is favorable to and required by many of the mesic forest herbs. It is usually associated with calcium-rich soils and canopy species like sugar maple, basswood, elm, birch, and wild cherry, species whose leaves decompose readily.

Mor humus is usually relatively acidic, only partially decomposed, and often from 3 to 7 inches deep. It is best tolerated by heath species and others common in oak and pine forests. It is most associated with acidic bedrock, cold climates, and areas that are poorly drained. Canopy species like the evergreens, beech, and oak also contribute to its development.

Regional Considerations

Deciduous forest communities range throughout the northeast and are the most characteristic plant communities of the entire area, with the possible exception of the prairie region of the midwest. The dominant hardwood communities in the central states and northward are those in which combinations of maple, beech, and basswood play a major role. In the midwest, oak communities predominate, and those of maple and basswood are relatively uncommon. To the east, oak communities again predominate in a mixture with eastern pines.

Communities dominated by pines are found most in the north and to the southeast along the Atlantic coast. In both regions, they are most common on sand and thin, dry soils, achieving major prominence in areas nearest the coast and where they have developed following lumbering and fire.

Communities dominated by hemlocks and spruces are common only in the coldest locales. Thus, while they do occur in the mountains south into Virginia and Kentucky, they are common only in the Northern Conifer–Hardwoods Region.

Design Considerations

Texture and color, major elements of design, are as varied in woodland communities as in grassland. Most prominent in the flowers, color also exists in the bark and foliage of trees and shrubs, and in the leaf litter on the forest floor. A textural element not available in grasslands is the bark of the trees. Extremely varied, it ranges from the rough, corkiness of the bur oak to the smoothness of the beech, paper birch, and musclewood (Figure 12.3).

These qualities, as well as the changing colors and bare branches of fall, lend themselves to conscious design effects. But while grassland design focuses on species whose maximum height for the most part is at or below eye level, forest design on all but the smallest sites involves canopy, middlestory, and forest floor layers.

Canopy   Canopy species in wild landscapes rarely reflect two of the most common features of conventional landscapes: uniform size and linear patterns. Most healthy woodlands support trees of different ages, and the spacing of trees is irregular and random. While species like oak and basswood resprout after cutting or fire and thus often appear as clusters of trunks, most forests are characterized by single trunks spaced at varying distances from one another. Few trees are so widely spaced that their branches have the broad spread characteristic of trees grown in the open. These natural patterns should be reflected in a landscape planting when possible, not only for the sake of natural aesthetics but also to simulate a community's environment as closely as possible. Trees spaced further apart than is normal for them may alter the nature of the canopy and thus the light levels reaching the lower layers.

Among the special design effects to be considered in planting canopy species are contrasts in the foliage and bark. Placing a sugar maple in a grove of hemlocks in a northern forest planting can provide a striking contrast of light and dark foliage (Figure 12.4).

Middlestory   Shrubs and vines are as much a part of woodland communities as flowers and ferns. So, too, are immature trees and understory tree species. With relatively few exceptions, such species can be found in any forest. Their numbers, however, vary from community to community. Those with the thinnest canopies usually have the greatest population of understory plants.

Many of these species contribute significantly to the diversity of color and texture in the forest planting. Common species like the dogwoods, laurels, rhododendrons, azaleas, and witch hazel flower add great beauty.

Shrubs and small trees in particular can also be used as screening,

Fig. 12.3 The light-colored bark of
the sugar maple contrasts with the
dark trunk of the white ash.

Fig. 12.4 The translucent leaves of
the sugar maple.

a major consideration in achieving the privacy characteristic of woodland plantings (Figure 12.5).

Forest Floor   If for no other reason than their great diversity and small size, the herbaceous species offer perhaps the greatest opportunity for design effects in creating a forest planting. In some communities, up to a dozen different species of plants occupy a single square foot of soil. As with the other forest layers, however, design of the herbaceous layer should follow natural patterns. Some species naturally produce clumps of plants, while others grow as scattered individuals. The random patterns of both clumps and individuals allow great variety in planting patterns (Figures 12.6 to 12.10).

There is one major caution in designing an herbaceous layer, however. Because of their size and colorfulness, forest herbs usually create a temptation to do more than the environment of the planting allows. For example, it may seem a good idea to take advantage of the shade on the north side of a building by planting ephemeral species like Dutchman's-breeches and trout lily. Such species, adapted to mesic deciduous forests, demand spring sunshine, a requirement that cannot be met in such settings. As a result, the planting will languish, wasting both effort and expense. It may also be tempting to increase the color of a hemlock-dominated landscape by adding species like large-flowered trillium. Again, planting species not well adapted to a given situation is in the long run a wasted effort (Figure 12.11).

Fig. 12.5   Mountain laurel in a
Connecticut oak forest.

Fig. 12.6 *The fine textures of this club moss ground layer contrast with accompanying starflowers.*

Fig. 12.8 *Clones of mayapple and toothwort.*

Fig. 12.9 *Clubmoss and trailing arbutus.*

Fig. 12.7 *Clones of white trout lily and mayapple.*

Given the popularity of maples in urban landscaping, a special caution deserves mention. Sugar maple is a shallow-rooted tree and, on sites drier than those natural for it, it will out-compete herbaceous species for moisture, gradually killing them. Thus, while herbaceous layers under maples are rich and diverse in most wild settings, the same does not hold true when the tree is inappropriately sited. (Figure 12.12).

Although rarely considered outside of rock-garden plantings, the forest floor includes a variety of additional elements that contribute to a diversity of life. Logs, rocks, and tip-ups (trees toppled by wind) all support unique groupings of plants. Logs, for example, may provide habitat for decay fungi or a cool microclimate for ground layer plants. Limestone rocks and tip-ups shelter ferns, hepaticas, mosses, liverworts, and lichens. Sandstone supports other mosses and ferns (Figures 12.13 to 12.16).

Mosses in particular can give the forest floor a quality of delicate richness. During early spring, for example, they are a brighter green than evergreens. Although they are not available commercially, they are relatively easy to propagate (see "Planting Techniques," p. 172).

Pathways

Woodland plantings lend themselves to two types of paths: those maintained with a lawn mower, and those composed of stones.

Mowing is appropriate on all but wet sites. On damp but not wet sites, mowed paths will eventually fill in with mosses if kept free of litter (Figures 12.17 and 12.18).

Stone, laid in a way that facilitates walking, is appropriate on all sites and is probably the best choice for overly wet soils. There, they should be set into a bed of gravel at least 4 inches deep. The stone chosen should complement the native bedrock. The pathway will look most natural if appreciably round or square stones are avoided. These are probably only appropriate if the path is to relate to an existing terrace or wall.

On wet sites, care should be taken to avoid blocking natural drainageways, where heavy runoff may wash even stonework away. Individual stones or bridges can be worked into drainageways safely, a technique Japanese landscapers have used to advantage (Figure 12.19).

Planting Techniques

Because of the relatively demanding nature of many forest species, establishing a woodland planting usually requires some care in preparing the site. Critical to the health of many species, especially the mesic forest herbs, is sufficient organic matter. If the proposed site supports a lush growth of bluegrass, it probably is sufficiently organic. If not, organic materials should be added by composting leaves from trees appropriate for the species being planted. Mesic species are accustomed to soils with an organic content that ranges

Fig. 12.10 *Bracken fern, blueberry, and twinflower in a forest recovering from fire.*

Fig. 12.11 *First-year planting on the north side of a residence. (John Diekelmann and Mark Allsup, landscape architects.)*

Fig. 12.12 *The sparse ground layer under an open-grown sugar maple.*

Fig. 12.13 *The delicacy of the maidenhair fern is enhanced through contrast with the rugged texture of rock.*

Fig. 12.14 *Polypody ferns in rocky woodland.*

Fig. 12.15 *Barren strawberry and moss in rocky woodland.*

Fig. 12.16 *Mosses provide an appealing contrast to a rock outcropping.*

from 10 to 33 percent of volume. However, clay soils may require more than 30 percent organic content, and sandy soils more than 20 percent.

It should be noted that organic materials must be replaced yearly if the natural accumulation of leaf litter is small.

Site preparation should probably also involve a consideration of soil organisms. Many of these organisms contribute to the production of humus and to the growth of some plant species. Because many of the factors involved are currently poorly understood, establishing a "complete" woodland soil is best assured through the addition of a small amount of soil brought in from a wild community like that being planted. It can be taken from the top 2 inches of forest soil, a layer which the great percentage of soil organisms inhabit.

If the site has been severely disturbed, mesic plantings at least will require that the lower soil layers be loosened to facilitate drainage. Again, large amounts of organic material should be added to ensure continued drainage.

Where a site is already sufficiently shaded either by existing mature trees or by buildings, these preliminary steps will probably be all that is necessary in preparation for planting. Unless highly shade-tolerant lawn grasses are present, existing sod will in most cases already be weakened by shade and will gradually disappear in competition with woodland species.

Sites with little or no shade present a greater challenge. On them, existing sod can be discouraged in either of two ways. Perhaps most effective is to mulch the site, much as is done for grassland plant-

Fig. 12.17 *And are a fine path surface.*

Fig. 12.18 *A mowed woodland pathway in Lincoln Gardens, Springfield, Ill. (Jens Jensen, landscape architect.)*

ings. Woodland plants can then be established the following spring. If this approach is taken, mulching around any existing trees should follow the recommendations offered in the last chapter. An alternative to mulching is to plant robust xeric forest species like Virginia creeper, wild strawberry, false Solomon's-seal, and mayapple. These will gradually out-compete the sod plants as tree plantings grow and cast more shade.

A larger question on unshaded sites is how to establish a tree cover. Where time is a major factor, most woodland plantings are established with relatively large plants, an expensive approach even on a moderately small site. An alternative is to plant pioneer tree species for relatively quick growth: paper birch, gray birch, quaking and bigtooth aspen, pitch pine, black cherry, and pin cherry. These can be purchased as small saplings or grown from seed. Desired species of trees can be started in the shade provided by the pioneers. Ground-layer species appropriate for the stage of forest development the planting represents are planted, and desired herbs are added as the planting matures.

Relatively untried is the option of beginning the entire planting, including trees, from seed. In the wild, however, old fields have been converted to forest by natural succession over periods ranging from 30 to 100 years, depending on habitat. While requiring generations, this approach may be of value in foresting large areas not critical in terms of immediate enjoyment.

Fig. 12.19 *Stepping-stones in a Japanese garden.*

While most other species lend themselves to a choice between purchase and seeding, mosses are not as yet commercially available. Establishing them in a planting, therefore, requires either of two approaches. Where extensive areas of moss are available in the wild and permission is obtained from a property owner, small patches of moss can be relocated to like environments. Critical to the success of transplantation is ensuring positive contact with the soil. Wire mesh weighted with stones or other heavy materials can be used to hold the mosses down, or alternatively the mosses can be attached to a substrate of clay with toothpicks. Such plantings will grow and spread successfully if kept moist.

An alternative is to propagate the moss in place or in flats by scattering over the soil pieces of moss that have been dried and ground. If flats are used, the planting medium should have a pH appropriate to the mosses used. Kept moist, the mosses will be growing successfully and can be transplanted within three months.

Maintenance

When appropriately sited, woodland plantings are probably more immune to early management problems than any other community. Few of the "weed" species that compromise grassland plantings survive with any success in appreciable shade. Some consideration should, however, be given to plants, both native and nonnative, that can be more long-term problems. Major pest species are listed in Table 12.1. It should be noted that while some of the species listed are in fact often recommended for attracting birds and other wildlife, they can reduce a diverse planting to relatively few species. In the long run, therefore, they may actually limit the variety of food available for wildlife.

Where such species plant themselves in a woodland landscape, they should perhaps be pulled from the soil immediately. Native species appropriate to the planting, however, might instead be monitored carefully. If they begin to spread rapidly at the expense of other plants, they should be removed or controlled. If not, they can probably be allowed to remain without jeopardy.

It should also be noted that shrubs often grow rapidly in young plantings, especially those with relatively high light levels. Usually when the planting is appropriate for the site, this is merely a temporary problem and will slowly disappear as the planting matures.

Of all of the communities discussed so far, woodland communities are most dependent on environmental buffers, including shade and protection from wind. If such buffers are inadequate, the planting may require extra maintenance as compensation. Good, organic soils can help but may not be enough to guarantee optimum results.

TABLE 12-1. *Woodland Problem Species*

Nonnative Trees

Acer platanoides (Norway maple)
Populus alba (White poplar)
Ulmus pumila (Siberian elm)

Nonnative Shrubs and Vines

Berberis thunbergii (Japanese barberry)
Celastrus orbicullatus (Oriental bittersweet)
Euonymus alatus (Winged euonymus)
Ligustrum vulgare (Common privet)
Lonicera japonica (Japanese honeysuckle)
Lonicera maackii (Amur honeysuckle)
Lonicera morrowii (Morrow honeysuckle)*
Lonicera tatarica (Tartarian honeysuckle)*
Rhamnus cathartica (Common buckthorn)
Rhamnus frangula (Glossy buckthorn)
Rosa multiflora (Multiflora rose)
Viburnum opulus (European highbush cranberry)

Nonnative Herbs

Arctium minus (Common burdock)
Glechoma hederacea (Creeping Charlie)
Leonurus cardiaca (Motherwort)
Vinca minor (Periwinkle)

Native Species**

Anemone canadensis (Windflower, Canada anemone)
Aralia nudicaulis (Wild sarsaparilla)
Asarum canadense (Wild ginger)
Eupatorium rugosum (White snakeroot)
Fragaria virginiana (Wild strawberry)
Gaylussacia baccata (Huckleberry)
Matteuccia struthiopteris (Ostrich fern)
Podophyllum peltatum (Mayapple)
Prunus serotina (Black cherry)
Pteridium aquilinum (Bracken fern)
Smilax rotundifolia (Greenbrier)
Solidago flexicaulis (Zigzag goldenrod)
Viola sororia (Hairy wood violet)

*Including hybrids.
**Potential problems in immature, poorly shaded plantings.

DURHAM AGRICULTURAL
COLLEGE LIBRARY BOOK

Additional Reading

Introductory

Benner, David, "The Moss Lawn," *Garden* 4(2):12–18, March–April 1980.

Birdseye, Clarence, and Eleanor G. Birdseye, *Growing Woodland Plants*, Dover, New York, 1972.

Farb, Peter, *Living Earth*, Harper Colophon Books, Harper & Row, New York, 1968.

Foster, F. Gordon, *The Gardener's Fern Book*, D. Van Nostrand, New York, 1964.

Sperka, Marie, *Growing Wildflowers: A Gardener's Guide*, Harper & Row, New York, 1973.

Taylor, Kathryn S., and Stephen F. Hamblin, *Handbook of Wildflower Cultivation*, Collier Books, Macmillan, New York, 1976.

Steffek, Edwin F., *Wild Flowers and How to Grow Them*, Crown, New York, 1954.

Wharton, Mary E., and Roger W. Barbour, *Trees and Shrubs of Kentucky*, University Press of Kentucky, Lexington, 1973.

chapter thirteen

Freshwater Wetland Landscapes

L ands saturated or covered with water have probably always been considered wasteland. In that belief, they have been drained and filled in phenomenal numbers for housing, farming, and transportation. It is only in the last few decades that we have begun to recognize that wetlands are a valuable resource in themselves, providing flood control, water purification, and wildlife habitat. Less appreciated is their landscaping value. As landscapes, they offer visual diversity, unique populations of plants, and the physical dynamics of water.

While preservation of existing wetlands is clearly the most desirable, wetland environments can be created. Doing so, however, may raise a number of economic and environmental issues. It is strongly recommended that no wetland project be undertaken without a full understanding of and sensitivity to its implications.

Perhaps the major issue is that of the potential water source. The use of municipal supplies is costly on all but the smallest scale and is objectionable for many of the same reasons as sprinkling. The use of well water, perhaps inexpensive, may divert water from natural wetlands and threaten their existence. For most purposes, therefore, creating a wetland requires natural sources of water like rainfall and runoff. And where utilizing them requires reshaping the land, even it may be costly and environmentally questionable.

Environmental Considerations

Among the major factors that shape wetland communities are topography, water level and quality, soil type, and light. One impor-

Fig. 13.2 *An upland wetland: a spring-fed fen.*

tant factor has not been included here: salt versus fresh water. The difference between saltwater ecology and freshwater and saltwater's applicability primarily to coastal areas places it beyond the scope of this book.

Topography For practical purposes, wetlands occur primarily where water is provided by runoff or a high water table. Such areas include general or local depressions in the landscape, stream courses, and ravines. Only under special conditions in which underground flowages are forced to the surface do wetlands occur in raised areas. Examples of these include areas fed by springs (Figures 13.1 and 13.2).

Water Level As suggested in Table 13.1, differences in water level favor distinct populations of wetland plants. Some species require standing water. Others tolerate periods of inundation but not permanent flooding. Still others require a high water table but can be killed even by brief flooding. These differences can be seen in the distinctions between pond and marsh communities, meadows, and wetland forests.

As a general rule, water levels do not change suddenly or dramatically in healthy wetlands. Changes that do occur are usually related to seasonal fluctuations. Water levels are naturally somewhat higher in spring during thaws and lower in the heat of late summer. Minor rises may also occur in fall. Major exceptions to this rule are the floodplains, where conditions range from flood to drought depending on weather.

TABLE 13-1. *Selected Wetland Species and Their Environment*

Species	Soil			Water Chemistry			Relationship to Water Level		
	Mineral	Muck	Peat	Soft	Hard	Alkaline	1–2 ft Below	0–1 ft Below	0–1 ft Above
Acorus calamus (Sweet flag)*		x		x	x			x	
Alisma plantago-aquatica (Common water plantain)			x	x	x			x	
Anacharis canadensis (Common waterweed)	x	x	x	x	x			x	
Brasenia schreberi (Water shield)		x	x	x	x	x	x		
Carex stricta (Tussock sedge)		x	x		x	x		x	x
Ceratophyllum demersum (Hornwort)‡	x	x	x	x	x		x		
Eleocharis acicularis (Noodle spike rush)		x			x			x	x
Iris shrevei (Blue flag iris)*		x	x	x	x			x	
Leersia oryzoides (Cut grass)	x	x		x				x	x
Najas flexilis (Slender naiad)	x	x	x		x	x	x		
Nelumbo lutea (Lotus)		x		x	x		x		
Nuphar advena (Yellow water lily)*‡		x	x		x		x		
Nymphaea odorata (White water lily)		x	x	x	x		x		
Peltandra virginica (Arrow arum)		x		x	x	x		x	
Phragmites communis (Common reed)*	x	x		x	x	x		x	
Polygonum coccineum (Water smartweed)	x	x		x	x		x		
Pontederia cordata (Pickerelweed)	x		x	x	x	x		x	
Potamogeton gramineus (Grass-leaved pondweed)‡		x			x		x		

TABLE 13-1 *Selected Wetland Species and Their Environment* (*continued*)

Species	Soil			Water Chemistry			Relationship to Water Level		
	Mineral	Muck	Peat	Soft	Hard	Alkaline	1–2 ft Below	0–1 ft Below	0–1 ft Above
Potamogeton natans (Common pondweed)‡		x	x	x	x		x		
Potamogeton nodosus (Long-leaved pondweed)‡	x	x			x		x		
Potamogeton pectinatus (Comb pondweed)†		x	x	x	x	x	x		
Potamogeton richardsonii (Richardson's pondweed)‡	x	x		x	x	x	x		
Sagittaria latifolia (Common arrowhead)*‡		x		x	x			x	x
Sagittaria rigida (Stiff arrowhead)‡	x	x	x	x	x		x		
Scirpus acutus (Hard-stemmed bulrush)	x			x	x	x	x		
Scirpus americanus (Chairmaker's bulrush)	x	x		x	x	x	x	x	
Scirpus fluviatilis (River bulrush)			x		x			x	x
Scirpus paludosus (Alkali bulrush)		x				x		x	x
Scirpus validus (Great bulrush)	x		x		x	x	x		
Sparganium eurycarpum (Common bur reed)*	x	x		x	x			x	
Typha angustifolia (Narrow-leaved cattail)*	x					x		x	x
Typha latifolia (Common cattail)*	x	x	x	x	x	x		x	x
Vallisneria americana (Eelgrass)‡	x	x	x	x	x	x	x		
Zizania aquatica (Wild rice)		x	x	x	x		x		

*Plants that are visually dominant.
‡Plants that indicate good wetland quality.

Water Chemistry The chemical nature of water further distinguishes the forms wetlands can take. Soft-water communities exist in an environment in which the pH is between 6.8 and 7.5, alkalinity less than 40 parts per million, and sulfate ion concentration less than 5 parts per million. Hard-water communities exist where pH ranges between 8.0 and 8.8, alkalinity between 90 and 150 parts per million, and sulfate ion concentration between 5 and 40 parts per million. Alkaline wetlands have a pH between 8.4 and 9.0, alkalinity greater than 150 parts per million, and a sulfate ion concentration greater than 125 parts per million. Tolerances for major species are listed in Table 13.1.

Public testing laboratories for determining the chemical nature of water are available in most states. Anyone considering a wetland planting is strongly advised to use their services before developing a planting plan.

Water Composition   Materials carried in water can have a great impact on the vegetation of standing-water communities. Three kinds are of major importance: silt, nutrients, and stains.

Silt can be defined as any kind of mineral soil in the water. Suspended, it shades and can kill submerged plants. Thus reducing the oxygen content in the water, it can also kill plants indirectly. Settling to the bottom in shallows, it changes the water depth and may increase the winterkill of shallow water species. Where deposited, it also favors species able to spread quickly and eliminates those requiring clean water and stable bottoms. Invaders in such areas include aliens like reed canary grass and purple loosestrife and natives like giant reed grass, water willow, arrowhead, and lotus (Figure 13.3).

Suspended nutrients are usually increased dramatically in association with runoff from fertilized fields, lawns, and gardens. Among the most important are nitrogen and phosphorus. Excesses of either can produce a dense growth of undesirable submerged species and algae, contributing to the filling of a body of water, a process known as *eutrophication*. While filling is a natural aging phenomenon, the speed at which it occurs can be accelerated rapidly where there is an extreme excess of nutrients. Phosphorus, in addition, favors the growth of blue-green algae. The blooms can cover the water's surface in extreme cases, leading to oxygen shortage and the subsequent death of aquatic plants and animals.

Stains, created by dissolved materials, are a normal part of the environment of communities like bogs and swamps. Where they occur, they absorb sunlight and thus reduce the growth of submerged species (Figure 13.4).

Soil   Wetland soils fall into two major categories: those composed primarily of organic materials—either decomposed (muck) or undecomposed (peat)—and those composed of mineral particles (silt, sand, and clay). Many species have strong preferences. In general, the sparsest growth occurs on highly acidic or highly alkaline mineral soils; the greatest on nearly neutral organic soils. However, fertility (an asset) and lack of oxygen (a liability) may be more important than pH in determining the amount of plant growth.

Physical Impact   Ice and water currents may also affect plants growing in standing water. Driven by wind and waves as it breaks up, ice can do extensive damage to the beds of submerged species. Ice sheets lifted by a sudden rise in water level in shallows can pull plants out of the soil. The physical action of ice at the water's edge often causes an annual setback of floating bog mats.

Fig. 13.3   Muddy water.

Fig. 13.4   Stained water.

Strong currents, on the other hand, can injure even established plants and set back plantings at almost any time of the year. In lakes, the areas most resistant are those in shallows along the shore.

Light   Light levels play as great a role in wetland communities as in nonwetlands. Above water level, the shade of swamp forests creates a different shrub and ground layer from that found in open wetlands. In deep-water areas, layers of plant life, ranging from emergents and floaters to submerged species, reflect the clarity of and the level of light in the water.

Regional Considerations

Wetland communities, like others, reflect regional differences, but for general purposes two major geographic divisions stand out. The bog and conifer swamp communities are the dominant wetlands in the Northern Conifer-Hardwoods region. Both are rare and found only on the coldest sites further south. More common in these other regions are the hardwood swamps, floodplain forests, marshes, meadows, and wet grasslands. From east to west, these communities retain a strong similarity. There is, however, a greater richness of species with increasing distance south.

Design Considerations

As a general rule, natural wetlands should not be altered merely for the sake of landscape design. Supporting unique populations of plants and animals in a balance with existing conditions, most should instead be utilized as they are.

Design is a more appropriate concern in areas in which the natural water supply is potentially adequate but which, for any of many reasons, do not support existing wetland communities. Where the land is undisturbed, these will be relatively low-lying areas and ravines. Increasingly, however, appropriate sites are also those affected by construction, ditching, and excavation.

Although wetlands are highly complex and varied, for purposes of design here they can be divided into two major groups: those in which water stands above the soil more or less permanently, and those in which standing or running water is a temporary phenomenon. An example of the former is marshland; of the latter, a wet ravine or grassland. For the sake of simplicity at least, they can be called aquatic and nonaquatic respectively. Permanent streams, if slow-moving, can be included in the first group. If fast-moving, they share characteristics of both groups.

Nonaquatic Wetlands   For the most part, nonaquatic wetlands carry water during and immediately after storms and remain wet between them. The physical impact of water is a major consideration in these areas and presents the landscaper with a choice: whether to protect the soil with nonvegetative means or to plant it.

The decision should be made on the basis of erosion damage. Where the slope is severe, dropping more than 1 foot for every 10 of distance, the potential for erosion is high, although it varies with soil type and the quantity of water flow. If they are eroded to the point that the topsoil has been lost, such sites probably require special protection.

One of the conventional solutions in urban areas, at least, has been to treat these areas as storm sewers and to line them with concrete to drain them as quickly as possible. Where they threaten buildings with flooding, this may be a valid approach. But where there is no threat, aesthetics are better served by other options.

A major alternative is to line the soil with rocks or stone, following a natural model. In unglaciated areas with a limestone bedrock, this may take the form of layers of limestone to simulate the natural strata. In glacial areas, it may include gravel or boulders to simulate a rocky stream bed. This treatment has two purposes in addition to aesthetics. First, it offers some protection from erosion. Second, it slows the flow of water and encourages it to move into the soil rather than overland (Figures 13.5 and 13.6).

If this seems a preferable treatment, it is advisable to consult a local office of the Soil Conservation Service for assistance.

Where erosion is not a problem, plantings may be more appropriate. Here, many of the same design considerations discussed in relation to nonwetland plantings apply. Again, the chemical nature of the habitat, the water level, and the availability of light will dictate species selection. The natural growth patterns of the plants should guide placement. If vegetation already exists, it may be best to leave it for the sake of erosion control. Where existing vegetation includes such aggressive wetland species as the nonnative reed canary grass and the more benign native giant reed grass, it may in fact be difficult to establish a more diverse planting. It may only be possible in this latter case to diversify with equally aggressive species like New England aster, the sunflowers, and the goldenrods.

Aquatic Wetlands Aquatic plantings are appropriate where there is sufficient runoff or an adequate water table to provide standing water. Often, such areas do not already hold water, owing to drainage ditching or to an insufficient depression in the landscape. Such areas require either damming or excavation. Before undertaking either of these often expensive procedures, it is advisable to make an appraisal of the potential volume and quality of water.

Potential water volume is determined by the area of the watershed and by precipitation. While it is best to consult an engineer or the Soil Conservation Service for assistance, it is possible to make a rough estimate of watershed area. Contour maps available from the United States Geological Survey may be helpful, although

Fig. 13.5 Water cascading slowly over limestone slabs in the Driftless Area of southwestern Wisconsin.

Fig. 13.6 A boulder-strewn stream bed.

Fig. 13.7 *A bank collapsing into an artificial pond.*

Fig. 13.8 *Plant distribution along a relatively abrupt environmental gradient.*

the scale of such maps is often too large for most sites. A second alternative is to step off the bounds of the watershed by starting at the proposed site and walking uphill to surrounding ridge lines. Unless ridges are obvious, it may be necessary to watch the direction of water flow during a storm or the spring thaw.

If the estimated water volume appears more than adequate in spring and inadequate in summer, it may be necessary to consider the addition of a storage pond for collection of water in wet seasons and release of it in dry ones.

Water quality is equally important. Quality may be excellent if the watershed is relatively undisturbed. Where it is not, however, pollutants may come from streets (sand, salt, asbestos, oil, and lead), fields (fertilizers and pesticides), lawns, and industries. If harmful materials are present, they should be diverted by ditching.

Where it is necessary to excavate or dam a proposed site, the landscaping needed should be made to resemble the natural terrain of the area. If the land is gently rolling, slopes should be kept gentle by spreading excavated materials evenly around the site. Many farm ponds, whether dammed or excavated, look artificial and detract from the landscape.

More gentle slopes have two other advantages as well. First, they are more stable and support a greater diversity of plant and animal life. And second, soil piled high above the water level is an invitation to unwanted species of trees and shrubs and to weeds like nettle (Figures 13.7 and 13.8).

With an artificial holding area, it is also necessary to find some way to ensure that water will not leak out in large volume. Unless the soil drains poorly, the bottom must be sealed. Choices include compacted clay, a plastic liner, or a material like Bentonite, a clay-like substance that swells when wet. All of these are expensive. Bentonite, in addition, will develop leaks when subjected to alternating periods of moisture and drought. Soil Conservation Service personnel, again, may be helpful in sealing a holding area.

A final concern is the possibility that an excess of water may occur following a major storm and may wash out the dam or cavity. For this reason, it is necessary to provide a properly designed outflow area with either outflow pipes or a vegetated spillway.

Design considerations in planning an aquatic planting are related to two major factors: water level and soil. As suggested in Table 13.1, most plants prefer certain depth ranges over others. It is necessary to make an estimate of water depth and of the fluctuations in it before selecting species. The original volume estimate can serve as a guide, but where water depths are marginal for a species, it may be best to observe the site for a year to gauge the effect of leaks and of evaporation.

Many wetland plants grow best in soils that are about half organic. If a site has a mineral soil bottom, desired species can be planted first on an experimental basis. If they fail to thrive, it may be helpful to provide a mixture of half organic material and half mineral to a depth of one foot. It is important to remember, however, that the pH of the organic material may be critical for some communities. Bogs, for example, require a highly acidic, sterile medium.

A last design consideration is one related to animal species. Although many wetland animals are beneficial to the health of the community, they may have no way to enter an isolated aquatic site. Some of the nurseries that supply wetland plants also offer animal species that are appropriate and useful; but if species are unavailable commercially, it may be necessary to consult local wetland experts for advice.

Pathway Design

Wetland landscapes need not be inaccessible. Boardwalks constructed on the same principles as piers or boat docks can provide access to areas of standing water, while conventional paths may work in nonaquatic areas. Boardwalks of decay-resistant woods like black locust are highly preferable to those of treated wood, however, because the preservatives in the latter may be toxic to plants and animals. Alternatives to wood include slabs of limestone in alkaline waters and granite in acidic waters.

There is one caution in providing access to wetlands. To avoid adversely affecting wildlife, especially birds, it is best not to intrude too far into an aquatic landscape, or to ring wetlands with paths, unless the landscape comprises 5 acres or more (Figures 13.9 and 13.10).

Fig. 13.9 A boardwalk permitting access to a wetland.

Fig. 13.10 Stepping-stone access in a Japanese garden.

Planting Techniques

Most nonaquatic wetland species can be planted using techniques already described. Dry seeds are broadcast onto a surface that has been textured when conditions allow by disking, dragging, or simply raking. Seedlings can be set out by hand or by machine, again when conditions allow, usually late in spring after high waters have receded or in fall. An alternative, where an area is already vegetated and erosion is a concern, is to use heavy sheets of wood or metal to smother existing plants. This technique can be used over small areas to introduce diversity.

Aquatic species require special techniques because of the relative permanence of water cover. One approach in deeper waters is to wrap a ball of clay around the lower ends of a group of 4 or 5 cuttings and to drop them onto a relatively soft bottom at 6-foot intervals. It is important that they make contact with the soil. A similar technique can be used to plant tubers. Although the tip of the tuber should be allowed to project from the ball, most of it should be placed below the surface of the soil. In shallow waters, plants can be placed directly into the soil without the use of a clay "sinker."

A second approach is direct seeding, which involves broadcasting soaked, saturated seed over the surface of the water. Buoyant seeds should be encased in clay before broadcasting. When seeds are scattered at 9-foot intervals, a bushel of them should be sufficient to plant an acre of wetland.

A final approach is more of a gamble but is also easier. It involves simply bringing in small amounts of bottom "mud" from comparable communities. Where seeds are present, some will grow.

Maintenance

While many of the maintenance problems in wetlands can, like those in other communities, be classified as either short or long term, the movement and periodicity of water in wetlands also creates a third category: intermittent problems.

Weeds Both a short-term and a periodic problem, rapidly spreading species like reed canary grass can be a major challenge in wetlands that are not permanently flooded. It, like a number of native species including reed grass, the cattails, and river bulrush, may crowd out more desirable species, especially in an early planting. The surest way to control them is to pull them from the soil before they can establish themselves in number. They, along with a number of trees and shrubs, are an especial problem along exposed shores and banks of marshes and meadows.

The remains of uprooted plants should not be allowed to remain in the planting because they may reroot. Perhaps more important, if allowed to remain they can deplete the oxygen in the water as they decompose.

An alternative to pulling, in short-term maintenance, is to keep the water level high for a full growing season.

Algae   Algae, plants which lack leaves, stems, and roots, are a basic food source in all wetlands and therefore are a normal and desirable part of the wetland environment. Explosions of algae populations, however, are a nuisance. They usually occur in warm water that contains an excess of nutrients, characteristics most common in small wetlands.

Controlling algae is often simply a matter of introducing animal species which feed on them, including daphnia, freshwater shrimp, tadpoles, snails, mussels, and freshwater clams. Many of these species can be purchased commercially, although as with plant purchases it is important to determine whether the seller propagates them or catches them in the wild at the expense of natural wetlands. It is also possible to introduce many of them by bringing in a cupful of water and mud from a nearby wetland.

Mammals   Mammals like muskrats eat great quantities of aquatic and emergent vegetation. Although this is a natural event, it can be catastrophic in small plantings. Managing this problem offers two choices. The first and easiest is simply to allow them to eat themselves out of food and to move on. The second is to live-trap them and transport the animals to the nearest large wetland. The disadvantage to this second approach is that animals introduced to another wetland may be forced out by an existing population. In such cases, trapping and transport are inhumane.

Of course, even removal is only a temporary measure. New populations may arrive every year.

Mosquitoes   Standing water is inevitable some time during the year in most wetlands. It is in these shallow, calm waters that mosquitoes breed. While it is a normal reaction to a mosquito problem to resort to pesticides, it is important to note that mosquito breeding grounds are also nurseries for desirable insects like dragonflies and damselflies, which prey on mosquito larvae and adults. These areas are also attractive to birds, which feed on adult mosquitoes. Where the shores slope gradually and the oxygen levels of the water are high, these predators often reduce mosquito populations to mere nuisance levels. Thus, unless mosquitoes are a health problem, it may be desirable to tolerate a little discomfort for the sake of preserving a diverse animal population. Predators like the dragonfly must have prey to survive.

Where mosquito populations are a serious problem, pesticides should still be a last resort. A more desirable solution is to stock permanent water communities with fish. Traditional garden-pond species like goldfish and guppies have proven to be effective mosquito controls. In natural wetlands, gambusia and surface-feeding minnows can be equally effective.

In areas where mosquitoes carry diseases like malaria, it is best to consult with experts like the Tennessee Valley Authority (TVA) for advice. The TVA in particular has carried out extensive research in the area of manipulating water levels for the control of mosquitoes.

Eutrophication   As suggested earlier, some wetlands change slowly over time because of the accumulation of plant materials and sediments. Open waters gradually fill in as a natural aging process. The process itself can be slowed by keeping waters as free of pollutants as possible. In waters that are clear and low in nutrients, the natural decay of plant materials is sufficient to prevent the accumulation of plant remains.

Where a water body has filled, the usual response is to dredge periodically, an expensive undertaking. Like all ecosystems, however, wetlands are dynamic and complex. The natural succession from open water to meadow or swamp is therefore an interesting phenomenon in itself and may make it desirable simply to allow the natural process to occur.

Additional Reading

Detailed

Bedford, B., E. Zimmerman, and J. Zimmerman, *Wetlands of Dane County, Wisconsin*, Dane County Regional Planning Commission, Madison, 1974.

Conard, Henry S., *How to Know the Mosses and Liverworts*, W. C. Brown, Dubuque, Iowa, 1956.

Fassett, Norman C., *A Manual of Aquatic Plants*, University of Wisconsin Press, Madison, 1957.

Fowells, H. A., *Silvics of Forest Trees of the United States*, Agriculture Handbook No. 271, U.S.D.A. Forest Service, Washington, D.C., 1965.

Lahti, T., "Restoration of a Small Suburban Southern Wisconsin Wetland," *Proceedings of the Waubesa Conference on Wetlands*, Calvin B. DeWitt and Eddie Soloway, eds., Institute of Environmental Studies, University of Wisconsin, Madison, 1978.

Moyle, John B., "Some Chemical Factors Influencing the Distribution of Aquatic Plants in Minnesota," *American Midland Naturalist* 34:402–420, 1945.

Muenscher, W. C., *Storage and Germination of Seeds of Aquatic Plants*, Cornell Agricultural Experimental Station Bulletin No. 652, 1936.

Muenscher, W. C., *Aquatic Plants of the United States*, Cornell University Press, Ithaca, N.Y., 1967.

Swenson, Allan A., *Cultivating Carnivorous Plants*, Doubleday, Garden City, N.Y., 1977.

chapter fourteen

Edges: Transitional Landscapes

I n the wild, transitions from one plant community to another reflect changes in environment. Usually, they occur so gradually and cover such distances that they are almost imperceptible to a casual observer. Exceptions do occur, however. Where moisture, soil, slope, or other environmental factors change abruptly, one community may give way to a second within a relatively short distance (Figures 14.1 and 14.2).

Fig. 14.1 Abrupt transition from dry prairie to maple–basswood forest.

Fig. 14.2   Abrupt transition from wet prairie to dry pine–oak forest.

Both situations are encountered in landscaping, although the latter are probably far more common given the scale and the nature of most developed areas. Buildings, for example, may produce complex environments in which both light and wind patterns change dramatically within a distance of several yards. Embankments cre-

Fig. 14.3   Dense shade on the north side of a residence.

Fig. 14.4   A narrow wind tunnel between buildings requires an edge to protect a woodland landscape.

ated for roads and drainageways condense moisture gradients, so that a change from wet soils to dry may occur much more quickly than usual. These conditions require relatively sharp transitions in vegetation because of habitat changes. Where they occur, plantings should be modeled after appropriate natural areas (Figures 14.3 to 14.5).

Some landscape transitions, however, are dictated by factors like property lines, recreation areas, and the need for screening. Such areas are artificial in the sense that they do not reflect environmental differences and usually require abrupt planting changes. For that reason, they present the landscaper who is interested in naturalizing with a number of unique problems.

Design Considerations

Traditionally, transitional areas—edges—have been treated in ways that pronounce a sense of artificiality. A familiar example is the hedgerow. Straight, often clipped, and planted with a single species, hedgerows often present themselves as merely another structural element like a wall or sidewalk and minimize the sense of dynamics that vegetation brings to a landscape. The same tradition often finds its way into naturalizing. Although less extreme than most hedges, many prairie plantings are laid out in rectangular beds or backed by a uniform wall of pines (Figures 14.6 to 14.9).

The challenge in naturalizing is to soften the artificiality of edges by blending two diverse plantings together in a way that eliminates the geometry of straight, simple lines. It requires visualizing the transition in two planes, one vertical and the other horizontal.

The vertical plane is most prominent when two plantings of dramatically different heights meet; for example, mowed lawn and

Fig. 14.6 *Plants treated like the wall of a house.*

Fig. 14.7 *A traditional, rectangular flower bed.*

Fig. 14.8 *Traditional geometry of landscape edges.*

Fig. 14.9 *A more complex naturalized edge.*

prairie or prairie and woodland. Plants whose form is rigidly vertical should not be allowed to dominate. Examples include young evergreen trees and dense bunches of little bluestem grass. Plantings of uniform height should also be avoided. More desirable in a woodland edge would be to plant horizontally branching trees and shrubs, which in time will spread out and create a varied, tunnellike effect. Where a grassland planting meets a lawn, plants of varying heights and those with some horizontal dimension, like northern dropseed, can be effective (Figures 14.10 and 14.11).

The horizontal plane, running the length of the edge, should be kept equally irregular. Rather than in a straight line, plantings should be placed so that the edge undulates in a series of gentle curves. It might, for example, be allowed to meander somewhat like a stream. Because the curves themselves can become too regular and predictable, however, some care should be taken to add variety. In a northern woodland planting, the regularity of an edge of evergreens can be broken with an occasional deciduous tree. Grassland edges should include a variety of species with different heights and textures (Figures 14.12 to 14.20).

Plant Selection

In nature, transitional areas between communities are in a constant state of flux as plants grow and modify their environment. While this dynamic quality is visually exciting and produces a mixed habitat favorable to many wildlife species, in landscaping it can also be a problem. On the small site, at least, the growth and spread of some species at the expense of others can dramatically affect the original design and the use of the site. The problem, of course, is minimized where the environment changes dramatically. But where environment is relatively uniform, the problem may increase the need for maintenance. Woodland plantings, whose species often invade open areas, offer the greatest challenge. Grassland plantings are a lesser problem, because they are controlled by shade at woodland edges and usually by mowing at lawn edges.

Most maintenance, then, is focused on woodland edges. Minimizing the need for it requires the selection of tree and shrub species which are slow-growing and do not spread vegetatively. Trees like

Fig. 14.10 *A future tunnel through a woodland–prairie edge. (John Diekelmann, landscape architect.)*

Fig. 14.11 *This distorted American beech provides an overhead enclosure at the edge of an old field.*

Fig. 14.12 *A flowering woodland–lawn grass edge.*

Fig. 14.13   Blended natural forms produce a naturalistic edge.

Fig. 14.14   A northern edge of conifers and paper birch.

Fig. 14.15   An edge of cedars and aspen.

bur oak and sourwood are especially desirable. Not only do they grow slowly, they also can be used like shrubs if planted densely enough so that crowding keeps them small. Table 14.1 lists other desirable woody species native to the northeast. Although the table has not been arranged by region or habitat, it should be understood that the community approach taken throughout the book also applies to edge plantings.

The choice of trees and shrubs should also include a consideration of species' tolerances for light and drought. Where a sheltered woodland edge faces north and east, plants less tolerant of sun and

Fig. 14.16   A gradual transition from prairie to open oak woodland.

Fig. 14.17   A complex landscape rhythm provided by birches along a forest-wet prairie edge.

low moisture levels are most appropriate. Where an edge faces south and west or is unsheltered, those more tolerant of sun and drought are needed. Table 14.1 identifies plants appropriate for each of these situations.

Different criteria apply to the selection of herbaceous species for a woodland edge. Ground layer plants which do spread vegetatively are most desirable, because they will fill in bare areas relatively quickly after planting. They also are often more flexible in the face of changing light levels than plants which reproduce primarily by seed and so are more likely to succeed. Table 14.2 lists a sampling

Fig. 14.18 Textural variety in a sedge meadow–dry prairie transition.

Fig. 14.18 *Textural variety in a sedge meadow–dry prairie transition.*

Fig. 14.19 *Oaks invading a prairie soften the transition from grassland to forest.*

of species which spread vegetatively and tolerate both full sun and partial shade on all but the driest sites. The list excludes several otherwise appropriate species like the wild grapes and the sunflowers because they are either overly aggressive or potentially toxic to other plants.

For diversity, herbaceous species which reproduce primarily by seed and do not spread rapidly, but which do tolerate both sun and some shade, can also be planted. In addition to the color and texture they add to a woodland edge, they contribute variety to the planting pattern because they occur as individuals rather than as colonies.

Table 14.3 lists a number of these species which can be used on all but the driest sites and in all but the deepest shade.

With an appropriate choice of species and careful observation of the transitions between wild communities of plants, landscape edges can be made something more than the high-maintenance, formal plantings they traditionally have been. The diversity of habitat that transition areas represent in the wild makes them perhaps the most dynamic of all natural settings, both for plants and animals. Some of the same qualities can be recreated even in the artificial edges of planted landscapes, heightening our enjoyment of them.

TABLE 14-1   *A Selection of Tree and Shrub Species for Woodland Edges*

Species	Size*			Optimal Orientation	
	Small Tree	Large Shrub	Small Shrub	N & E Facing	S & W Facing
Acer pensylvanicum (Moosewood)	x			x	
Acer spicatum (Mountain maple)	x			x	
Amelanchier arborea (Downy serviceberry)	x			x	
Amelanchier laevis (Allegheny serviceberry)	x			x	
Amorpha fructiosa (Indigobush)		x			x
Aronia arbutifolia (Red chokeberry)		x		x	x
Betula lenta (Sweet birch)	x			x	x
Betula nigra (River birch)	x			x	x
Betula papyrifera (Paper birch)	x			x	

Species	Size*			Optimal Orientation	
	Small Tree	Large Shrub	Small Shrub	N & E Facing	S & W Facing
Betula populifolia (Gray birch)	x				x
Calycanthus floridus (Carolina allspice)			x	x	
Ceanothus americanus (New Jersey tea)			x		x
Cephalanthus occidentalis (Buttonbush)		x		x	x
Cercis canadensis (Redbud)	x			x	
Chionanthus virginicus (White fringe tree)	x			x	
Cladrastis lutea (Yellowwood)	x			x	
Clethra alnifolia (Summer sweet)		x		x	
Cornus alternifolia (Alternate-leaved dogwood)	x			x	
Cornus florida (Flowering dogwood)	x			x	
Crataegus crus-galli (Cockspur hawthorn)	x				x
Crataegus mollis (Downy hawthorn)	x				x
Crataegus phaenopyrum (Washington hawthorn)	x				x
Crataegus punctata (Dotted hawthorn)	x				x
Crataegus viridus (Green hawthorn)	x				x
Euonymus atropurpureus (Burning bush)	x				x
Fothergilla major (Large fothergilla)		x			x
Glymnocladus dioica (Kentucky coffee tree)	x			x	
Hamamelis virginiana (Common witch hazel)		x		x	
Hydrangea arborescens (Snowhill hydrangea)			x	x	x
Hypericum densiflorum (Bushy St. Johnswort)			x		x
Hypericum prolificum (Shrubby St. Johnswort)			x		x
Ilex opaca (American holly)	x			x	
Ilex verticillata (Common winterberry holly)		x		x	
Juniperus communis (Common juniper)			x		x
Juniperus virginiana (Eastern red cedar)	x				x
Kalmia latifolia (Mountain laurel)		x		x	
Leucothoe editorum (Drooping leucothoe)			x	x	

Species	Size*			Optimal Orientation	
	Small Tree	Large Shrub	Small Shrub	N & E Facing	S & W Facing
Magnolia virginiana (Sweet bay magnolia)	x			x	
Malus coronaria (Garland crab)	x				x
Malus ioensis (Prairie crab)	x				x
Morus rubra (Red mulberry)	x			x	
Ostrya virginiana (Ironwood)	x			x	
Oxydendrum aboreum (Sourwood)	x			x	x
Physocarpus opulifolius (Ninebark)		x			x
Pieris floribunda (Mountain pieris)			x	x	
Potentilla fructiosa (Bush cinquefoil)			x		x
Ptelea trifoliata (Hop tree)	x			x	
Quercus ellipsoidalis (Jack oak)	x				x
Quercus illicifolia (Scrub oak)	x				x
Quercus imbricaria (Shingle oak)	x				x
Quercus laevis (Turkey oak)	x				x
Quercus laurifolia (Laurel oak)	x				x
Quercus macrocarpa (Bur oak)	x				x
Quercus marilandica (Black-jacket oak)	x				x
Quercus phellos (Willow oak)	x				x
Rhamnus carolinianus (Carolina buckthorn)	x			x	
Rhododendron calendulaceum (Flame azalea)		x		x	
Rhododendron nudiflorum (Pinxter bloom)			x	x	
Ribes americanum (Wild black currant)			x		x
Ribes cynosbati (Prickly gooseberry)		x		x	
Ribes missouriense (Missouri gooseberry)		x		x	
Sambucus canadensis (American elderberry)		x		x	x
Sambucus pubens (Red-berried elder)		x		x	
Sorbus americana (American mountain ash)	x			x	
Sorbus decora (Mountain ash)	x			x	
Taxus candensis (Canada yew)			x	x	
Thuja occidentalis (American arborvitae)	x			x	
Vaccinium corymbosum (Highbush blueberry)		x			x
Viburnum dentatum (Arrowwood)			x		x
Viburnum lentago (Nannyberry viburnum)		x		x	x

TABLE 14-1 *A Selection of Free and Shrub Species for Woodland Edges* (*continued*)

	Size*			Optimal Orientation	
Species	Small Tree	Large Shrub	Small Shrub	N & E Facing	S & W Facing
Viburnum nudum (Southern withe rod)		x		x	
Viburnum prunifolium (Black haw)		x		x	x
Viburnum rafinesquianum (Downy arrowwood)		x		x	
Viburnum trilobum (Highbush cranberry)		x		x	

*Small tree 15–25 ft in height; large shrub 6–15 ft in height; small shrub 2–6 ft in height.

TABLE 14-2. *A Selection of Woodland-Edge Ground Layer Species Which Reproduce Vegetatively*

Apocynum androsaemifolium (Spreading dogbane)
Carex pensylvanica (Pennsylvania sedge)
Dennstaedtia punctiloba (Hay-scented fern)
Eupatorium rugosum (White snakeroot)
Fragaria virginiana (Wild strawberry)
Galium boreale (Northern bedstraw)
Parthenocissus vitacea (Virginia creeper)
Penstemon digitalis (Smooth beardtongue)
Polygala senega (Seneca snakeroot)
Potentilla simplex (Common cinquefoil)
Pteridium aquilinum (Bracken fern)
Smilacina stellata (Starry Solomon's-plume)

TABLE 14-3. *A Selection of Woodland-Edge Ground Layer Species Which Do Not Spread Rapidly*

Anemone cylindrica (Thimbleweed)
Aquilegia canadensis (Columbine)
Asclepias purpurescens (Purple milkweed)
Aster azureus (Sky-blue aster)
Aster laevis (Smooth blue aster)
Campanula rotundifolia (Harebell)
Claytonia virginica (Spring beauty)
Dodecatheon meadia (Shooting star)
Epilobium angustifolium (Fireweed)
Euphorbia corollata (Flowering spurge)
Geranium maculatum (Wild geranium)
Heliopsis helianthoides (Oxeye)
Heuchera richardsonii (Alumroot)
Hypoxis hirsuta (Yellow star grass)
Hystrix patula (Bottlebrush grass)
Krigia biflora (Two-flowered Cynthia)
Monarda fistulosa (Bergamot)
Pedicularis canadensis (Wood betony)
Phlox glabberrima (Smooth phlox)
Phlox paniculata (Perennial phlox)
Phlox pilosa (Prairie phlox)
Polygonatum canaliculatum (Great Solomon's-seal)
Ranunculus fascicularis (Early buttercup)
Ratibida pinnata (Yellow coneflower)
Silene stellata (Starry campion)
Silene virginica (Fire pink)
Smilacina racemosa (Solomon's-plume; false Solomon's-seal)
Taenidia integerrima (Pimpernel)
Thalictrum dasycarpum (Purple meadow rue)
Veronicastrum virginicum (Culver's root)
Viola cucullata (Marsh violet)
Viola papilionacea (Butterfly violet)
Viola sororia (Woolly blue violet)
Zizia aptera (Heart-leaved golden Alexanders)

Additional Reading

Introductory

Hightshoe, Gary L., *Native Trees for Urban and Rural America*, Iowa State University Research Foundation, Ames, 1978.
Mooberry, F. M., and Jane H. Scott, *Grow Native Shrubs in Your Garden*, Brandywine Conservancy, Chadds Ford, Penn., 1980.

Detailed

Rosendahl, Carl Otto, *Trees and Shrubs of the Upper Midwest*, University of Minnesota Press, Minneapolis, 1955.

part four

Evaluating the Results— Examples of Naturalizing

chapter fifteen

Private Residential Landscapes

T his chapter and the final two are devoted to examples of naturalistic design in a variety of locations. The examples are hypothetical and have been chosen to be as representative as possible of
a wide range of landscaping situations.

Each covers the period from the beginning of a project to the
point at which it can be considered completed—that is, when major
changes are no longer needed in the plantings. In them, you will
find the kinds of problems to be expected in real life as well as hints
on how to deal with them. Our hope is that you will gain some
insight into working with nature as well as people.

This chapter presents two examples of privately owned, residential sites, one small and one medium-size. The first is located in the
eastern part of the United States; the second in the central states.
Both are occupied by adults and children.

Example One: A Small, Eastern Residential Site

A couple with a 4-year-old child have recently moved into the corner
unit of a townhouse development in an urban area. They find the
buildings attractive and well constructed. The landscaping, however, is extremely formal, with clipped lawns, trimmed hedges, and
regularly spaced trees along the streets. Maintenance is done by an
outside contractor, and the owners are assessed for their share of
the cost. Included are substantial expenditures needed to modify the

soil to encourage a lush growth of lawn grass. While pleased with their new home and their neighbors, the couple are not happy at the effort and money needed to maintain what they feel is a static and uninteresting landscape.

A dramatic transformation would, they know, be impossible socially, given the urban setting. But they feel that modest steps toward a more natural landscape might be acceptable. The process would have to be carried out gradually in order not to antagonize the other residents.

Site Analysis   As they study the site, three major things stand out. First, there is not enough room for active group sports, although with the proper planning there could be enough space for relaxation and small group entertainment. Second, the complex is located on an intersection between a busy major street and a small local thoroughfare. Traffic noise is modest but noticeable. Third, the combined driveway and parking area takes up much of the rear lot and offers a rather unpleasant contrast to the modern buildings themselves. There are also two plantings of oriental bittersweet on fences along the sides of the lot. The lot itself is relatively level, with moderately deep soils and a slightly acidic pH of between 5.0 and 6.0 (Figure 15.1).

Planning   Because the sides and rear of the lot are too small to be of much use to all of the residents, the couple decide to concentrate on developing the front of the lot. They know that as it is, it is too noisy to be a pleasant area for sitting. Located between the brick buildings and the street, it is probably also too warm during the

Fig. 15.1   Site analysis plan.

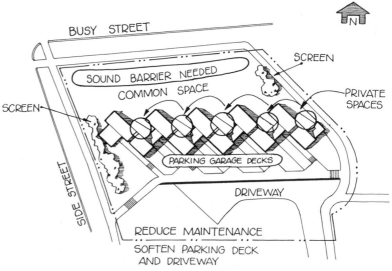

summer. Their problem is that if they were to plant enough trees to shade the entire area and enough shrubbery to deaden the street sounds, there would be little space left for recreation of any sort.

Consequently, after considerable debate, they decide on a compromise. Rather than leaving a large, open common space that would be hot and uncomfortable, their plan is to plant a landscape of scattered trees much like a savanna. Small groups of people would be able to sit in the shade of individual trees during the summer and to enjoy the sunlight in spring and fall. The children could also use the shade as play areas. A second attraction of the savanna design, they feel, is that each group of residents could feel as if it had its own area of sunlight and shade and thus could have a sense of personal space even without major provisions for privacy. The variety of plantings possible in the mixed sun and shade would also be pleasing.

Reducing the street noise is a second problem. While a tall board fence would help, the sense of enclosure would not be consistent with the open feeling of the savanna. They decide instead to create an earth berm just high enough to block the noise and add to the privacy of the front of the lot. They decide, too, to plant it with a scattering of trees like those in the savanna in order to make it appear as though the landscape continues beyond. Because the berm would be a difficult place for the periodic maintenance needed to keep it free of small trees and shrubs, they decide to work with the natural succession of plants in the east and plant slow-growing shrubs under the trees.

As substitutes for the vine-covered fences lining the sides of the lot, they decide to plant the edges of their property much as the berm is planted. The mixture of trees and shrubs, they decide, will have the same visual effect there as in the front of the lot and will also provide adequate privacy.

The remaining problem is the parking area in the rear. Because the back of the lot is too small to be of much use for recreation or utility, they decide to plant it in trees and woodland plants. A woodland planting, they reason, would not only require no regular maintenance, it would also soften the lines of the pavement. As a transition to the plantings in front, they decide to create a small savanna area along the side of the lot facing the street (Figure 15.2).

At this point, they decide to approach the other residents of the complex with their plan. To minimize adverse reactions, they suggest transforming the existing landscape in stages small enough to be maintained in a traditional "weed-free" manner. They also suggest continuing traditional lawn maintenance in selected areas as a transition from the street to the landscape and for recreation areas. As a selling point, they present a slide show to illustrate some of the trees and shrubs they have found growing naturally in their region of the country in relatively sunny areas.

In our example, the residents of the complex are favorably impressed with the couple's efforts and interested in their ideas for

Fig. 15.2   Site use plan.

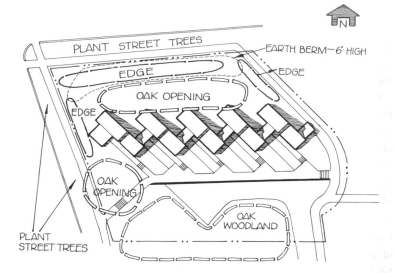

the front of the lot, but they are also apprehensive about the reaction of other residents in the neighborhood. Nevertheless, they agree to let the couple experiment with an area of the west side of the lot adjacent to their own townhouse.

Planting Plan   Encouraged, the couple begin to search for information about the savanna communities in their area. They find some limited descriptions of two types in several books about the natural vegetation of the east: a cedar savanna growing on limestone and a pine savanna growing on the sandy plains of New Jersey. Neither is exactly what they want. Not only are the soils inappropriate, the evergreens would not give them the sense of open spaces they want. They also find references to deciduous savannas of oak that probably grew in the region before the land was intensively settled, but unfortunately there is little information about the plants that grew in them.

Relying on information about midwestern oak openings, the work in progress at the Connecticut Arboretum, all of the wildflower guides they can find, and their own observations of how plants native to their area are distributed in various areas of light and shade, they decide to experiment.

Knowing that both scarlet and chestnut oaks are tolerant of a wide range of conditions, they decide to use them for their trees. Finding that many of the taller heath shrubs like mountain laurel tolerate some sunlight as well as shade, they decide to use heaths and feel fortunate in the choice because of the attractive foliage and flowers of the heath plants.

The ground-layer plants are a more difficult problem. They know that both hay-scented fern and the lowbush blueberries grow

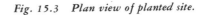

Fig. 15.3   Plan view of planted site.

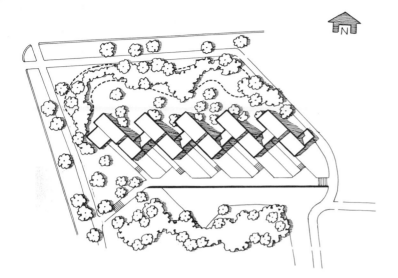

throughout their area in sunlight as well as light shade, but they also want to add a few plants with moderately showy flowers. After talking to a local naturalist, they decide to plant local sun-loving species like butterfly weed, coreopsis, and black-eyed Susan in the open areas between trees, and woodland species like phlox, columbine, and false Solomon's-seal in the shade. To soften the transition from sun to shade, they also plan to use a medium-size grass that tolerates some shade, little bluestem (Figure 15.3).

Reviewing the planting plan, the other residents are happy with the selection of plants, especially the colorful grassland species, and give a final approval to the project.

Establishment   Ready for planting, the couple begin to look for plant sources. Local nurseries sell most of the tree and shrub species on the couple's plan. The lowbush blueberries and hay-scented ferns are also available. The other species are sold only through wildflower nurseries and are relatively expensive. Agreeing that they want the planting to look like their plan as quickly as possible, they decide to purchase expensive but relatively large trees and a few large shrubs. They also decide to purchase enough of the other species to plant one small area and plan to expand it every year by growing plants from seed.

They begin their planting by mulching small circles around the areas where they want to plant the trees and shrubs. To save the time and effort needed to remove the lawn sod, they leave it in place and cover it with a thick layer of newspapers. To make these mulched areas more attractive for the neighbors, they cover the newspapers with woodchips. After two months, the grass under the mulch is dead.

Fig. 15.4   View of planted site.

Because of the size of the trees, the couple decide to have the nursery plant them, but to save additional cost by planting the shrubs and other plants themselves. They find, in fact, that several of the other residents are anxious to help.

The results are attractive even though limited in scale. The shade under the trees is a welcome addition late in the summer. The flowers and ferns attract a lot of attention, and the couple find that the plantings have become a focal point for conversation (Figure 15.4).

Example Two: A Medium-Size Central Residential Site

In this example, a couple with two school-age children have purchased a house on a good-size lot in a quiet residential area. They had been fairly warned by the former owners that it was impossible to grow a good lawn and that a deep ravine behind the house had been known to flood occasionally after exceptionally heavy spring rains. The couple found the purchase price attractive, however, and liked the house.

Looking the lot over more carefully after moving in, the couple find the warnings to be accurate. The lawn at the front of the lot is brown and patchy. The ravine is steep and was cleared by the builders.

Site Analysis Wanting to landscape, the couple immediately contact the local county extension office to see if they can discover why the existing lawn is doing so poorly. They find that much of their area is underlain by sandstone and the soils are quite thin and acidic. A soil test confirms the information. The pH of their soil is quite sour at between 4.5 and 5.5. Local landscapers inform them that their only choice if they want a healthy lawn is to have a thick covering of topsoil brought in and that it would be a good idea to give it periodic applications of lime to keep the soil sweet.

They also conclude that the ravine behind the house is too steep to be used for any kind of regular outdoor activities.

Despite these shortcomings, the couple feel satisfied with their purchase. The neighborhood is quiet and peaceful. The street running by the front of the house is used only by local residential traffic. And the front yard is spacious enough to serve their recrea-

Fig. 15.5   Site analysis plan.

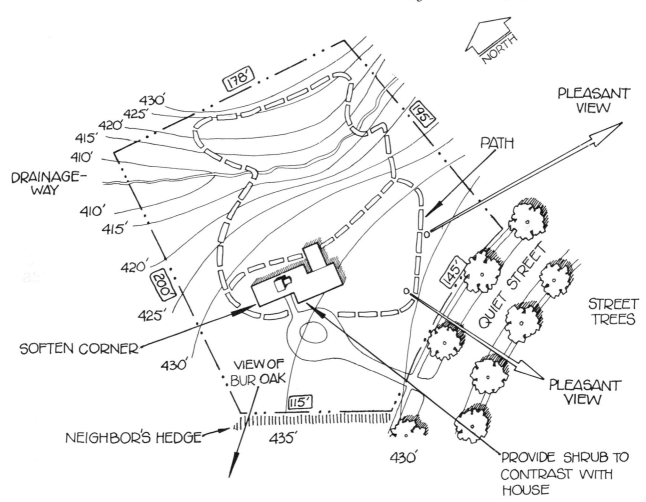

tional needs. Except for a neighbor's hedge along one edge, the views from the yard and house are attractive (Figure 15.5).

Planning The couple struggle with the question of what to do about the lawn. While they know that most of the neighbors make an attempt to maintain the traditional mowed front yard, they feel that the results are neither successful nor in keeping with the natural character of the area. They feel, too, that the expense of purchasing topsoil and maintaining the lawn would be objectionable.

They decide instead to accept their lot as it is and to plant species tolerant of the existing conditions. Because of the pleasant views they have from the front and sides of their site, they decide to keep the landscape open. For privacy, they plan to plant a few trees along the front and a variety of shrubs along the edges of the lot. The shrubs have the added benefit of softening the effect of the neighboring hedge. They decide to keep one small area at the front of the house open for activities like volleyball and plan to surface it with

Fig. 15.6   Site use plan.

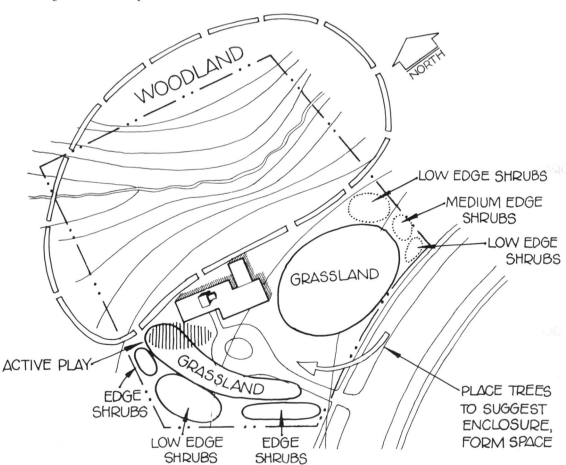

woodchips. The deck at the back of the house can be used for eating and entertaining.

The ravine presents a different problem. Because of its terrain, it can only be used for activities like walking and bird-watching. Because maintenance would be difficult if not impossible on the steep slopes, they decide to create a woodland landscape that could be essentially maintenance-free (Figures 15.6 and 15.7).

Planting Plan Although the couple know that deciduous forests with ground layers of Dutchman's-breeches and other spring ephemerals are typical of their region of the country, they also realize that the underlying sandstone and the builders' activities would make it difficult to grow many of them. Instead, they plan to plant trees tolerant of the acid soils, such as the oaks, near the top of the ravine. Further down, in the shelter of the slopes, they plan to plant a few hemlocks available from a friend who grew them from seed obtained from a local hemlock forest. Because the

Fig. 15.7   Large-scale site use plan.

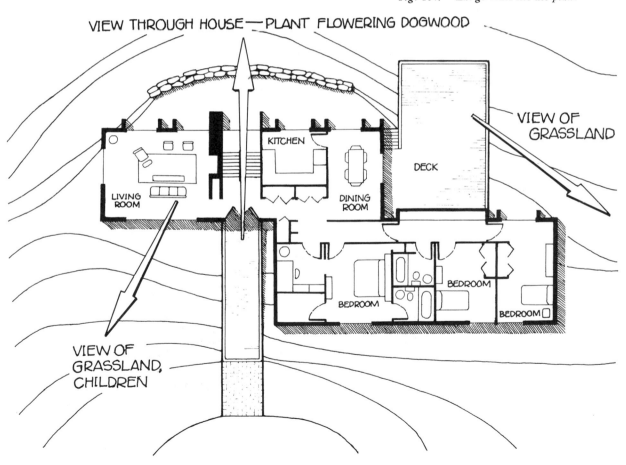

expense of planting such a large area could be prohibitive, they decide to do it in stages from one year to the next, concentrating for the first few years on the trees. Their hope is that after a number of years, the humus will build up in places so that a patchwork of herbs like mayapple and painted trillium can be started where light allows.

The front yard is more of a concern. Although they have visited tallgrass prairie plantings in Ohio, they realize that their thin soils will not support a lush tallgrass prairie. They decide to plant grassland species growing in the rocky areas they have seen along ridgetops in their area, among them puccoon, bird's foot violet, bush clover, blazing star, spiderwort, and butterfly weed. Among the grasses themselves, they decide to plant medium-size species like little bluestem and June grass. To continue the flowering into fall, they also plan for a variety of asters and goldenrods.

To complement these plants, they decide to use trees like pitch pine and chestnut oak, which they know will grow on thin, infertile soils. Among the shrubs, they decide to plant a few heath species along with flowering dogwood and redbud, both common throughout the area. As a transition between the grassland plantings and the shade of the trees, they plan to use savanna species like coreopsis, lupine, and Solomon's-plume for the ground layer.

Fig. 15.8   Plan view of planted site.

Establishment In deciding how to begin planting, the couple realize that they face one major problem. Because the soils are thin and underlain by rock, large trees will be difficult to establish. Behind the house, the problem is not as critical because they have already decided to develop the area slowly. Small trees are as acceptable there as larger ones and might in fact grow more rapidly. The screening in front is a different matter. Although the neighborhood is quiet, the couple prefer to begin with larger plants for the sake of screening. After discussing the problem with a number of nurseries, they decide to plant larger specimens in holes as large as possible and to add a large mixture of sphagnum moss.

The grassland plantings present a different problem. Most are not available from local nurseries, and those that are are expensive, up to $4 per plant. For that reason, the couple decide to gather seeds whenever they find desired plants growing along roadsides and to sow some directly into the soil as an experiment, while starting oth-

Fig. 15.9   Large-scale plan view of planted site.

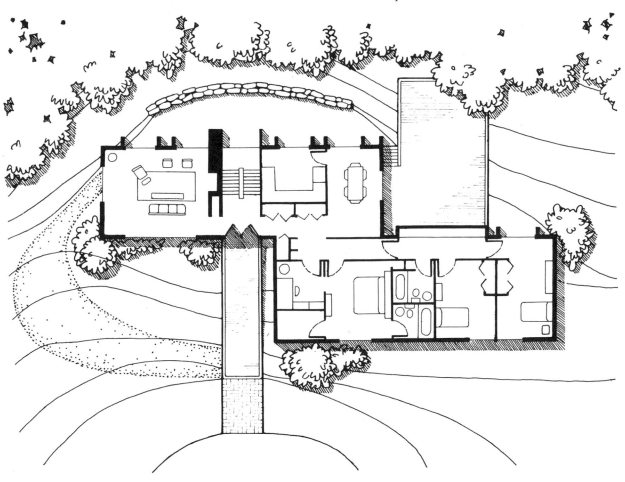

Fig. 15.10   View of planted site.

ers indoors. For the sake of having something to look at the first year, however, they decide to compromise and to buy a few of the plants that are available.

Ready to begin planting, the couple find that mulching is not even necessary. Much of the lawn grass can be removed with vigorous raking, leaving the soil free for planting. They conclude that the major disadvantage of the site might in the long run be an advantage. Weeds might not even be a problem during the first years of the planting.

They conclude, too, that even though their landscape will require a number of years to be fully established, the process of gathering seeds and the satisfaction of growing their own plants will have its own compensations as a learning experience for themselves and their children (Figures 15.8 to 15.10).

chapter sixteen

Public Landscapes

T his chapter turns from private landscaping projects to public to illustrate the process of naturalizing. Two examples, a public park in a small city and a schoolyard, have been chosen to convey some of the advantages that an alternative approach to landscaping can have for larger groups of people.

Example One: A Midwestern Community Park

A tornado has inflicted damage on a part of the central business district of a small, midwestern community. Before the storm, the river that bisects the city was lined with a variety of small manufacturing businesses, but the storm has completely leveled some of them and badly damaged others.

The city has decided to purchase the area and to devote the space to public use. To attract people to the community and its shopping areas, the intent is to develop a nontraditional park area using federal funds. A planning committee has been appointed.

Site Analysis   The site lies in the middle of town and straddles a ridge that runs east and west. To the north, it slopes down to the river, which has never been known to flood. To the south, the site slopes more gradually to the street on which many of the city's remaining businesses are located. To the east and west of this slope are a number of two- and three-story buildings left standing by the storm.

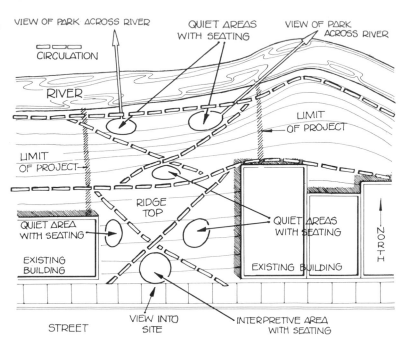

Fig. 16.1   Site analysis plan.

Below the debris of the buildings that were destroyed, the soil is found to be a mixture of broken bricks, concrete, and clay. Extensive cleanup appears necessary to remove the storm debris as well as the earlier building materials (Figure 16.1).

Planning   The committee are at a loss as to what might be done with the site to make it a regional attraction. Suggestions like major water fountains and extensive stone work are rejected because of the expense and because of their visual conflict with the stream and its natural topography. It is decided instead that plantings would be more appropriate.

Although a traditional planting of flowers and ornamental shrubbery would be possible, the committee feel that it would not be novel enough to benefit the business district. For that reason, the committee plan to recommend a park in which the plantings will recreate the natural vegetation of the area before its settlement. Because the area is intensively farmed, very little remains of the native vegetation with the exception of a single, state-owned prairie preserve an hour's drive to the north.

The committee ask for the assistance of the local university botany department in trying to identify the plants native to the area. Several members of the botany faculty present a program to them, explaining that while much of the area was covered with rolling tallgrass prairie, local differences in topography produced wide variations in vegetation. North slopes, like that proposed for the park, and especially those protected from fire by lakes and rivers, provided the unique habitat required in the midwest to support forest species like those found in the rich forests of Ohio and Kentucky. On south slopes, especially those where the soil was poor, dry prairies and dry oak forests often took the place of the tallgrass prairie. In many places, oak forests or oak openings provided a transition from grassland to maple forest.

The committee consequently decide that the rarity of maple forests in their area and the favorable topography of the site should be made the cornerstone of their plan. Furthermore, to capture some sense of the more representative prairie, the committee feel a grassland planting should also be included. They devote the north slope of the ridge to forest. The inner two-thirds of the slope is reserved for maples and basswoods as well as for a variety of appropriate spring flowers. The edges and the ridge top are reserved for a transitional planting of oaks. The south slope closest to the street is laid out as a prairie area. To soften the transition between the prairie plantings and the buildings, the committee plan to plant a few oaks and shrubs like those intended for the ridge top.

To enable people to enjoy the plantings, the committee also plan a system of paths leading from the street to the river, with a longer path following the river edge itself the length of the business district. To ensure that tired shoppers will have a place to rest and enjoy the park, they plan also to include strategically placed benches throughout the park (Figure 16.2).

At the hearing held to give the residents of the city a chance to respond to the plan, the committee also suggest a number of other ideas. They recommend incorporating interpretive materials to explain the concept behind the design, inviting civic groups like the Rotary Club as well as organizations like the Boy Scouts to contrib-

Fig. 16.2 Site use plan.

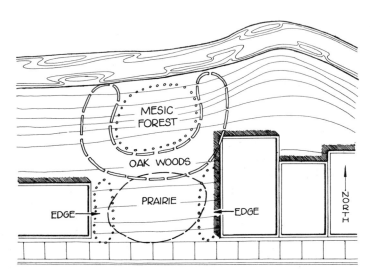

ute to the planting and management of the park, and encouraging science classes in the city schools to use the park as a living laboratory.

While many of those attending the hearing are familiar with many of the woodland flowers, few recognize the prairie species the committee are recommending. The committee consequently present a series of slides showing some of the species found in both plantings, explaining the character of both types of native communities. Their presentation focuses on the prairie itself, detailing its seasonal changes, brilliant floral shows, and physical characteristics.

Reactions range from moderately positive to negative, but most of those attending express some interest. The committee offer to schedule a visit to the prairie preserve north of the city to allow those with doubts an opportunity to see for themselves what a prairie looks like.

At a second hearing, most townspeople approve the planting. Civic groups volunteer their labor to assist in planting. The Chamber of Commerce agrees to publicize the plans for the park.

Planting Plan With the help of consultants from the university, the committee develop its planting plan. While no relics of mesic forest remain in the vicinity of the community, extensive information is available about the composition of maple–basswood forests in the midwest. The committee plan to plant relatively mature trees and shrubs to speed the development of the park. They also plan to emphasize the understory, and, in keeping with the general character of mature mesic forests, to leave the planting relatively open visually. They favor the showiest herb species, including large-flowered trillium, bloodroot, jack-in-the-pulpit, trout lily, and columbine

Fig. 16.3 Plan view of planted site.

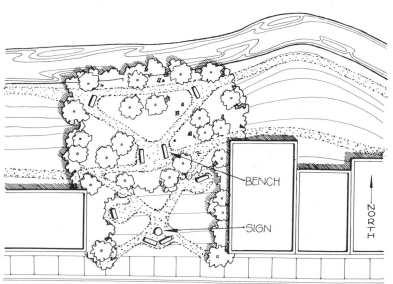

as well as a variety of ferns including the small, delicate maidenhair.

They also find that the midwestern prairies have been extensively studied despite their modern rarity. In keeping with their philosophy in designing the forest planting, they plan on including a variety of showy forbs: shooting stars, phlox, wild indigo, and purple prairie clover. Because they want to keep the planting relatively open to the street, they also plan to emphasize the medium-size grasses like northern dropseed and little bluestem. For the sake of representing the diversity of the prairie species, however, they also plan to include a representative number of taller species like big bluestem, Indian grass, and compass plant as well as less conspicuous forbs like yellow star grass and blue-eyed grass (Figure 16.3).

Establishment   The committee promote the planting phase as a civic project, encouraging garden clubs, senior-citizen groups, conservation organizations, and local schools to join in gathering seeds and growing prairie seedlings.

A local nursery volunteers to contribute the needed trees at cost. Wood chips, the surface planned for the paths, are collected from city tree-trimming operations. Organic materials needed to improve the soils on the north slope are obtained during the citywide pickup of leaves during the fall and composted in unused bins at the city incinerator.

These preparations made, one problem remains: what to do with the building debris left on the site following the storm. At the suggestion of a local conservation group, the decision is made to turn the debris to advantage by using it to accentuate the shape of the ridge. Planting soil for the south slope is provided in the form of mixed sand and gravel unused by the county in the construction of roadbeds and too infertile to be used as topsoil for turf grass. It is, however, perfect for the proposed dry prairie plantings.

The same groups volunteering to plant the park also agree to provide needed maintenance through the most difficult first 3 years of the project.

Within 3 years, the park is relatively permanently established. Weed problems in the woodland section of the park are nearly non-

Fig. 16.4   View of planted site.

existent. In the prairie, they are limited to a few woody plants and several persistent patches of lawn grass. Both problems are controllable through a single mowing every spring and hand-clipping of the invading shrubs every fall.

The community, meanwhile, has received statewide attention through the newspapers and garden clubs, and the project has become a demonstration site for others interested in more natural alternatives in landscaping (Figure 16.4).

Example Two: A Central States Schoolyard

A medium-size school in the western portion of the Central Hardwoods Region is facing problems, common today, of decreasing enrollments and increasing costs. It has extensive grounds, most of them in athletic fields. The remainder is mowed turf grass. A few traditional shrubs and trees grow near the front of the building.

Two movements exist within the school: one, to cut the landscape maintenance budget, and the other, to beautify the school grounds. Because these aims seem incompatible, faculty and administration are in a quandary.

A new idea, however, is suggested by an art teacher, who has visited a large prairie park in Central Ohio that utilizes a variety of sculptures to interpret the movement and colors of the tall prairie grasses. Since the sculptures have been attracting considerable favorable attention, he suggests, perhaps the plants which inspired them might also be well received. The art teacher is supported by another faculty member. Projects of this sort, he argues, are beginning to take hold throughout the midwest.

Strong support comes from another source. The biology teacher is enthusiastic about the opportunity to demonstrate on the school grounds themselves the interrelationships that exist in biological systems. She also proposes that the needed plants be propagated by the school's science classes as an ongoing special project designed to acquaint students with native species of plants.

Site Analysis   Several aspects of the site stand out. The school is located in a quiet residential area of medium-size lots that are, like the schoolyard itself, relatively unenclosed.

Much of the site is already devoted to uses that do not lend themselves to change. Among them is a large, paved parking area and a short drive. Athletic fields take up much of the southwestern corner of the property.

But perhaps the most notable feature is a broad drainageway running behind the school on the northwest corner of the site. It has a history of periodic severe flooding and has been recommended by the city engineering department as a candidate for lining with concrete. Lying between the bottom of the drainageway and the build-

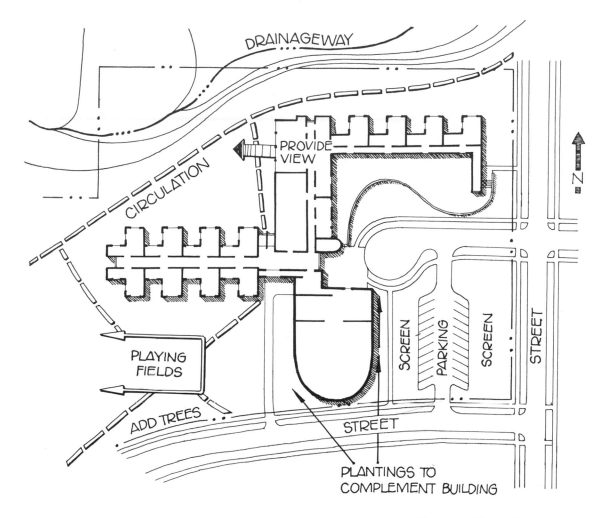

Fig. 16.5 Site analysis plan.

ing itself is a fairly abrupt slope leading up to a level area adjacent to the school.

Although the soils are found to be disturbed, tests show that they are relatively fertile, deep, and generally moist (Figure 16.5).

Planning Various items must be considered: circulation, active play, maintenance, safety, appearance, and education.

Circulation is noted by observing the routes that students take to school. Over the first winter, tracks in the snow are checked in both circulation and general play areas.

The maintenance staff, at first skeptical of the naturalistic planting proposal, are gradually won over. They feel that "mow" and "no-mow" areas should be clearly delineated, perhaps by a gravel path, and request that the width and turning radius of their mowing and snowplowing equipment be considered in laying out spaces.

They ask that sidewalks be widened to eliminate the current turf destruction and resulting erosion and mud, and that snow storage be considered in the placement of trees and shrubs.

Although the school fortunately has no serious safety problem, it is felt that all major areas should be kept visible from the school or at least from one of the surrounding residences. Vandalism problems are minimal, because the school is bordered on all sides by houses.

Three aspects of landscaping are considered for the sake of appearance. First, the site development should be as orderly as possible. Because unanimous support for the project has not yet been achieved, areas put into natural succession should be inconspicuous. Second, the volume of the building should be softened by nearby vegetation. Third, the site should offer a large open area in the midst of extensive residences. Leaving most of the site unplanted would be consistent with many of these objectives, although its rectangularity might be modified with plantings to present a more parklike appearance.

The educational aspects of the project will benefit from a diversity of plantings. The slope to the drainageway offers an opportunity to illustrate how plant communities change along a moisture gradient from the wet bottom of the ditch to the mesic upper slope. Other areas lend themselves to demonstrating stages in the development of various plant communities.

Based on these considerations, a plan is developed for the site. Because relatively little of the schoolyard on the east and south sides lends itself to extensive changes, it is decided that an area of prairie will be planted in the curve of a low wall bordering the entrance to the school. Though the planting will be relatively small, it is felt that this can be turned to an advantage. Because of its scale, it can be carefully weeded during the first few years of the planting and maintained as a showpiece for visitors.

Major attention is given to the drainage area. Because it presents a maintenance problem and is little used as a path to the building, the decision is made to create a small woodland. The lower, wetter areas lend themselves to floodplain species like river birch and sycamore. The more mesic upper slopes and level ground adjacent to the school seem perfectly suited for the mesophytic forest community now rare in the area.

It is decided that the parking lot can be visually softened with plantings of shrubbery edge species small enough to keep the site open to the south and east. These same species can be used as a transition to the mesic forest plantings.

A system of paths is also provided for. It is designed to provide for circulation along the top of the drainageway. Leading past the playing fields and through the mesic forest planting, it circles the school building, allowing access to all but the floodplain area at the bottom of the ditch.

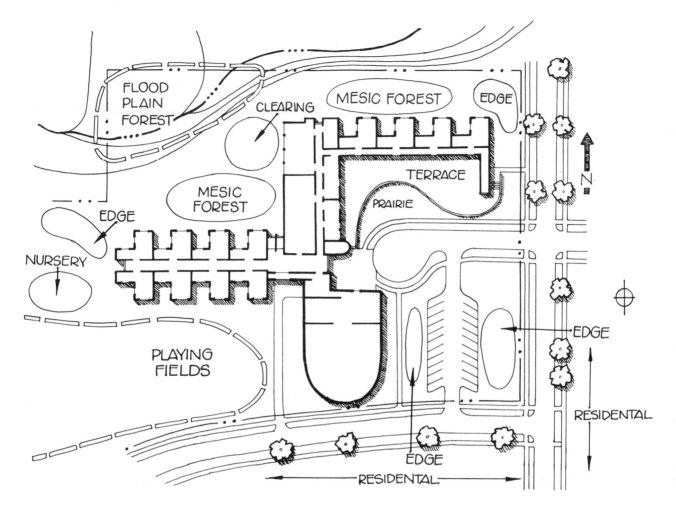

Fig. 16.6 *Site use plan.*

Finally, a small corner of the playing fields is reserved as a nursery area for seedlings started by the science classes (Figure 16.6).

Planting Plan   The composition of the proposed plantings is relatively easy to determine. As in the midwest, extensive studies have been made of the beech-maple and prairie communities in the Central Hardwoods Region. It is decided to plant as great a variety of both forest and grassland species as space and plant sources will allow, not only to reflect the diversity inherent in the communities, but also to give the students a wide exposure to the native plant species.

While it is felt that the forest plantings should look as natural as possible, that approach is tempered on the more public sides of the building. The plan is to plant those areas in a "loosely formal" way, using native species but arranging them in more obviously struc-

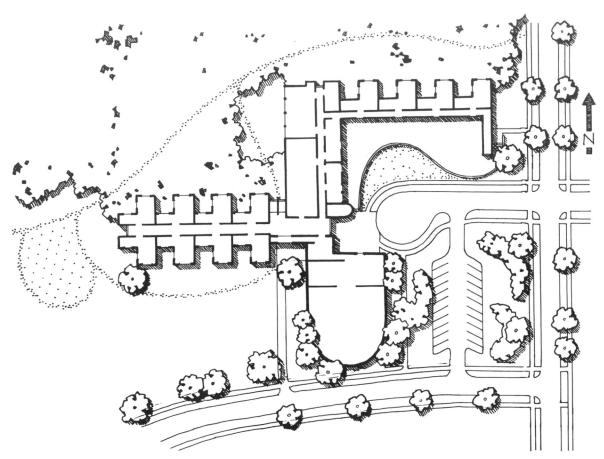

Fig. 16.7 Plan view of planted site.

tured groupings as a transition to the more traditional neighborhood landscapes (Figure 16.7).

Establishment The rationale for the project, engaging students in the study of native vegetation, is allowed to guide its establishment. With the exception of a few trees and shrubs purchased from local nurseries, all of the plants are grown by the students from seeds gathered on science field trips to natural areas. As an experiment, two approaches are taken. Most of the plants are started in the nursery and moved to their appropriate locations when large enough. Some of the forest seeds, however, are planted as seeds in the landscape itself to see how successfully they will grow. Their success or failure is discussed in class as a way of studying the requirements plants have for survival in the wild (Figure 16.8).

The site, always used for a range of activities, has the potential

Fig. 16.8 View of planted site.

more than ever of becoming a neighborhood focal point. Places are provided for relaxation in the shade of the large trees. The trail system is used for quiet evening walks as well as jogging. And bird watchers find near at hand an interesting array of songbirds attracted to the maturing grassland and woodland plantings.

chapter seventeen

Corporate/Commercial Landscapes

I n this chapter we turn again to examples of private landscapes, this time nonresidential sites utilized by relatively large numbers of people. The examples are the grounds of a manufacturing firm in the Eastern Oak Region of the country and a small medical office building in the Northern Conifer–Hardwoods Region.

Example One: Medium-Size Corporate Grounds

The annual review of the company's budget shows that the cost of maintaining the firm's grounds in a traditional manner is steadily rising. On examination, the rising cost is linked to the rising cost of petroleum products directly connected with the use of fertilizers and gasoline for lawn mowing and grooming. But more important is the growing cost of labor.

During a meeting, an officer of the firm points out that the company has emphasized adaptability in most other areas in the belief that you succeed in business by recognizing and adapting to change. "You don't always do today what you did yesterday." As a further example, he reminds his colleagues that they are now driving smaller, more efficient cars than they would have considered only 5 years ago. He recommends that they redesign their grounds to be more consistent with maintenance economy.

Site Analysis   Several features of the site stand out. To the north, a rail line borders the property and runs relatively close to the building itself. The firm has wanted to screen it from view for a number of years but the cost of doing so with attractive fencing has been prohibitive.

The boulevard to the west is undergoing strip development and a variety of small franchises have located there. While the firm does not feel it should concern itself with the appearance of the street, it does want its building to be easily visible.

South of the building, a large employees' parking lot, though attractively designed, adds to the visual sprawl of the building and detracts from its appealing architecture.

The site itself slopes gradually to the southwest, rising steeply only in the northeast corner near the railroad tracks. The soil, on testing, proves to be moderately infertile and slightly acidic. The entire site is relatively dry (Figure 17.1).

Planning Turf management procedures currently used on the grounds are reviewed formally and bear out the earlier perception

Fig. 17.1 Site analysis plan.

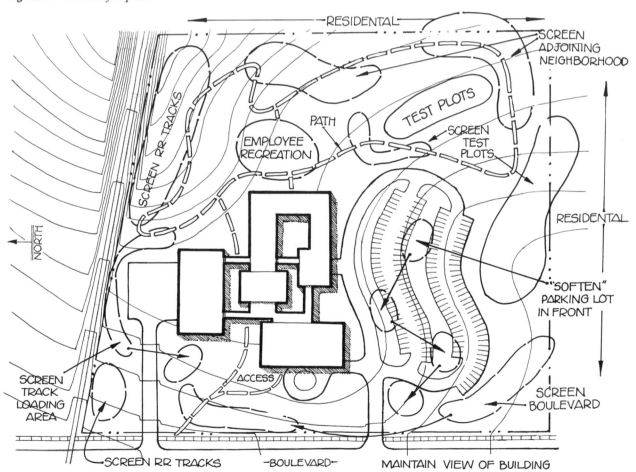

of their expense. Because they are dependent on labor, require petroleum-related products, and involve power machinery, it is also anticipated that costs will continue to rise rapidly.

Ground covers popular among some landscapers are reviewed as an alternative. Like turf, however, they are expensive to establish, require regular maintenance, including weeding, and are prone to problems of disease just as is lawn.

The example of some of the more rural roadsides in the area is then suggested. An attractive variety of wildflowers, grasses, and ferns grows along many of them in areas left unmaintained by highway crews. Several of the officers also cite the example of Shenandoah National Park, where meadows dating back to the native Americans are flourishing and greatly admired. The question is raised why, if these areas left relatively unmaintained are considered appealing, the company itself cannot incorporate some of the same plants into its landscape.

The board meets with local landscape architects who have been experimenting with work of this nature. They cite some discouraging points. Most work with open communities is being done in the midwest. The behavior of similar plants might be completely different in their area, and the professionals feel it unwise to use plant materials not adapted to local conditions. Seeds are difficult to locate, and, even if available, are in short supply. Also, seed mass-produced in the midwest remains the subject of many unanswered genetic and ethical questions.

But the meeting ends positively. It is decided to start work on several trial sections at remote areas of the site, both to develop demonstration plots and to provide sources of future seed. The landscape architects explain that they have been able to harvest dozens of seeds from a single plant of native grass in only its third year of growth, and they report that very large prairie restorations in the midwest depend on quite small areas for seed production. The initial sites, the firm decides, should have low visibility in terms of appearance, but high visibility in terms of publicity, and they would cost little. In fact, if the project fails, the space could easily be converted back to sod fairly cheaply.

The landscape architects are directed also to develop a design for the entire site so that the trial plantings will fit logically into a total scheme.

They begin their design by noting that site conditions favor a combination of grassland, oak savannas, and oak forest. Grassland will do well on the west-tending slope. Oak savannas can be used to soften the view toward the boulevard while keeping it somewhat open, and will tolerate the relatively dry site conditions and provide needed screening.

Employees use the grounds for lunchtime relaxation and exercise. A jogging trail, perhaps with some exercise stations along it, would be a desirable morale builder and would be consistent with modern corporate practices.

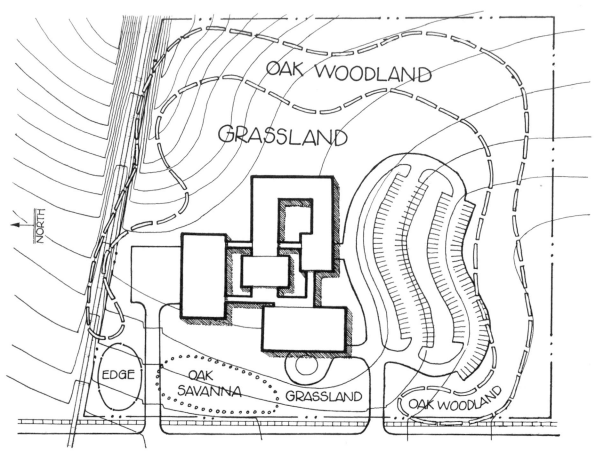

Fig. 17.2   Site use plan.

These factors in mind, they develop a plan that calls for screening the three edges of the company's grounds facing away from the boulevard. Oak woodland plantings, relatively reliable to establish, will serve that purpose. The front of the grounds requires a more elaborate planting scheme. For variety, and because of the need to keep the building visible, they decide to combine an area of savanna with a larger open area. The savanna can be used to give the grounds a sense of distance from the street while not removing the building entirely from view.

Their plan calls for placing the test plots and the recreation and exercise trail toward the rear of the property where they will be screened on all sides and given a sense of privacy (Figure 17.2).

Planting Plan   The savanna is designed to begin with large specimen trees placed so as to interrupt the view of the building from the opposite side of the boulevard but not from the street. The overhead tree canopy has the immediate advantage of providing a dark contrast to the light building materials and therefore will call attention to the building itself. The plan calls for the use of three species of oak: chestnut, white, and black.

The plan for the woodland screen takes advantage of the often dense growth of heaths that characterizes the eastern oak forest; it calls for masses of mountain laurel. Using a variety of dry oak species on the upper slope and a gradual transition to more mesic species like tulip tree and red oak further down the slope, the plan provides for some diversity in the plantings as well. Small, understory trees like ironwood and flowering dogwood contribute to the diversity by adding bark texture and flower color respectively.

Although grassland forms the major portion of the ultimate plan, the immediate planting plan calls for a series of plots, each covering about 100 square feet. To avoid having them seem too formal and thus out of keeping with the rest of the plantings, straight-lined borders are avoided. Instead, they are to parallel the contours of the site so that they take on a gently curving shape. The initial plan calls for a variety of low-growing species like little bluestem, butterfly weed, blueberry, sweet fern, coreopsis, and aster to minimize

Fig. 17.3 Plan view of planted site.

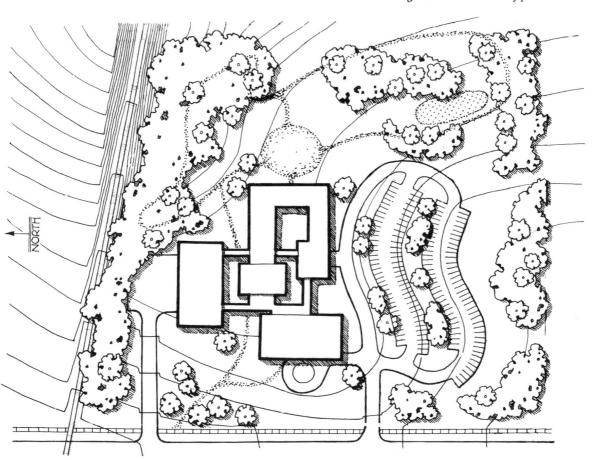

abrupt transitions from the remaining areas of mowed lawn. A few taller species like bush clover, big bluestem, Indian grass, and milkweed are included for variety (Figure 17.3).

The officers of the company are pleased by the plans and decide to go ahead with the savanna and woodland plantings immediately. Although they are anxious to transform the lawn areas as soon as possible, they decide to follow the plan calling for test areas until the success of the grassland plantings is evaluated.

Establishment   Mature trees and shrubs are purchased from area nurseries and are planted following traditional nursery practices, except that instead of being placed in formal rows they are staggered in irregular groups to give a more natural feel to the planting. Underneath, the ground is covered annually with a continuous mulch of woodchips. The edges of the mulch are allowed to curve in graceful arcs, moving out into the lawn areas in places and falling back to the trees in others.

Beneath the trees in the savanna planting, the ground is mulched as well but left free of other plantings pending the success of the test plots.

Fig. 17.4   View of planted site.

The plants for the test plots are purchased from wildflower nurseries when possible, but unavailable species are begun in a greenhouse from seed collected in the wild.

Within the first year, the success of the test plots is evident. Expansion of the plots to form a more continuous planting is planned for the fall of the third year. The advantage of this gradual approach to the grassland planting is obvious. A variety of lawn weeds as well as a few woody plants have shown up in the test areas and the landscape architect estimates that they will require annual mowing and clipping for 2 or 3 years. By expanding the test areas year by year, maintenance can be kept to a minimum (Figure 17.4).

Example Two: Small Medical Office Building Grounds

A group of medical practitioners have established a private practice devoted to preventive medicine. The associates have converted an old farmhouse on the edge of the community into their medical clinic and are concerned about landscaping the site.

One of the associates, an environmental toxicologist, suggests a landscape which would remain free of chemical fertilizers, herbicides, and insecticides, all of which are suspected of having an adverse effect on health. She argues that landscapes like those she has canoed, fished, and hiked in are probably not only physically better for the group's clientele but also symbolic of a healthier life style.

A second associate, an allergist, agrees, reminding the group that of the common allergen-producing plants few are native, the major exception being ragweed. The much maligned goldenrods, he points out, not only have little effect on allergy sufferers but are also among the most colorful species of the area's countryside. Most common native grasses like the bluestems produce too little pollen to be troublesome, while on the other hand Eurasian grasses like timothy, red-top, and the popular Kentucky bluegrass are often associated with allergy problems. He recommends using native species in the landscape.

The group agree to develop a plan for naturalizing the clinic site. Such an approach would not only better represent their professional philosophy; they feel it would also better complement the rural character of their setting than would a formal lawn.

Site Analysis The site is relatively flat and is landscaped with mowed lawn, one large lilac bush, and two mature white pines. Toward the rear, a few established pines offer shade but insufficient screening to block an undesirable view. The soils are extremely sandy and relatively dry. A paved walk leads directly to the clinic from the sidewalk, and a drive leads behind the building to a small parking lot (Figure 17.5).

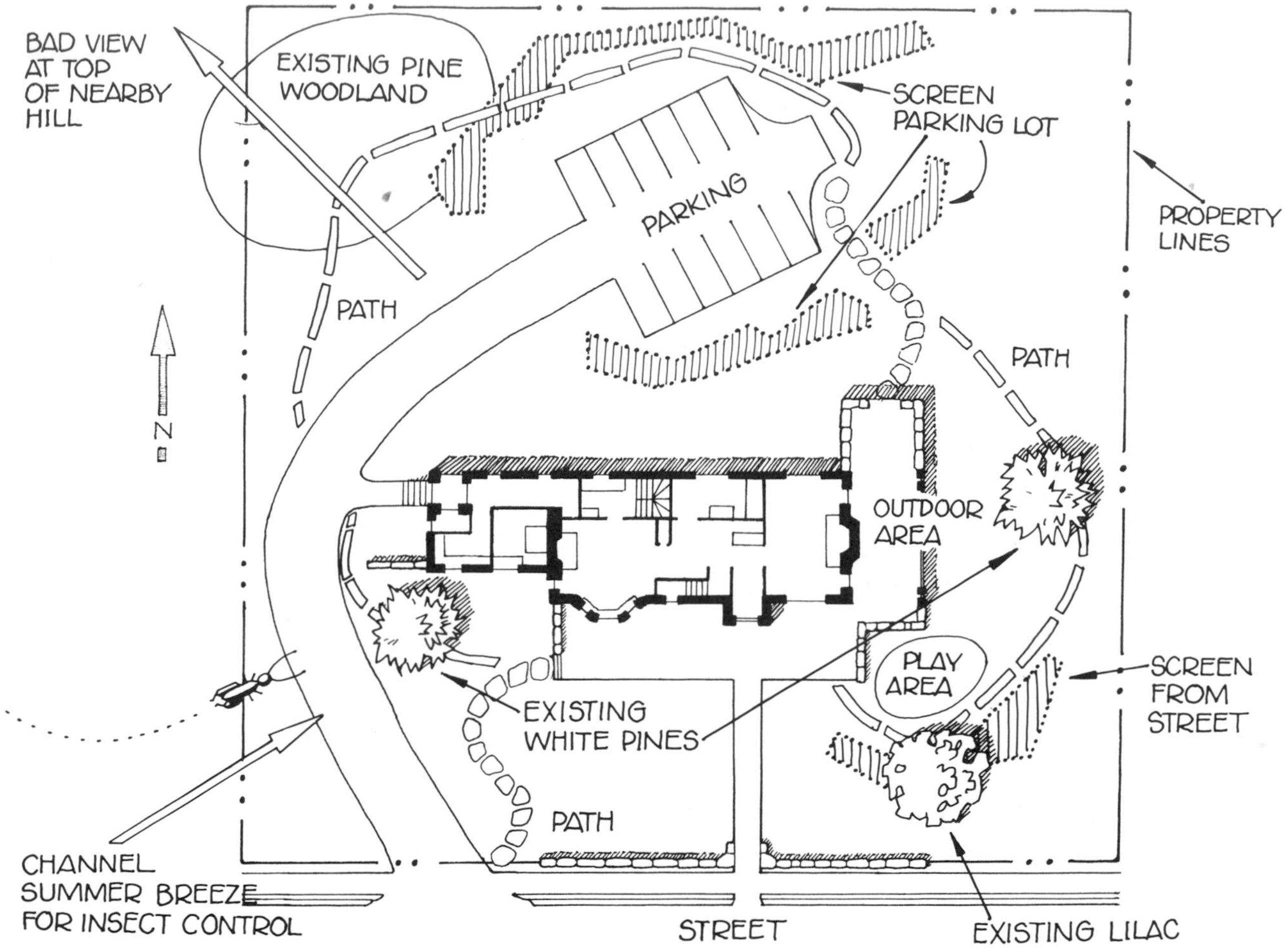
BAD VIEW AT TOP OF NEARBY HILL
EXISTING PINE WOODLAND
SCREEN PARKING LOT
PARKING
PROPERTY LINES
PATH
N
PATH
OUTDOOR AREA
PLAY AREA
SCREEN FROM STREET
EXISTING WHITE PINES
PATH
CHANNEL SUMMER BREEZE FOR INSECT CONTROL
STREET
EXISTING LILAC

Fig. 17.5 Site analysis plan.

Planning The major activity occurring on the site is the coming and going of the clinic's clients. Because the clinic is family-oriented, it is felt that a play area for preschool and school-age children would be highly desirable. It is felt that while the parking area should be retained, the play area should be separated from it and located in front of the clinic for the children's safety. Also for the sake of safety, it should be enclosed on the street side while remaining open and in view of parents waiting in the clinic. Because a fence is felt to be out of keeping with the site and a traditional stone wall might itself be a safety hazard for young children, the associates decide to partly enclose the play area with dense, nonprickly shrubs.

Two other activities are also considered. Provision should be made for outdoor adult seating for clients and clinic staff. To make it possible for adults and children to enjoy the plantings, a system of

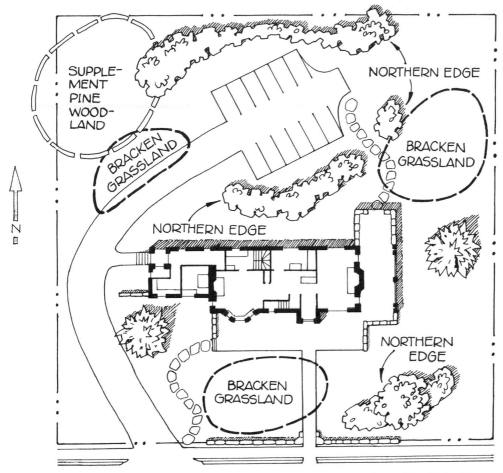

Fig. 17.6 Site use plan.

paths would also be desirable. The paths might include outdoor "learning" areas where clients can be familiarized with the common native plants they might encounter in the wild.

Because of the area's northern location and the site's sandy soils, logical choices for plantings include a pine forest community for needed privacy or screening. To keep much of the rest of the site relatively open, bracken grassland plantings are selected (Figure 17.6).

Planting Plan Because the entire area is relatively rural and undeveloped, the associates have little trouble identifying existing models for their proposed landscape. They find that many of the mature pine forests are relatively open in the understory, and they decide they enjoy the effect of tall, nearly limbless tree trunks reaching up to a pine canopy. Major shrubs like beaked hazelnut and

DURHAM AGRICULTURAL
COLLEGE LIBRARY BOOK

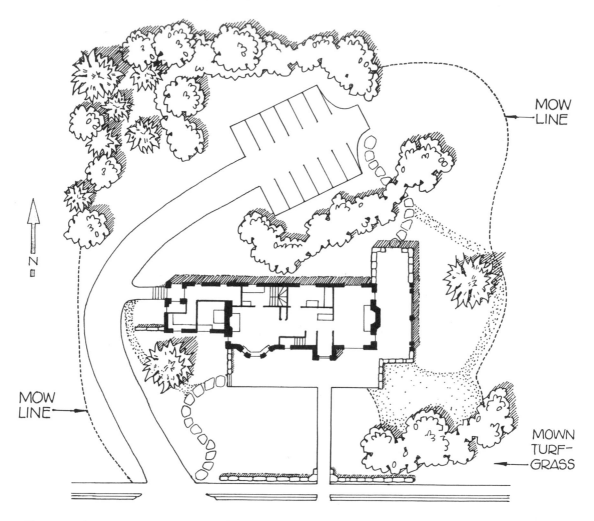

MOW
LINE

MOW
LINE

MOWN
TURF-
GRASS

Fig. 17.7 Plan view of planted site.

round-leaved dogwood are scattered throughout the forests and lend themselves well to their plans. Masses can be used as screening along the rear of the lot and adjoining the parking area to hide it from view. The same species can be used as screening for the play area in front.

Models for the grassland area, too, are abundant in the area. Several large areas nearby, once pine forest, had burned 10 years earlier and are now grown up in species like bracken fern, the small, shrubby sweet fern, little bluestem, wild strawberry, and a variety of asters. The associates decide that they enjoy the color and textures of these plants and decide to use the same species (Figure 17.7).

Establishment To their delight, the associates find that many of the species on their planting plan are relatively easy to establish,

Fig. 17.8   View of planted site.

requiring only careful monitoring during the first few summers for drought. The shrub and tree species are available from local nurseries in all sizes. The grassland species, however, are not available commercially. While most can be grown from seed, a few, like sweet fern, are relatively difficult.

After asking some of the local residents, they locate an area dairy farmer whose fields support large colonies of bracken fern and sweet fern. Because his cows will not graze on them, he is only too happy to allow the associates to attempt to transplant them to the clinic site.

The associates decide to make the project an all-clinic one. All join in the spring and fall plantings and in the summer maintenance, and enjoy the common bond. Within 3 years, the grassland planting, with a growing colony of sweet fern and a scattering of bluestem, is doing well and requires little maintenance on the dry, sandy site.

Although out of the ordinary, the landscape is well accepted by the clinic's clients, who enjoy looking at the wildflowers while waiting to be seen. Children enjoy the play space provided for them and the pathways through what they have come to call the "wilderness" (Figure 17.8).

Representative Species of the Major Plant Communities

The following lists, synthesized from personal observations and much of the literature suggested for further reading, are intended as general guides and should be used only as a point of departure. For the most part they include only those species which seem to occur in a given community type. Those identified as dominants are visually dominant in season. A number of the species listed—those identified with an asterisk (*)—are representative of their communities but may be difficult to grow. Most of them require an optimal environment for success.

It is worth repeating that the study of plant communities is not an exact science. Species with broad geographic ranges may behave differently from one region to another. In addition, no two examples of a given community are ever exactly alike. For these and other reasons, it is best to develop a personal knowledge of communities occurring in your area.

Mesic Forest (Central) (Throughout, but with important regional variations)

Canopy Trees

Acer nigrum	Black maple
Acer saccharum	Sugar maple
Aesculus octandra	Sweet buckcyc
Betula lutea	Yellow birch
Carya cordiformis	Yellow bud hickory
Fagus grandifolia	American beech

Fraxinus americana	White ash
Liriodendron tulipfera	Tulip tree
Nyssa sylvatica	Black gum
Quercus alba	White oak
Quercus borealis	Northern red oak
Tilia americana	American basswood
Tilia heterophylla	White basswood

Understory Trees

Carpinus caroliniana	Musclewood
Magnolia acuminata	Cucumber magnolia
Magnolia fraseri	Fraser's magnolia
Ostrya virginiana	Ironwood

Small Trees and Shrubs

Asimina triloba	Papaw
Cercis canadensis	Redbud
Cornus alternifolia	Alternate-leaved dogwood
Cornus florida	Flowering dogwood
Dirca palustris	Leatherwood
Hamamelis virginiana	Witch hazel
Hydrangea arborescens	Wild hydrangea
Lindera benzoin	Spicebush
Stewartia ovata	Mountain camellia*
Viburnum acerifolium	Mapleleaf viburnum

Ground Layer

Common Plants

Arisaema triphyllum	Jack-in-the-pulpit
Carex laxiflora	Sedge
Carex plantaginea	Plantain-leaved sedge
Claytonia virginica	Virginia spring beauty
Dentaria laciniata	Cut-leaved toothwort
Dicentra canadensis	Squirrel corn
Dryopteris spinulosa	Spinulose wood fern
Erythronium albidum	White trout lily
Erythronium americanum	Yellow trout lily
Galium aparine	Shining bedstraw
Osmorhiza claytoni	Hairy sweet cicely
Parthenocissus quinquefolia	Virginia creeper
Podophyllum peltatum	Mayapple
Polygonatum pubescens	Downy Solomon's seal
Smilacina racemosa	Solomon's-plume; false Solomon's-seal
Solidago flexicaulis	Zigzag goldenrod
Viola eriocarpa	Smooth yellow violet
Viola pubescens	Downy yellow violet

Others

Actaea alba	White baneberry
Adiantum pedatum	Maidenhair fern
Allium tricoccum	Wild leek
Amphicarpa bracteata	Hog peanut
Anemone quinquefolia	Wood anemone
Anemonella thalictroides	Rue anemone

Aplectrum hyemale	Adam-and-Eve orchid*
Aralia nudicaulis	Wild sarsaparilla
Aralia racemosa	Spikenard
Aralia spinosa	Hercules'-club
Arisaema draconitum	Green dragon
Aristolochia durior	Dutchman's-pipe
Aristolochia serpentaria	Virginia snakeroot
Asarum canadense	Wild ginger
Astilbe biternatum	False goat's beard
Aster cordifolius	Heart-leaved aster
Aster divaricatus	White wood aster
Aster shortii	Short's aster
Athyrium filix-femina	Lady fern
Athyrium pycnocarpon	Gladefern
Athyrium thelypteroides	Silvery spleenwort
Blephilia hirsuta	Wood mint
Botrychium virginianum	Rattlesnake fern
Brachyelytrum erectum	Long-awned wood grass
Cardamine douglassii	Purple cress
Carex davisii	Sedge*
Carex deweyana	Sedge*
Carex hirtifolia	Sedge*
Carex pensylvanica	Pennsylvania sedge
Carex rosea	Sedge*
Caulophyllum thalictroides	Blue cohosh
Cimicifuga racemosa	Black snakeroot
Circaea quadrisulcata	Enchanter's nightshade
Claytonia caroliniana	Carolina spring beauty
Clematis virginiana	Virgin's bower
Collinsonia canadensis	Horse balm
Conopholis americana	Squawroot*
Cryptotaenia canadensis	Honewort
Cubelium concolor	Green violet
Delphinium tricorne	Dwarf larkspur
Dentaria diphylla	Crinkleroot
Dentaria heterophylla	Slender toothwort
Dentaria maxima	Toothwort
Diarrhena americana	Beak grass
Dicentra cucullaria	Dutchman's-breeches
Disporum lanuginosum	Yellow mandarin
Disporum maculatum	Spotted mandarin
Dryopteris marginalis	Marginal shield fern
Epifagus virginiana	Beechdrops*
Erigenia bulbosa	Harbinger-of-spring
Eupatorium purpureum	Purple Joe-Pye weed
Euonymus obovatus	Running strawberry-bush
Floerkea proserpinacoides	False mermaid*
Galium circaezans	Wild licorice
Galium lanceolatum	Lance-leaved wild licorice
Galium triflorum	Sweet-scented bedstraw
Geranium maculatum	Wild geranium
Habenaria viridis	Bracted orchid*
Hepatica acutiloba	Hepatica
Hydrophyllum appendiculatum	Great waterleaf
Hydrophyllum canadense	Canada waterleaf
Hydrophyllum macrophyllum	Large-leaved waterleaf

Hydrophyllum virginianum	Virginia waterleaf
Impatiens pallida	Pale touch-me-not
Isopyrum biternatum	False rue anemone
Jeffersonia diphylla	Twinleaf
Lonicera canadensis	Fly honeysuckle
Medeola virginiana	Indian cucumber root
Menispermum canadense	Moonseed
Mitella diphylla	Bishop's-cap; mitrewort
Monotropa uniflora	Indian pipe*
Orchis spectabilis	Showy orchid*
Osmorhiza longistylis	Sweet cicely
Osmunda claytoniana	Interrupted fern
Panax quinquefolium	Ginseng
Panicum latifolium	Broad-leaved panic grass
Passiflora lutea	Passionflower
Phacelia bipinnatifida	Purple phacelia*
Phlox divaricata	Woodland phlox
Phryma leptostachya	Lopseed
Pilea pumila	Clearweed
Poa sylvestris	Woodland bluegrass
Polygonatum pubescens	Downy Solomon's-seal
Polystichum acrostichoides	Christmas fern
Prenanthes alba	Lion's foot
Prenanthes altissima	Tall white lettuce
Sanicula canadensis	Canadian black snakeroot
Sanicula trifoliata	Large-fruited black snakeroot
Sanguinaria canadensis	Bloodroot
Smilax ecirrhata	Upright carrion flower
Smilax rotundifolia	Greenbrier
Smilax taminoides	Bristly greenbrier
Solidago caesia	Blue-stemmed goldenrod
Stachys riddellii	Riddell's hedge-nettle
Stellaria pubera	Star chickweed
Stylophorum diphyllum	Celandine poppy
Thalictrum dioicum	Early meadow rue
Thelypteris noveboracensis	New York fern
Tiarella cordifolia	Foamflower
Trillium erectum	Wake-robin
Trillium gleasoni	Gleason's trillium
Trillium grandiflorum	Large-flowered trillium
Trillium recurvatum	Prairie trillium
Trillium sessile	Toad trillium
Trillium viride	Green wake-robin
Triphora trianthophora	Three birds orchid*
Uvularia grandiflora	Large-flowered bellwort
Uvularia perfoliata	Perfoliate bellwort
Viola canadensis	Canada violet
Viola rostrata	Long-spurred violet
Viola stoneana	Stone's violet

Oak-Hickory Forest (Central and Midwest)

Canopy Trees

Dominants

Quercus alba	White oak
Quercus velutina	Black oak

Others

Carya glabra	Pignut hickory
Carya laciniosa	Big shellbark hickory
Carya ovata	Shagbark hickory
Carya tomentosa	Mockernut hickory
Quercus borealis	Northern red oak
Quercus ellipsoidalis	Northern pin oak
Quercus imbricaria	Shingle oak
Quercus macrocarpa	Bur oak
Quercus marilandica	Blackjack oak
Quercus muhlenbergii	Chinquapin oak
Quercus stellata	Post oak

Shrubs

Cornus alternifolia	Alternate-leaved dogwood
Cornus racemosa	Gray dogwood
Corylus americana	Hazelnut
Prunus americana	American plum
Prunus virginiana	Chokecherry
Ribes cynosbati	Prickly wild gooseberry
Ribes missouriense	Wild gooseberry
Sambucus canadensis	Elderberry
Viburnum lentago	Nannyberry
Viburnum rafinesquianum	Downy arrowwood

Ground Layer

Common Plants

Amphicarpa bracteata	Hog peanut
Carex pensylvanica	Pennsylvania sedge
Circaea quadrisulcata	Enchanter's nightshade
Desmodium glutinosum	Tick trefoil
Galium concinnum	Shining bedstraw
Geranium maculatum	Wild geranium
Osmorhiza claytoni	Hairy sweet cicely
Parthenocissus vitacea	Virginia creeper
Smilacina racemosa	Solomon's-plume; false Solomon's-seal

Others

Adiantum pedatum	Maidenhair fern
Agrimonia gryposepala	Agrimony
Anemone cylindrica	Thimbleweed
Anemone quinquefolia	Wood anemone
Apocynum androsaemifolium	Spreading dogbane
Aralia nudicaulis	Wild sarsaparilla
Arisaema triphyllum	Jack-in-the-pulpit
Aster sagittifolius	Arrowleaf aster
Athyrium filix-femina	Lady fern
Botrychium virginianum	Rattlesnake fern
Celastrus scandens	Bittersweet
Cypripedium pubescens	Large yellow lady's slipper
Euphorbia corollata	Flowering spurge
Fragaria virginiana	Wild strawberry
Geum canadense	Wood avens
Helianthus strumosus	Pale-leaved sunflower

Hystrix patula	Bottlebrush grass
Lactuca biennis	Tall blue lettuce
Lonicera prolifera	Yellow honeysuckle
Monarda fistulosa	Bergamot
Phryma leptostachya	Lopseed
Podophyllum peltatum	Mayapple
Polygonatum canaliculatum	Large Solomon's-seal
Potentilla simplex	Common cinquefoil
Prenanthes alba	White lettuce
Pteridium aquilinum	Bracken fern
Pyrola elliptica	Large-leaved shinleaf
Rosa spp.	Rose
Sanicula gregaria	Clustered black snakeroot
Smilacina stellata	Starry Solomon's-plume
Smilax ecirrhata	Upright carrion flower
Smilax herbacea	Carrion flower
Uvularia grandiflora	Large flowered bellwort
Veronicastrum virginicum	Culver's root
Viola cucullata	Marsh violet
Vitis aestivalis	Summer grape
Vitis riparia	Riverbank grape

Chestnut Oak Forest (Central and East)

Canopy Trees

Dominants
Acer rubrum	Red maple
Quercus alba	White oak
Quercus borealis	Northern red oak
Quercus prinus	Chestnut oak

Others
Acer pensylvanicum	Moosewood
Carya glabra	Pignut hickory
Carya ovalis	Small-fruited hickory
Fraxinus pennsylvania	Red ash
Juglans cinerea	Butternut
Quercus coccinea	Scarlet oak
Quercus velutina	Black oak
Sassafras albidum	Sassafras

Understory Trees
Amelanchier arborea	Serviceberry; shadbush
Cornus florida	Flowering dogwood
Oxydendrum arboreum	Sourwood

Shrubs
Hamamelis virginiana	Witch hazel
Kalmia latifolia	Mountain laurel
Rhododendron calendulaceum	Flame azalea
Rhododendron maximum	Great rhododendron
Rhododendron nudiflorum	Pinxter bloom

Ground Layer

Common Plants

Chimaphila maculata	Spotted wintergreen
Potentilla simplex	Common cinquefoil
Thelypteris noveboracensis	New York fern

Others

Aralia nudicaulis	Wild sarsaparilla
Aster paternus	Aster
Carex cephalophora	Woodbank sedge*
Cypripedium acaule	Moccasin flower*
Galax aphylla	Galax
Gaultheria procumbens	Wintergreen
Gerardia tenuifolia	Slender false foxglove*
Gillenia trifoliata	Bowman's root
Lysimachia quadrifolia	Whorled loosestrife
Medeola virginiana	Indian cucumber root
Monarda clinopodia	Wild bergamot
Parthenocissus quinquefolia	Virginia creeper
Polystichum acrostichoides	Christmas fern
Pteridium aquilinum	Bracken fern
Silene virginica	Fire pink
Smilacina racemosa	Solomon's-plume; false Solomon's-seal
Thelypteris hexagonoptera	Broad beech fern
Uvularia sessilifolia	Sessile bellwort

Pitch Pine Forest (Central and East)

Canopy Trees

Dominant

Pinus rigida	Pitch pine

Others

Acer rubrum	Red maple
Betula lenta	Sweet birch
Betula populifolia	Gray birch
Pinus echinata	Yellow pine
Quercus prinoides	Chestnut oak

Small Tree and Shrub Layer

Amelanchier laevis	Allegheny shadbush
Aronia melanocarpa	Black chokeberry
Diervilla lonicera	Dwarf bush honeysuckle
Gaylussacia baccata	Huckleberry
Kalmia angustifolia	Sheep laurel
Kalmia latifolia	Mountain laurel
Quercus ilicifolia	Bear oak
Vaccinium angustifolium	Early low blueberry

Ground Layer

Aralia nudicaulis	Wild sarsaparilla
Carex pensylvanica	Pennsylvania sedge

Solidago odora	Sweet goldenrod
Solidago puberula	Downy goldenrod
Solidago rugosa	Rough-stemmed goldenrod
Solidago speciosa	Showy goldenrod
Sorghastrum nutans	Indian grass
Spiranthes tuberosa	Ladies' tresses*
Spirea latifolia	Meadowsweet
Tephrosia virginiana	Goat's rue
Trichostema dichotomum	Blue curls
Vaccinium vacillans	Late low blueberry
Viola fimbriatula	Sand violet
Viola latiuscula	Broad-leaved wood violet
Viola pedata	Bird's-foot violet

Mesic Grassland (East)

Allium cernuum	Nodding wild onion
Amianthium muscaetoxicum	Fly poison
Andropogon gerardi	Big bluestem
Andropogon scoparius	Little bluestem
Apocynum androsaemifolium	Spreading dogbane
Apocynum cannabinum	Indian hemp
Asclepias incarnata	Marsh milkweed
Asclepias syriaca	Common milkweed
Asclepias tuberosa	Butterfly weed
Aster laevis	Smooth blue aster
Aster patens	Late purple aster
Aster pilosus	Frost aster
Aster simplex	Panicled aster
Astragalus canadensis	Canadian milk vetch
Baptisia australis	Wild blue indigo
Baptisia tinctoria	Yellow wild indigo
Bromus ciliatus	Prairie brome
Cacalia atriplicifolia	Pale Indian plantain
Carex lanuginosa	Woolly sedge
Carex pensylvanica	Pennsylvania sedge
Cassia fasciculata	Partridge pea*
Ceanothus americanus	New Jersey tea
Cicuta maculata	Water hemlock
Cirsium discolor	Pasture thistle
Coreopsis verticillata	Whorled coreopsis
Dennstaedtia punctibula	Hay-scented fern
Euphorbia corollata	Flowering spurge
Fragaria virginiana	Wild strawberry
Galium boreale	Northern bedstraw
Gentiana andrewsii	Bottle gentian
Gentiana quinquefolia	Stiff gentian*
Gentiana saponaria	Soapwort gentian
Geranium maculatum	Wild geranium
Helianthus decapetalus	Thin-leaved sunflower
Helianthus divaricatus	Woodland sunflower
Helianthus strumosus	Pale-leaved wood sunflower
Heliopsis helianthoides	Oxeye
Heuchera pubescens	Alumroot
Houstonia caerulea	Bluets

Hypoxis hirsuta	Yellow star grass
Lespedeza hirta	Hairy bush clover
Liatris graminifolia	Grass-leaved blazing star
Liatris spicata	Marsh blazing star
Lilium philadelphicum	Wood lily
Lilium superbum	Turk's-cap lily
Lithospermum canescens	Puccoon*
Monarda fistulosa	Bergamot
Oenothera biennis	Evening primrose
Oenothera tetragona	Glandular sundrops
Oxalis violacea	Violet wood sorrel
Oxypolis rigidior	Cowbane
Parthenium integrifolium	Wild quinine
Pedicularis canadensis	Wood betony*
Penstemon digitalis	Smooth beardtongue
Penstemon canescens	Gray beardtongue
Penstemon hirsutus	Hairy beardtongue
Phlox paniculata	Garden phlox
Phlox subulata	Moss phlox
Polygonatum canaliculatum	Great Solomon's-seal
Potentilla canadensis	Dwarf cinquefoil
Potentilla simplex	Common cinquefoil
Pteridium aquilinum	Bracken fern
Pycnanthemum incanum	Hoary mountain mint
Pycnanthemum virginianum	Virginia mountain mint
Rosa carolina	Carolina rose
Rosa palustris	Swamp rose
Rudbeckia hirta	Black-eyed Susan
Salix humilis	Prairie willow
Satureja vulgaris	Wild basil
Senecio pauperculus	Balsam ragwort
Silphium trifoliatum	Whorled rosinweed
Sisyrinchium atlanticum	Eastern blue-eyed grass
Sisyrinchium graminoides	Blue-eyed grass
Smilacina racemosa	Solomon's-plume; false Solomon's-seal
Solidago arguta	Sharp-leaved goldenrod
Solidago juncea	Early goldenrod
Sorghastrum nutans	Indian grass
Spiraea latifolia	Meadowsweet
Stenanthium gramineum	Feather-fleece
Taenidia integerima	Pimpernel
Tephrosia virginiana	Goat's rue
Thalictrum coriaceum	Meadow rue
Thalictrum polygamum	Tall meadow rue
Thaspium barbinode	Meadow-parsnip
Thaspium trifoliatum	Purple-flowered meadow parsnip
Thaspium trifoliatum flavum	Yellow-flowered meadow parsnip
Vernonia noveboracensis	New York ironweed
Veronicastrum virginicum	Culver's root
Viola papilionacea	Butterfly violet
Viola pedata	Bird's-foot violet
Viola sororia	Woolly blue violet
Zizea aptera	Heart-leaved golden Alexanders
Zizea aurea	Golden Alexanders

Xeric Prairie (Midwest)

Common Plants

Amorpha canescens	Leadplant
Andropogon gerardi	Big bluestem
Andropogon scoparius	Little bluestem
Antennaria neglecta	Pussytoes
Aster ericoides	Heath aster
Aster sericeus	Silky aster
Bouteloua curtipendula	Side oats grama
Coreopsis palmata	Prairie coreopsis
Euphorbia corollata	Flowering spurge
Helianthus laetiflorus	Prairie sunflower
Liatris aspera	Rough blazing star
Liatris cylindracea	Dwarf blazing star
Panicum perlongum	Long-stalked panic grass
Petalostemum purpureum	Purple prairie clover
Rosa spp.	Rose
Solidago nemoralis	Old-field goldenrod
Sporobolus heterolepis	Northern dropseed
Stipa spartea	Needlegrass

Others

Anemone cylindrica	Thimbleweed
Anemone patens	Pasqueflower
Artemisia caudata	Beach wormwood
Artemisia frigida	Prairie sagebrush
Artemisia ludoviciana	White sage
Asclepias syriaca	Milkweed
Asclepias tuberosa	Butterfly milkweed
Asclepias verticillata	Whorled milkweed
Aster azureus	Sky-blue aster
Aster laevis	Smooth blue aster
Aster oblongifolius	Aromatic aster
Aster pilosus	Hairy aster
Aster ptarmicoides	Stiff aster
Astragalus crassicarpus	Ground plum
Callirhoe triangulata	Clustered poppy mallow
Cassia fasciculata	Partridge pea*
Cirsium hillii	Hill's thistle*
Cirsium discolor	Pasture thistle
Commandra richardsiana	Toadflax*
Delphinium virescens	Prairie larkspur
Erigeron strigosus	Daisy fleabane
Gentiana quinquefolia	Stiff gentian*
Hedeoma hispida	Rough pennyroyal
Helianthus occidentalis	Naked sunflower
Koeleria cristata	June grass
Kuhnia eupatorioides	False boneset
Lactuca ludoviciana	Western wild lettuce
Lespedeza capitata	Roundheaded bush clover
Liatris punctata	Dotted blazing star

Linum sulcatum	Grooved yellow flax*
Lithospermum canescens	Puccoon*
Lithospermum incisum	Gromwell*
Microseris cuspidata	Prairie dandelion*
Monarda fistulosa	Bergamot
Muhlenbergia cuspidata	Prairie satin grass
Oenothera biennis	Evening primrose
Orobanche fasciculata	Clustered broomrape*
Panicum leibergii	Prairie panic grass
Panicum oligosanthes	Few-flowered panic grass
Petalostemum candidum	White prairie clover
Physalis virginiana	Lance-leaved ground-cherry
Plantago rugelii	Red-stalked plantain
Potentilla arguta	Prairie cinquefoil
Prenanthes aspera	Rough white lettuce
Ratibida pinnata	Yellow coneflower
Rudbeckia hirta	Black-eyed Susan
Scutellaria leonardi	Skullcap*
Sisyrinchium campestre	Blue-eyed grass
Solidago rigida	Stiff goldenrod
Sorghastrum nutans	Indian grass
Tradescantia ohiensis	Spiderwort
Viola pedata	Bird's-foot violet
Viola pedatifida	Prairie violet

Mesic Prairie (Midwest)

Common Plants

Amorpha canescens	Leadplant
Andropogon gerardi	Big bluestem
Andropogon scoparius	Little bluestem
Aster ericoides	Heath aster
Aster laevis	Smooth blue aster
Comandra richardsiana	Toadflax*
Coreopsis palmata	Prairie coreopsis
Desmodium illinoense	Illinois tick trefoil
Eryngium yuccifolium	Rattlesnake master
Euphorbia corollata	Flowering spurge
Helianthus laetiflorus	Prairie sunflower
Lespedeza capitata	Roundheaded bush clover
Liatris aspera	Rough blazing star
Monarda fistulosa	Bergamot
Panicum leibergii	Prairie panic grass
Phlox pilosa	Prairie phlox
Ratibida pinnata	Yellow coneflower
Rosa spp.	Rose
Solidago rigida	Stiff goldenrod
Sporbolus heterolepis	Northern dropseed
Stipa spartea	Needlegrass
Tradescantia ohiensis	Spiderwort

Others

Allium cernuum	Nodding wild onion
Anemone cylindrica	Thimbleweed
Antennaria neglecta	Pussytoes
Apocynum androsaemifolium	Spreading dogbane
Apocynum cannabinum	Indian hemp
Asclepias syriaca	Milkweed
Aster azureus	Sky-blue aster
Astragalus canadensis	Canadian milk vetch
Baptisia leucophaea	Cream wild indigo
Ceanothus americanus	New Jersey tea
Convolvulus sepium	Hedge bindweed
Desmodium canadense	Showy tick trefoil
Dodecatheon meadia	Shooting star
Echinacea pallida	Pale purple coneflower
Elymus canadensis	Canada wild rye
Eupatorium altissimum	Tall boneset
Fragaria virginiana	Wild strawberry
Galium boreale	Northern bedstraw
Gaura biennis	Biennial gaura
Gentiana puberula	Downy gentian*
Gentiana saponaria	Soapwort gentian
Helianthus grosseserratus	Sawtooth sunflower
Helianthus occidentalis	Naked sunflower
Heliopsis helianthoides	Oxeye
Hypericum canadense	Canadian Saint-John's-wort
Hypericum multilum	Weak Saint-John's-wort
Lactuca canadensis	Wild lettuce
Lathyrus venosus	Veiny pea
Liatris ligulistylis	Blazing star
Lilium philadelphicum andinum	Prairie lily
Oxalis violacea	Violet wood sorrel
Parthenium integrifolium	Wild quinine
Penstemon digitalis	Smooth beardtongue
Petalostemum purpureum	Purple prairie clover
Physalis virginiana	Lance-leaved ground-cherry
Potentilla arguta	Prairie cinquefoil
Rudbeckia hirta	Black-eyed Susan
Silphium integrifolium	Wholeleaf rosinweed
Silphium laciniatum	Compass plant
Solidago juncea	Early goldenrod
Solidago missouriensis	Missouri goldenrod
Solidago speciosa	Showy goldenrod
Sorghastrum nutans	Indian grass
Vicia angustifolia	Narrow-leaved vetch
Viola pedatifida	Larkspur violet
Zizia aptera	Heart-leaved golden Alexanders

Hydric Prairie (Midwest)

Common Plants

Andropogon gerardi	Big bluestem
Andropogon scoparius	Little bluestem
Asclepias syriaca	Common milkweed

Aster azureus	Sky-blue aster
Calamagrostis canadensis	Bluejoint grass
Comandra richardsiana	Toadflax*
Dodecatheon meadia	Shooting star
Euphorbia corollata	Flowering spurge
Equisetum arvense	Common horsetail
Fragaria virginiana	Wild strawberry
Galium boreale	Northern bedstraw
Helianthus grosseserratus	Sawtooth sunflower
Liatris pychnostachya	Blazing star
Panicum leibergii	Prairie panic grass
Phlox pilosa	Prairie phlox
Pychanthemum virginianum	Mountain mint
Ratibida pinnata	Yellow coneflower
Rosa spp.	Rose
Rudbeckia hirta	Black-eyed Susan
Salix humilis	Prairie willow
Silphium terebinthinaceum	Prairie dock
Solidago gigantea	Large goldenrod
Solidago rigida	Stiff goldenrod
Spartina pectinata	Prairie cord grass
Thalictrum dasycarpum	Purple meadow rue
Veronicastrum virginiam	Culver's root

Others

Allium canadense	Wild garlic
Amorpha canescens	Lead plant
Artemisia serrata	Sawtooth wormwood*
Asclepias purpurescens	Purple milkweed
Aster ericoides	Heath aster
Aster laevis	Smooth aster
Aster novae-angliae	New England aster
Baptisia leucantha	White wild indigo
Blephilia ciliata	Downy wood mint
Cacalia tuberosa	Tuberous Indian plantain
Camassia scilloides	Wild hyacinth
Carex bicknelli	Sedge
Cicuta maculata	Water hemlock
Cirsium discolor	Old-field thistle
Desmodium canadense	Showy tick trefoil
Elymus canadensis	Canada wild rye
Equisetum laevigatum	Scouring rush
Gentiana andrewsii	Bottle gentian
Gentiana crinita	Fringed gentian*
Habenaria flava	Tubercled orchid*
Habenaria leucophaea	Prairie fringed orchid*
Helianthus laetiflorus	Stiff sunflower
Heuchera richardsonii	Alumroot
Lactuca canadensis	Tall wild lettuce
Lathyrus palustris	Marsh vetchling
Lathyrus venosus	Veiny wild pea
Lespedeza capitata	Roundheaded bush clover
Lilium michiganense	Michigan lily

Lithospermum canescens	Puccoon*
Lythrum alatum	Winged loosestrife
Monarda fistulosa	Bergamot
Napaea dioica	Glade mallow
Oxybaphus nyctaginea	Wild four-o'clock
Oxypolis rigidior	Cowbane
Polytaenia nuttallii	Prairie parsley*
Prenanthes crepidinea	Great white lettuce*
Prenanthes racemosa	Smooth white rattlesnake root
Rudbeckia subtomentosa	Sweet black-eyed Susan
Silphium integrifolium	Rosinweed
Smilacina stellata	Starry Solomon's-plume
Solidago gramnifolia	Grassleaf goldenrod
Sorghastrum nutans	Indian grass
Spirea alba	Narrowleaf meadowsweet
Sporobolus heterolepis	Northern dropseed
Tradescantia ohiensis	Spiderwort
Vernonia fasciculata	Western ironweed
Vicia americana	American vetch
Zizia aurea	Golden Alexanders

Boreal Forest (North)

Canopy Trees

Dominants

Abies balsamea	Balsam fir
Abies fraseri (east)	Fraser fir
Picea glauca	White spruce
Picea rubens (east)	Red spruce

Others

Acer pensylvanicum	Moosewood
Acer spicatum	Mountain maple
Betula papyrifera	Paper birch
Pinus banksiana	Jack pine
Pinus resinosa	Red pine
Pinus strobus	White pine
Populus grandidentata	Large-toothed aspen
Populus tremuloides	Aspen
Prunus pensylvanica	Pin cherry
Quercus borealis	Northern red oak
Sorbus americana	American mountain ash

Shrubs

Amelanchier spp.	Serviceberry; shadbush
Cornus rugosa	Round-leaved dogwood
Corylus cornuta	Beaked hazelnut
Diervilla lonicera	Dwarf bush honeysuckle
Nemopanthus mucronata	Mountain holly
Rhododendron roseum	Rose azalea
Sambucus pubens	Red-berried elder
Taxus canadensis	Canada yew

Vaccinium angustifolium	Early low blueberry
Viburnum alnifolium	Hobblebush
Viburnum cassinoides	Withe rod

Ground Layer

Apocynum androsaemifolium	Spreading dogbane
Aralia nudicaulis	Wild sarsaparilla
Aster macrophyllis	Large-leaved aster
Carex debilis	Sedge
Chimaphila umbellata	Pipsissewa
Clintonia borealis	Bluebead lily
Coptis trifolia	Goldthread
Cornus canadensis	Bunchberry
Dryopteris austriaca	Shield fern
Epigaea repens	Trailing arbutus
Fragaria virginana	Wild strawberry
Galium triflorum	Sweet-scented bedstraw
Gaultheria hispidula	Snowberry
Gaultheria procumbens	Wintergreen
Gymnocarpium dryopteris	Oak fern
Hepatica americana	Round-leaved hepatica
Linnaea borealis	Twinflower
Lonicera canadensis	American fly honeysuckle
Lycopodium clavatum	Running ground pine
Lycopodium lucidulum	Shining club moss
Lycopodium obscurum	Ground pine
Mitchella repens	Partridgeberry
Oxalis acetosella	True wood sorrel
Polygala paucifolia	Gaywings
Pteridium aquilinum	Bracken fern
Pyrola secunda	One-sided shinleaf
Rubus pubescens	Dwarf raspberry
Smilacina racemosa	Solomon's-plume; false Solomon's-seal
Streptopus roseus	Twisted-stalk
Thelypteris hexagonoptera	Broad beech fern
Trientalis borealis	Starflower
Trillium undulatum	Painted trillium*
Uvularia sessilifolia	Wild oats
Viola rotundifolia	Round-leaved yellow violet
Waldsteinia fragaroides	Barren strawberry

Hemlock Ravine (Central)

Canopy Trees

Dominant
| *Tsuga canadensis* | Hemlock |

Others
Acer pensylvanicum	Moosewood
Betula lenta	Sweet birch
Betula lutea	Yellow birch
Fagus grandifolia	Beech

Shrubs

Common Plant
Rhododendron maximum	Great rhododendron

Others
Corylus cornuta	Beaked hazel
Kalmia latifolia	Mountain laurel
Ilex montana	Mountain winterberry
Rhododendron arborescens	Smooth azalea
Rhododendron calendulaceum	Flame azalea
Viburnum alnifolium	Hobblebush

Ground Layer
Actaea alba	White baneberry
Aralia nudicaulis	Wild Sarsaparilla
Athyrium filix-femina	Lady fern
Carex debilis	Sedge
Carex laxiculmis	Sedge
Carex rosea	Sedge
Carex scabrata	Sedge
Carex styloflexa	Sedge
Cinna arundinacea	Woodreed
Clintonia borealis	Bluebead lily
Gaultheria procumbens	Wintergreen
Glyceria striata	Fowl meadow grass
Habenaria fimbriata	Large purple fringed orchid*
Habenaria orbiculata	Round-leaved orchid*
Lycopodium lucidulum	Shining club moss
Lygodium palmatum	Climbing fern
Maianthemum canadense	Canada mayflower
Medeola virginiana	Indian cucumber root
Mitchella repens	Partridgeberry
Monotropa uniflora	Indian pipe*
Osmunda cinnamomea	Cinnamon fern
Oxalis acetosella	True wood sorrel
Stenanthium gramineum	Feather bell
Tiarella cordifolia	Foamflower
Trillium erectum	Wake-robin
Trillium undulatum	Painted trillium*
Viola blanda	Sweet white violet
Viola hastata	Halberd-leaved violet
Viola rotundifolia	Round-leaved yellow violet

Bog (North)

Pool
Brasenia scheberi	Water shield
Nuphar advena	Yellow water lily
Nuphar variegatum	Yellow water lily
Nymphaea odorata	White water lily

| *Pontederia cordata* | Pickerelweed |
| *Sparganium americanum* | American bur reed |

Pioneer Mat

Outer Edge

Calla palustris	Water arum
Carex lasiocarpa	Sedge
Decodon verticillatus	Swamp loosestrife
Hypnum spp.	Hypnum moss
Menyanthes trifoliata	Bogbean
Potentilla palustris	Marsh cinquefoil
Rhynchospora alba	Beak rush
Vaccinium macrocarpon	Cranberry
Vaccinium oxycoccos	Small cranberry

Inner Portion

Andromeda glaucophylla	Bog rosemary
Arethusa bulbosa	Dragon's-mouth*
Calopogan pulchellus	Grass pink
Carex disperma	Sedge
Carex lasiocarpa	Sedge
Eriophorum spissum	Dense cotton grass
Eriophorum virginicum	Rusty cotton grass
Habenaria leucophaea	Prairie fringed orchid*
Iris versicolor	Blue flag
Leersia oryzoides	Cut-grass
Potentilla palustris	Marsh cinquefoil
Pogonia ophioglossoides	Snakemouth*
Sarracenia purpurea	Pitcher plant
Thelypteris palustris	Marsh fern
Vaccinium macrocarpon	Cranberry
Viola pallens	Wild white violet

Moss Heath

Andromeda glaucophylla	Bog rosemary
Chamaedaphne calyculata	Leatherleaf
Kalmia polifolia	Swamp laurel
Ledum groenlandicum	Labrador tea
Vaccinium oxycoccus	Small cranberry
Aronia prunifolia	Purple chokeberry
Cypripedium acaule	Moccasin flower*
Decodon verticillatus	Swamp loosestrife
Gaylussacia baccata	Huckleberry
Nemopanthus mucronatus	Mountain holly
Osmunda regalis	Royal fern
Rosa spp.	Rose
Sphagnum spp.	Sphagnum moss
Spirea tomentosa	Hardhack
Thelypteris palustris	Marsh fern
Vaccinium macrocarpon	Cranberry

Bog Forest

Tamarack Parkland

| *Larix laricina* | Tamarack |

Aralia nudicaulis	Wild sarsaparilla
Carex disperma	Sedge
Clematis virginiana	Virgin's bower
Cornus canadensis	Bunchberry
Cypripedium calceolus	Yellow lady's slipper*
Cypripedium reginae	Showy lady's slipper*
Fragaria virginiana	Wild strawberry
Gaultheria hispidula	Creeping snowberry
Kalmia angustifolia	Sheep laurel
Ledum groenlandicum	Labrador tea
Linnea borealis	Twinflower
Lonicera dioica	Wild honeysuckle
Rubus pubescens	Dwarf blackberry
Sarracenia purpurea	Pitcher plant
Sphagnum spp.	Sphagnum moss
Vaccinium myrtilloides	Canada blueberry
Vaccinium oxycoccus	Small cranberry
Viburnum cassinoides	Withe rod
Viola canadensis	Canada violet
Viola pallens	Wild white violet

Spruce Woods

Picea mariana	Black spruce
Abies balsamea	Balsam fir
Aralia nudicaulis	Wild sarsaparilla
Athyrium filix-femina	Lady fern
Botrychium virginianum	Rattlesnake fern
Caltha palustris	Marsh marigold
Clintonia borealis	Bluebead lily
Coptis trifolia	Goldthread
Cornus canadensis	Bunchberry
Gaultheria hispidula	Creeping snowberry
Ledum groenlandicum	Labrador tea
Linnea borealis	Twinflower
Maianthemum canadense	Canada mayflower
Mitella nuda	Small bishop's-cap
Onoclea sensibilis	Sensitive fern
Osmunda cinnamomea	Cinnamon fern
Osmunda regalis	Royal fern
Rubus pubescens	Dwarf blackberry
Smilacina trifolia	False mayflower
Sphagnum spp.	Sphagnum moss
Trientalis borealis	Starflower

Moat

Alnus rugosa	Speckled alder
Calamagrostis canadensis	Bluejoint grass
Carex stricta	Sedge
Fraxinus nigra	Black ash
Glyceria canadensis	Rattlesnake grass
Ilex verticillata	Black alder
Myrica gale	Sweet gale
Onoclea sensibilis	Sensitive fern
Osmunda cinnamomea	Cinnamon fern
Matteuccia struthiopteris	Ostrich fern
Rhamnus alnifolius	Alder buckthorn
Thelypteris palustris	Marsh fern
Typha latifolia	Common cattail
Viola pallens	Wild white violet

Places to Visit

The sites that are suggested in the following table represent only a small sampling of the places available to visit. It is recommended that local preservation organizations such as The Nature Conservancy and Audubon Society be contacted. Often these organizations conduct field trips to areas with restored or intact native plant communities. State and federal natural resource agencies can be helpful in giving information on the location of high-quality, visitable sites.

Examples of intact or representative plant communities are listed in the left-hand column of the table. Places to see individual plants are listed in the right-hand column (some of these include community restoration and preservation projects).

State or Province	Plant communities	Individual plants
Connecticut	Greenwich Audubon Center, Greenwich	Connecticut College Arboretum, New London
	Nipmuck Laurel Sanctuary, Union (dry oak community)	Greenwich Audubon Center, Greenwich
	Platt Hill Park, Winchester (dry oak community)	
	Sleeping Giant State Park, Hamden (oak community)	
Delaware		Winterhur Gardens, Winterhur

State or Province	Plant communities	Individual plants
District of Columbia		United States National Arboretum, Washington
Illinois	Goose Lake Prairie State Park, Morris (prairie community)	Morton Arboretum, Lisle
	Apple River Canyon State Park, Apple River (mesic forest community)	Lincoln Gardens, Springfield
	Shawnee National Forest, Harrisburg (mixed forest community)	
	Woodworth Prairie Preserve, Glenview (prairie community)	
	Illinois Beach State Park, Waukegan (prairie and savanna communities)	
Indiana	Turkey Run State Park, Marshall (mesic forest community)	
	Versailles State Park, Versailles (mesic forest community)	
	Spring Mill State Park, Lawrenceport (mesic forest and prairie communities)	
	Hoosier Prairie, Highland (prairie, wetlands, and savanna communities)	
	Indiana Dunes National Lakeshore, Michigan City (mixed forest community)	
	Harrison-Crawford State Forest, Corydon (prairie and mixed forest communities)	
Iowa	Cayler Prairie, Wahpeton (prairie community)	Bickelhaupt Arboretum, Clinton
	Hayden Prairie, Saratoga (prairie community)	Loveland Overlook, I-80, Loveland
	Yellow River State Forest, Waterville (mixed forest community)	Cornell College Prairie, Mt. Vernon
	Spirit Lake/Okoboji State Parks, Spirit Lake (mixed forest community)	University of Northern Iowa, Cedar Falls
	Sheeder Prairie, Guthrie Center (prairie community)	
	Waubonsie State Park, Waubonsie (prairie community)	

State or Province	Plant communities	Individual plants
Kentucky	Daniel Boone National Forest, Winchester (mixed forest community)	
	Mammoth Cave National Park, Brownsville (mixed forest community)	
Maine	Acadia National Park, Bar Harbor (northern forest and wetland communities)	Wild Gardens of Acadia, Acadia National Park, Bar Harbor
Maryland	Sandy Point State Park, Anne Arundel County (mixed forest community)	
	St. Mary's River Park, St. Mary's County (mixed forest community)	
Massachusetts	Bartholomew's Cobble, Ashley Falls (cliff community and cedar glade)	Arnold Arboretum, Jamaica Plain
	Bear Swamp Reservation, Ashfield (mixed forest community)	Phillips Andover Succession Project Charles Ward Reservation, Andover
	Menemsha Hills Reservation, Martha's Vineyard (mixed forest community)	Garden in the Woods, Framingham
	Stoneybrook Nature Center and Wildlife Sanctuary, Norfolk (northern mixed forest community)	
	Milestone Road Preserve, Nantucket (heath scrub oak community)	
	Westfield River Wilderness, Hampshire County (northern hardwood community)	
	Elliott Laurel Reservation, Phillipston (dry oak community)	
	Leominster State Park, Leominster (northern hardwood community)	
Michigan	Pictured Rocks National Lakeshore, Munising (northern forest and wetland communities)	Fernwood, Inc., Niles
	Manistee National Forest, Cadillac (mixed forest community)	Michigan Nature Association, Avoca
Minnesota	Lake Itasca State Park, Park Rapids (northern forest and wetland communities)	Hennepin County Park System, Hennepin County

State or Province	Plant communities	Individual plants
	Cedar Creek National Area, Cedar (savanna and wetland communities)	
	Glacial Lake State Park, Starbuck (prairie community)	
	Nerstrand Woods, Northfield (mesic forest community)	
Missouri	Taberville Prairie, St. Clair County (prairie community)	St. Louis Botanical Gardens, St. Louis
New Hampshire	Rhododendron State Park, Fitzwilliam (mixed forest community)	
New Jersey	Wharton State Forest, Burlington County (pine barrens community)	
	Lebanon State Forest, Burlington County (pine barrens community)	
	Bass River State Park, Burlington County (sand plains and bog communities)	
	High Point State Park, Sussex County (mixed hardwood community)	
	Poricy Park, Middletown (beech and oak forest and marsh communities)	
New York	Baltimore Woods, Onondaga County (meadow and mixed forest communities)	Brooklyn Botanical Gardens, Brooklyn
	Central Park, Schenectady (mixed forest community)	
	Hoyt Preserve, Smithtown (open forest community)	
Ohio	Castalia Prairie, Castalia (prairie community)	Aullwood Audubon Center, Dayton
	Lynx Prairie, Lynx (prairie and wetland communities)	
	Buzzardroost Rock, Adams County (prairie and mixed forest communities)	
	The Wilderness, Adams County (prairie and mixed forest communities)	

State or Province	Plant communities	Individual plants
Ontario	Algonquin Provincial Park, Huntsville (mixed forest and wetland communities)	
	Point Pelee National Park, Leamington (prairie and wetland communities)	
Pennsylvania	Allegheny National Forest, Warren (mixed forest and savanna "orchards" communities)	Bowman's Hill Wildflower Preserve, Washington Crossing Park
	Jennings Blazing Star Nature Preserve, Butler County (prairie community)	Longwood Gardens, Kennett Square
	Presque Isle State Park, Erie (prairie community)	John Tyler Arboretum, Lima
		Morris Arboretum, Philadelphia
		Brandywine Conservancy, Chadds Ford
Vermont	White Mountain National Forest, Waterville (mixed forest community)	
	Glenlake Property, Rutland County (mixed forest community)	
	McKnight Property, Windsor County (red pine forest)	
	Gifford Woods State Park, Sherburne (northern hardwood community)	
Virginia	Shenandoah National Park, Front Royal (grassland and mixed forest communities)	
	Jefferson National Forest, Roanoke (mixed forest community)	
West Virginia	Monongahela National Forest, Elkins (mixed forest community)	Core Arboretum, Morgantown
Wisconsin	Avoca Public Hunting and Fishing Grounds, Avoca (prairie community)	University of Wisconsin Arboretum, Madison (prairie restoration)
	Wyalusing State Park, Bagley (mixed forest and cedar glade communities)	The Clearing, Ellison Bay
	Ridges Sanctuary, Bailey's Harbor (boreal forest and alder thicket communities)	Wyalusing State Park, Bagley (prairie restoration)

State or Province	Plant communities	Individual plants
	Peninsula State Park, Door County (boreal and northern hardwood forest communities)	Necedah Wildlife Refuge, Necedah (prairie/pine savanna restoration)
	Council Grounds State Roadside Park, Merrill (pine forest community)	Madison Audubon Goose Pond Refuge, Arlington (wetlands and prairie restoration)
	Waupun Park, Waupun (mesic forest community)	Boerner Botanical Gardens, Hales Corners
	Sanders Park, Racine County (mesic forest community)	Schlitz Audubon Cenner, Brown Deer

Glossary

Algae: Any of various primitive, chiefly aquatic plants that lack true stems, roots, and leaves but usually contain chlorophyll.

Alien: A plant native to one region but brought to another as a result of human activity.

Allelopathy: Condition in which one plant produces antibiotic chemicals which repress its growth or that of other plants.

Aggregated: Crowded or massed into a cluster.

Aquatic Plant: Living or growing in or on the water.

Barrens: A plant community with either a low total coverage or with stunted individuals of species which elsewhere reach considerable size.

Berm: A mound of earth, gravel, sand, or rocks for protection or concealment.

Boreal: Northern biogeographical region.

Canopy: The overhead branches of trees together with their complement of leaves. Said to be a closed canopy when the ground is completely hidden by the leaves when viewed from above.

Clay: A fine-grained, firm, natural material, plastic when wet, that consists primarily of silicates of aluminum.

Conglomerate: A rock consisting of pebbles and gravel embedded in a loosely cementing material.

Coniferous: Of or composed of evergreen, cone-bearing trees, such as pine, spruce, hemlock, or fir.

Contour Lines: A line on a map representing elevations and surface configurations.

Deciduous: Shedding or losing foliage at the end of the growing season.

Dominant: Designating or pertaining to the species that is most characteristic of a habitat and that may determine the presence and type of other species.

Drumlin: A streamlined hill or ridge composed of glacial drift.

Ecosystem: An ecological community together with its physical environment, considered as a unit.

Ecotype: The smallest taxonomic subdivision, consisting of subspecies or varieties adapted to a particular set of environmental conditions.

Ephemeral: Spring-blooming herb, mostly of mesic deciduous forests.

Esker: A long, narrow ridge of coarse gravel deposited by a stream flowing in an ice-walled valley or tunnel in a decaying glacial ice sheet.

Exotic: From another part of the world; not indigenous; foreign.

Faulting: Fracturing of a rock formation, caused by a shifting or dislodging of the earth's crust.

Floodplain: A plain bordering a river, subject to flooding.

Fold: A bend in a stratum of rock.

Forb: A specialized term for any nongrassy herbaceous plant. Used particularly for the broad-leaved plants of prairies.

French Drain: A hole dug downward through poorly drained soils and filled with gravel to facilitate drainage.

Frost Pocket: Low places in landscapes where heavier cold air settles. Many years will have temperatures below freezing throughout the growing season.

Fungi: Any of numerous plants lacking chlorophyll, including the yeasts, molds, and mushrooms.

Gneiss: A banded metamorphic rock, usually of the same composition as granite, in which the minerals are arranged in layers.

Grassland: An area, such as a prairie or meadow, of indigenous grass or grasslike vegetation.

Ground Layer: The herbs, shrubs, and woody vines found beneath the trees in a forest. Excludes seedlings and saplings of the overhead trees.

Habitat: The area or type of environment in which an organism or biological population normally lives or occurs.

Herbaceous: Pertaining to or characteristic of a plant that has a fleshy stem, as distinguished from a woody plant.

Horticultural Species: A species of plant that is not indigenous to an area. This may include native species that are commercially vegetatively propagated or are ecotypes different from those of local populations.

Humus: A brown or black organic substance consisting of partially or wholly decayed vegetable matter that provides nutrients for plants and increases the ability of soil to retain water.

Hybrid: The offspring of genetically dissimilar parents or stock; especially the offspring produced by breeding plants of different varieties, species, or races.

Hydric: Pertaining to, characterized by, or requiring considerable moisture.

Indigenous: Occurring or living naturally in an area; not introduced; native.

Intergrade: To merge or grow into each other in a series of stages, forms, or types.

Kame: A small conical hill or short ridge of sand and gravel deposited during the meeting of glacial ice.

Kettle: A depression left in a mass of glacial drift, apparently formed by an isolated block of glacial ice.

Lichen: Any of numerous plants consisting of a fungus in close combination with certain of the green or blue-green algae, characteristically forming a crustlike, scaly, or branching growth on rocks or tree trunks.

Litter Layer: The uppermost layer of the forest floor consisting chiefly of freshly fallen and decaying organic matter.

Loam: Soil, consisting mainly of sand, clay, silt, and organic matter.

Loess: A gray-to-buff-colored, fine-grained, calcareous silt or clay, thought to be a deposit of windblown dust.

Macroclimate: The climate of a large geographical area.

Mesic: Conditioned by temperate and/or moist microclimate, neither xeric or hydric.

Microclimate: The climate of a specific place within an area, contrasted with the climate of the area as a whole.

Metamorphic: Characteristic of, pertaining to, or changed by any alteration in composition, texture, or structure of rock masses, caused by great heat or pressure.

Moraine: An accumulation of boulders, stones, or other debris carried and deposited by a glacier.

Mor Humus: A thick mat of partially decomposed and fibrous organic matter, comprising the remains of several years' leaf litter, as found on the surface of the soil especially in conifer forests.

Mulch: A protective covering of various substances, especially organic, placed around plants to prevent evaporation of moisture and freezing of roots and to control weeds.

Mull Humus: An intimate mixture of organic and mineral matter, as in the uppermost soil layer of mesic hardwood forests.

Nutrient: Something that nourishes; having nutritive value.

Peat: Partially carbonized vegetable matter, usually mosses, found in bogs.

pH: A measure of the acidity or alkalinity of a solution, numerically equal to 7 for neutral solutions, increasing with increasing alkalinity and decreasing with increasing acidity.

Phenology: The study of periodic biological phenomena, such as flowering, breeding, and migration, especially as related to climate.

Phenotype: The environmentally and genetically determined observable appearance of an organism, especially as considered with respect to all possible genetically influenced expressions of one specific character.

Photosynthesis: The process by which chlorophyll-containing cells in green plants convert incident light to chemical energy and synthesize organic compounds from inorganic compounds, especially carbohydrates from carbon dioxide and water, with the simultaneous release of oxygen.

Podzolic: Characteristic of a leached soil formed mainly in cool, humid climates.

Relief: The variations in elevation of any area of the earth's surface.

Sand: Loose, granular, gritty particles of worn or disintegrated rock, finer than gravel and coarser than dust.

Savanna: Transitional zone between grasslands and forests, on which there are scattered individual trees and/or clumps of trees and shrubs.

Schist: Any of various medium- to coarse-grained metamorphic rocks composed of laminated, often flaky, parallel layers of chiefly micaceous minerals.

Sedge: Any of numerous plants, resembling grasses but usually having triangular solid stems rather than hollow round stems.

Sedimentary: Of or pertaining to rocks formed from sediment or from transported fragments deposited in water.

Serpentine: Winding.

Shale: A rock composed of laminated layers of claylike, fine-grained sediments.

Silt: A sedimentary material consisting of fine mineral particles intermediate in size between sand and clay.

Siltation: The process of becoming filled with a sedimentary material consisting of fine mineral particles intermediate in size between sand and clay.

Slope: A stretch of ground forming a natural or artificial incline.

Sphagnum: Any of various pale or ashy mosses, the decomposed remains of which form peat.

Substrate: A surface on which an organism grows or is attached.

Topography: The exact physical configuration of a place or region and the art of graphically representing it on a map.

Transition: The process or an instance of changing from one type of vegetation to another or from one plant community to another.

Weed: A plant considered undesirable, unattractive, or troublesome.

Water Table: Water level.

Xeric: Of, characterized by, or adapted to an extremely dry habitat.

Index

ABOUT THE AUTHORS

JOHN DIEKELMANN *is both a licensed architect and a graduate landscape architect. His undergraduate work was done at the Illinois Institute of Technology in Chicago. As an architect, he has worked as a project designer on numerous projects including the Adler Planetarium Extension, which won a Chicago Chapter AIA award. During his graduate studies at the Department of Landscape Architecture in Madison, he coauthored two master plans for the Wisconsin chapter of The Nature Conservancy, and was awarded a national stewardship award.*

ROBERT SCHUSTER *is an instructional communications specialist with the University of Wisconsin School of Medicine. He holds B.A. and M.A. degrees in English from that university. Having actively assisted in the restoration of a variety of natural plant communities, Mr. Schuster has also been involved in naturalizing a number of private landscapes including his own home.*